LOST CRUSADE

LOST CRUSADE

America's Secret Cambodian Mercenaries

Peter Scott

Naval Institute Press

ANNAPOLIS, MARYLAND

Library of Congress Cataloging-in-Publication Data

Scott, Peter, 1945–
   Lost Crusade : America's secret Cambodian mercenaries / Peter Scott.
    p. cm. — (Naval Institute special warfare series)
   ISBN 1-55750-846-1 (alk. paper)
   1. Vietnamese Conflict, 1961–1975—Personal narratives, American.
2. Counterinsurgency—Cambodia. 3. Vietnamese Conflict 1961–1975—
Underground movements. 4. Cambodia—History—1953–1975. 5. Scott,
Peter, 1945– . I. Title. II. Series.
DS559.5.S39   1998   98-20797
959.704'38—dc21

Maps by John Tottenham

Printed in the United States of America on acid-free paper ∞

98 99 00 01 02 03 04 05   9 8 7 6 5 4 3 2

First printing

To my children—Jacob, Sarah, and Michael—
and to the children of my Khmer Krom friends,
who we hope will never know war

Acknowledgments

The story of the Khmer Krom and their American friends told here is drawn almost entirely from the memories of the survivors I could find. It is not a definitive history, but a story told by the participants and arranged by me.

I am especially grateful to those who sat for many long, often laborious interviews: Chau Reap, Thach Quyen, Sem Ly, Ha Son, Rinh Kien, Sa Abdul Aziz, Thach Tan, Thach Prum Sira, Thach Thuong, Michael Healy, Frank Brown, John Strait, Richard Sirois, H. H. McGuffin, Greg Horan, Larry Caber, Richard Vela, Lloyd Thyen, Peter Krawtzow, and the unnamed sergeant.

Tim O'Brien encouraged me to tell this story and helped with the final draft. Anthony Schneider, Dale Andrade, and Mark Gatlin also helped guide me through various stages of the manuscript.

For their assistance and support I would also like to thank Dr. Thach Bunroeun, Robert Topp, Art Kong, Le Nguyen Binh, Herbert Martin, Richard Steppe, Steve Sherman, Bill Laurie, Mark Moyar, William Tucker, John Tottenham, Nick Garbarino, the Counterparts Association, the National Archives, the Special Forces Association, and the United States Department of State's Office of Freedom of Information.

Hawken School gave me time and financial support for work and travel, which proved invaluable.

Above all I am grateful to Holly Scott, my wife and best friend, who advised and encouraged me every step of the way.

LOST CRUSADE

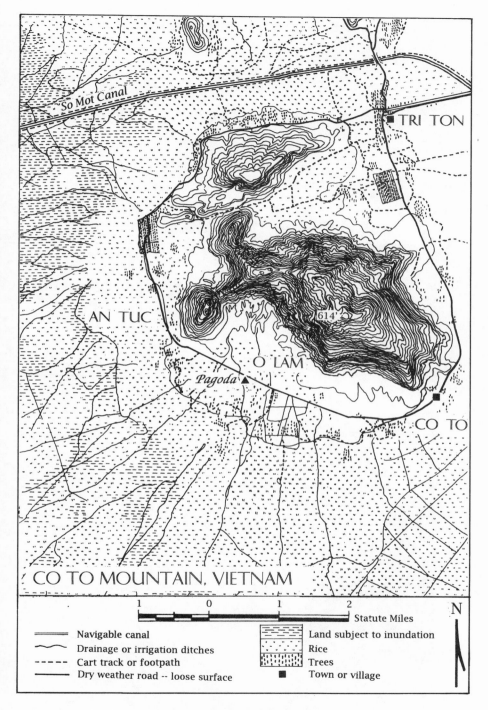

So Mot Canal

TRI TON

AN TUC

614'

O LAM

Pagoda

CO TO

CO TO MOUNTAIN, VIETNAM

1   0   1   2

Statute Miles   N

Navigable canal   Land subject to inundation
Drainage or irrigation ditches   Rice
Cart track or footpath   Trees
Dry weather road -- loose surface   Town or village

Coto Mountain, Vietnam

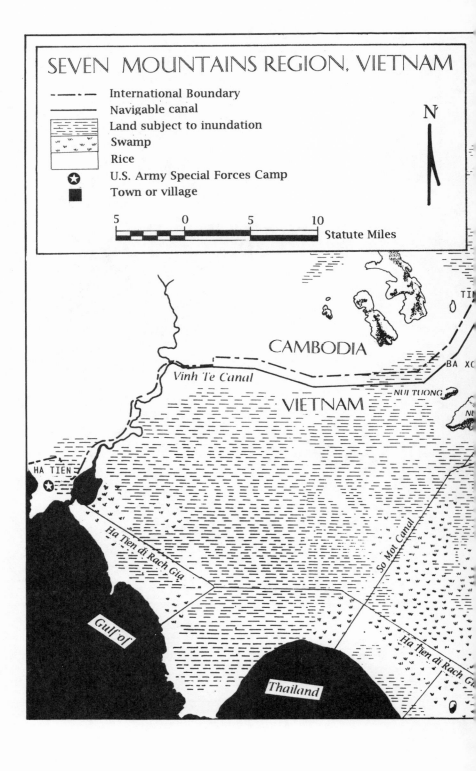

SEVEN MOUNTAINS REGION, VIETNAM

— ⋅ — ⋅ — International Boundary
——————— Navigable canal
Land subject to inundation
Swamp
Rice
⭐ U.S. Army Special Forces Camp
◼ Town or village

5   0   5   10
                                Statute Miles

N

CAMBODIA

Vinh Te Canal

VIETNAM

NUI TUONG

BA XO

TI

HA TIEN

Ha Tien di Rach Gia

So Mot Canal

Gulf of

Thailand

Ha Tien di Rach Gi

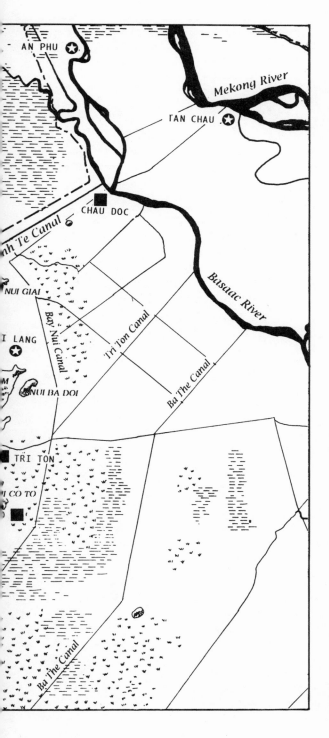

**Seven Mountains
Region, Vietnam**

ONE · MESSIAH

The organization, clandestine or otherwise, is the arena in which the struggle for power takes place. . . . No organization is ever completely disguised. All consist of at least two parts, the overt face and the secret apparatus; but the best, in addition to the covert leadership . . . has a third layer, which is reality. . . . Members assemble around individual leaders rather than around an ideology or political platform. The best leader is paternalistic, sly, skilled at intrigue, master of the deceptive move, possessor of untold layers of duplicity, highly effective in the world in which he moves. Sagacity in the follower consists of knowing whom to join and when, for timing is all important.

DOUGLAS PIKE, *Viet Cong*

1

—

IN THE COURTYARD in the middle of the sleeping outpost, I watched as twelve dark men and boys stood shoulder to shoulder for inspection. The moon was high and full but shed little light through the haze that had risen from the rice paddies since nightfall. They wore the distinctive tiger fatigues of American Special Forces mercenaries; they were armed with new AR 15s, grenade launchers, AK 47s, and hand grenades. Chau Got, their leader, approached them as quietly as the *kmauit*, the dark spirits that awaited them beyond the outpost walls. Other than the terrible teeth that protruded from the shadow of his hat brim like splayed bony fingers, his face was hidden. His right hand rested on his holster, and though he seemed to be at ease, the men awaiting his inspection knew that he could lash out with sudden startling violence for the slightest reason. He faced the first man, looked him over closely, then stepped back while the man hopped up and down; when he was satisfied that he could hear nothing, no sound at all from the man or his equipment, he nodded and moved on to the next, without so much as a whisper. When he'd finished his inspection, he reported briskly to Major Quyen, the district chief. In the shadow of the command bunker, only the major's immaculate white T-shirt was visible; his bodyguard and Chau Got were vague forms. And only the major spoke, quietly, reminding, admonishing. Chau Got pulled his hat string tight under his chin and waved to the first man to lead off.

One behind the other they followed the first. When six had gone, Chau Got joined the file, and I fell in behind him. Breathing a prayer, I left the last Americans behind and followed my team of former communists into the dark world only they knew. As each man passed through the gate, he pulled a bundle of charms from beneath his shirt to let it hang outside where the bullets could see it.

Beyond the village of Tri Ton, we broke into a steady trot; little Krech, the running point man, turned onto a paddy dike that ran along a fetid canal toward the looming shapes of the Cambodian mountains across the border. The paddy dike was wide, slapped firm and flat by a million bare feet. Out in the open on the raised dike, we were clear silhouettes for any eyes that might be watching from the wood line. In the middle of the line, one silhouette, my own, was a foot taller than the others, an obvious target.

"We can't cross the rice paddies because the mud is too deep and thick," Chau Got had told me earlier. "In the paddies we'd be trapped if we got ambushed. It's almost planting time; the mud is the worst now."

So we ran exposed. To the east, under the moon, the paddies were flat and gray, with here and there a distant flicker of lantern light amidst a dark hamlet. To our left and behind were the forested slopes of the mountain called Coto, "the place where Buddha never walks." We ran at an easy pace, about twenty feet apart. At the front of the file, tiny Krech and Ut Le picked up their pace and pulled away from us to scout ahead. It was a cool night, but my shirt was heavy with sweat.

We were going north to Cau Giai hamlet, which lay on the Vinh Te Canal, a few hundred meters from the Cambodian border. We were out to find Nguyen Xuan, a ranking member of the communist District Committee, whom every man running on the dike but me knew by sight.

We had been told by what I hoped were reliable sources that Xuan would be spending the night with his sister in the third house on the eastern path to the canal. He had as many as four bodyguards, all armed with AK 47s, and a reputation as a ruthless tax collector. Our mission was to surprise him and his men, overcome them, and induce them to forsake the communists and bear arms for the government of South Vietnam, to *chieu hoi*, as Chau Got and his men had just done. If Xuan refused, we were to arrest him and his men and bring them back for trial, or kill them if need be. Captured, he'd be a prize; dead or alive, his elimination would swell our reputation.

I was alone in enemy territory with twelve men who only months before had been Viet Cong themselves. We had no radio, no compass, and no map.

"A map," Chau Got had said before we left the compound, "needs a light to see it by. Light attracts bullets. You have to study it here and remember it."

It was March 1969. I was twenty-three years old, an infantry lieutenant with less than four months in Vietnam. I was a regular army officer, Airborne and Ranger qualified. I had been to Special Warfare School for counterinsurgency, language school, and the CIA agent-handling school in Vung Tau. The language I had learned was Vietnamese. The men I was with that night were Cambodians, Khmer Krom; they understood the language of their ancient enemies, but they were loath to speak it. They could not make sense of my Vietnamese, and I could only understand a few words of theirs. None of us carried any identification or wore a conventional uniform.

Without insignia or rank on my fatigues, I was out of uniform in enemy territory. I prayed for courage, and for the ability to kill my fellow man.

Chau Got and his team did not need identification, because everybody in the area knew who they were. Everybody on both sides. Among the twelve of them they were related to half the local population. They had gained a reputation for ferocity when they were with the Viet Cong in the caves on Coto Mountain. Chau Got had been assistant company commander; Sinh had been the mortar platoon leader and Ut Le the political officer; the others were all Khmer Krom and loyal to Chau Got. After they defected, they were trained by the Americans to target and "neutralize" members of the communist infrastructure in the villages of their home district for the Phoenix Program. When they reappeared wearing the tiger fatigues of American mercenaries, the communist District Committee sentenced them to death, and offered a price for their heads. Though I had been in the district for less than a month, and was generally in uniform, it was known that I was working for the CIA and paying the team of traitors. The District Committee offered a thousand piasters, about fifty dollars, for my head.

That night we knew that the communist C-805 Company had moved back across the border, and there were no elements of any other main force enemy unit in the area. Except for the local militia companies and a small force of mercenaries in a Special Forces fighting camp at nearby Ba Xoai, there were no American or South Vietnamese units within a hundred miles. While we were in no danger of crossing minefields because we knew where they were, we might run into an ambush set by zealous local guerrillas, or bump into enemy scouts, even with Krech and Ut Le sniffing up ahead.

Our route of march took us between Olam village west of the mountain, and the camp at Ba Xoai beyond. In Olam there were three companies of native Khmer Krom troops holding that village and two others at the foot of the mountain for the South Vietnamese government. We had visited them that afternoon, conferring with their officer Lieutenant Reap (pronounced Rep) and his American advisor, Captain Strait. They too had heard rumors that Xuan would be visiting his sister sometime soon, and they wished us luck. We didn't need to worry about bumping into friendly patrols from the mercenary camp.

"You can bet your ass anything out there tonight is hostile," Strait told me.

We slowed to an easy shuffle, passing in and out of warm banks of earth-smelling mist. I concentrated on keeping as close as I could to the man in front of me. When I did look around, I tried to orient myself with the shadows of the singular mountains, naming them to myself—Sam, Giai, Cam —but their silhouettes changed, or were hidden by the thick mists that shrouded their hillsides.

We had been running for about an hour when I heard angry whispering behind me. Surprised by a breach in noise discipline, I looked around to see that another man had caught up with Con and was running by his side. When he saw me turn, Con pushed the other man out of the way. A minute later, I felt Con closing in on me; he ran six feet behind me for a while, then dropped back to his position. Shadows of the mountains loomed in the middle distance across the border.

As we drew closer, we could see two distant communist signal fires that marked the way for the lead elements of the North Vietnamese Army who were beginning to filter across the border into the area. Until recently the war in the Mekong Delta of Vietnam had been a contest between local communist guerrillas and militia units loyal to the government of South Vietnam. Our province, like many others, was considered "contested," which meant that the communists controlled the villages at night and the South Vietnamese controlled them in daylight. Now North Vietnamese regulars were beginning to fill the ranks of local guerrilla units and appeared to be moving their own units into the delta, using the mountains as temporary strongholds in their southward push.

I heard Con closing on me again, but this time he ran past me to Chau Got. With a sudden noise like air rushing from a slashed tire, Chau Got halted us. We took cover on both sides of the paddy dike, keeping our intervals. Had Con seen or heard something? This stop had not been part of the plan, but perhaps it was part of one they had made without me. This was my first mission with them as their "control officer," and their first with an American. Had they told the truth when they had said they had been betrayed by the communists, and sworn allegiance to us? They had new weapons, uniforms, boots, and money; they could easily disarm me and deliver me or my head to this Xuan for the reward, and return to the communists as heroes. Nothing scared me more than the prospect of being captured, led away, tortured at every step of the way for information I did not have. I watched and listened for movement in the paddy behind me. Across the dike, Sinh's floppy hat and head appeared, then quickly drew back down.

Moments later Chau Got and Con were back up on the dike, and the others scrambling up to join them. Their silhouettes were uncertain in the pale, moonlit haze. They quickly surrounded me, corralling me with my back to the canal bank, whispering earnestly among themselves. Then they fell silent when Chau Got stepped forward. He gestured impatiently with his grenade launcher.

Here it comes, I thought. Christ God help me.

Chau Got said something to me in Cambodian; he held his nose and shook his head, making a noise of disgust. Sinh made a barking noise, a sudden yap that made me jump, and another chuckled softly. With gestures and an explanation I could not understand, Chau Got told me to get into the canal and submerge myself, holding his nose and pushing his own head down with his hand to show me how I should do it.

They could shoot me there and lug my body back, claiming I had gone down in a firefight. They could kill me and let my body settle in the canal, never to be recovered. Or perhaps it was some strange ritual. I had to prove to them that I trusted them and their judgment, and I could not show fear. If it was a test of some kind, I hoped it would be painless, and one I could endure without shaming myself.

Chau Got spoke rapidly, his voice sharp and eager. He poked Sinh with his thumb. Sinh reached out for my grenade launcher. When I handed it to him, I hoped he could not see that I was trembling. He took my bandoleers as well, and motioned me into the water. I slipped down the bank gingerly, expecting to slide down onto poisoned punji stakes in the water, but found only a muddy bottom and the palpable stench of warm rotting fecal matter. As they watched from above in a dark silent line, I ducked under and surfaced, fully expecting to see the muzzle flash of the bullet that would strike my forehead.

Instead I saw Sinh motioning to me that I should scrub under my arms, saying *buku*, very much, as he demonstrated. When I did so, Sinh looked at Chau Got for approval, then he and another scurried down the bank to help me out. They planted their feet on the slippery bank and hauled me up, encouraged by comments from the others above.

Someone gave me his shirt to dry my head and face. Another sniffed at my armpits and said something that brought whispered sounds of approval and, apparently, relief. Sinh returned my weapon and bandoleers; someone behind me patted my shoulder. The point men started out and the rest of the line followed. As I shuffled along, squishing in the dark, Sinh ran by my side to make sure I understood. With a pantomime that included a sleeping, then barking, dog, he made me understand that the unfamiliar odor of my deodorant and shampoo, my "parfum," would have roused the dogs in the village we were about to skirt. I could not understand his words, but the tone of his voice was apologetic. He patted my shoulder reassuringly and smiled. Only then did I believe that it was over; I fought to keep a sob of relief from escaping my throat. It was not until later that I understood how embarrassed they had been for me, and how relieved they had been that I had not been offended.

When the shadows of the tall sugar palms and houses of Cui Giai hamlet were in view, we halted and crouched in the undergrowth. I had dried off as we traveled, but now began to sweat again, making my shirt sticky with mud and shit. As rehearsed, Chau Got clapped once and we approached the hamlet in two files, one from the south, the other from the paddies to the east, both downwind. It was too dark for hand signals, and as the village lay silent, no place for noise of any kind. Several of the men had removed their boots and wore them hanging from their necks with their amulets. From the tail of each file, two men dropped off and spread out to protect our rear. Four others surrounded the three houses on the path to the canal. No dogs barked. The air smelled of smoldering charcoal and rotten vegetation. The four disappeared in the dark, and the rest of us approached the third house. It was built of thatch, and would slow no bullet, but it was likely that there was a bunker inside from which Xuan and his men could surprise us or offer a fight. When we came to the front, we saw no sign of bodyguards. I could see only the shape of the hut, and beside me Chau Got's hat, which I knew I did not dare lose sight of. If shooting broke out now, I would be blinded by muzzle flashes, lost in the chaos.

He pushed me aside gently, toward Ut Le on my left, and he and Krech disappeared inside. Ut Le put his amulet into his mouth to have his charms and little ivory Buddha closer to his soul; its strings curved downward from his lips like fangs. Angry whispering and scuffling inside were followed by a sharp shout, voices. Then a curse from Krech, which was a signal for the others to rush the two nearby houses.

A moment later two of our men brought in four women and a boy about twelve years old. They were Vietnamese peasants, thin, slightly built, and of a fairer complexion than our men. Sinh and Con probed the floor with bayonets for a tunnel or bunker. By the light of the candle on the floor, Con politely interrogated the women, while Krech held his grenade launcher against the boy's temple, his finger on the trigger, pushing cruelly for emphasis. The younger women were weeping; the old toothless one hugged herself and rocked on her heels, moaning to the candle. The boy stood upright, placid despite the huge barrel that Krech held against his head. They knew nothing, they said. The women begged us not to hurt them, to please leave them alone. They knew nothing about anyone named Xuan. They were not related to him, they said; they didn't even know the name.

With obvious delight, Krech held the boy at arm's length and shouldered the grenade launcher as if to fire. Tiny beads of sweat, oily yellow in the light, popped out on the boy's upper lip, but his face was blank, his frame perfectly still. He was perhaps three years younger than Krech, but a head taller; only his eyes moved, from me to Chau Got and back, flashing with hatred. The younger woman, his mother, fell to Chau Got's feet, weeping, pleading in a sad, incessant whisper, calling him *Ong*, master. He pushed her away and said something to me to make me understand that we were not going to find our man here. Did I want to take these back for questioning?

All I wanted was to get the hell out of there. I said we should take them if he thought it advisable.

"They're nobody," he said.

Outside a dog barked once, yelped, and was silent. Chau Got led us out. In the darkness he said something to the others, who hurried away. Behind us, just outside the doorway, framed in the candlelight, Krech held the boy at arm's length. Chau Got tugged on my shirt sleeve to get me to follow him. I stumbled, recovered, my eyes adjusting to the dark again. On firm ground, a raised path perhaps, we had run about fifty meters when we heard a muffled *thump*, like an explosion under water, then a piteous wail, followed by shouts and a few bursts of automatic weapons fire. Chau Got picked up his pace, and I stuck with him.

As planned, we assembled at a little shrine on the road south of the hamlet. There was murmured excitement and chatter when Krech caught up with us. Chau Got counted heads, whispered orders, and to me said, "Okay." In the same shuffling run, we started back to the outpost, but soon our file veered off the prearranged route; we passed through a deserted hamlet, and skirted the base of a dark wooded hill. The moon was down and I could see only the moving shadow of Chau Got ahead of me. I guessed by the vague shapes of the mountains ahead that he had chosen a more easterly return route, perhaps to pass through Khmer Krom villages, perhaps to take advantage of the darkness among the increasing trees. I wanted to run ahead and ask him, as best I could, where we were going, but decided to trust him.

We stopped at an old French colonial school building on the edge of a tiny hamlet. Chau Got sent Ut Le and Krech in to reconnoiter the hamlet. While we waited, squatting against the stucco wall, the cool night grew colder. A lizard the size of a house cat waddled past me. Sinh swatted at him with his M16 and taunted him with his own noise: "Gek-ko! Gek-ko!"

only to be hushed by Chau Got. When the two returned, they assured Chau Got that the village was safe.

Several of the men gathered around Krech, talking in rapid Khmer, excited, pleased, but a little apprehensive of Chau Got, who stood to the side with me. Krech was reenacting his adventure. He mimicked the boy's defiant stance—then *Boom!* he pulled the trigger of his grenade launcher, recoiling with it; *Whoosh!* his arms flew apart to show how the boy's head had exploded; and then arms apart, palms upward with an expression of disgust, he looked down at his own soiled shirt front. It must have been a shotgun round in the grenade launcher, a 40-millimeter handful of ball bearings the size of baby garden peas at two paces. Ut Le touched Krech's cheek with his finger, then licked it, laughing. Someone repeated a phrase in Vietnamese, something with the word *Ong* in it, in a mocking tone. Another said it again, this time with conviction, a defiant growl.

When he thought they had had enough fun, Chau Got quieted them and sent Krech to the well to clean himself. I would have to wait until we got back to the compound and an interpreter before I could get a full account, but I wanted then to be assured that the boy had been killed in self-defense. With the few simple words we had in common, I asked Chau Got why Krech had killed the kid.

He said the boy fought. He was a communist.

Fought? How could he have fought? Chau Got had said that he was nobody, not worth arresting, not a communist. He was only a boy. And why the celebration, the childish pleasure, afterward? The exultation. Not adrenaline, certainly. Not an hour later. What the hell was going on? Was it revenge for something? Could it be political? It seemed murder without a motive, for pleasure. I had heard that the Vietnamese called the Cambodians "children" because they could be tender at one moment, savage the next. I would have to report that we had killed the boy, and I needed to believe that it had been in self-defense. I felt then that I would never understand, felt afraid that I had already failed terribly somehow.

Chau Got said we would spend the rest of the night there behind the schoolhouse, so we moved into a little dry wooded area to sleep. With whispered orders, he dispersed half of the team to form a defensive perimeter. On his knees in the midst of those of us who remained, Sinh rolled two joss sticks between his palms, releasing a sweet scent to please the protective spirits. Then we lay down in the shape of a star on our backs with our heads together, our legs radiating to twelve points. Around us, perhaps twenty meters out from each point, the others lay awake listening. Should an enemy patrol pass by, we could whisper in each other's ears, and either lie still and let them pass, or explode outward at them when detected. We lay awake fitfully at first, shivering on the hard ground, hardly expecting rest, but soon we had turned on our sides and were sound asleep. When Ut Le came to wake us at dawn, he found our formation had folded like a fan as we had nestled together, front to back, for warmth.

2

IN THE DROWSY sulfurous heat before the afternoon rain, Lt. Sa Abdul Aziz, my counterpart, or the officer I was meant to advise, invited me to meet with him and Chau Got in the briefing room for just one more session. The room was a concrete rectangle built against the old French headquarters building of the district compound; opposite the doorway a small window opened onto the little ghetto of ramshackle enlisted housing built of thatch and flattened Budweiser cans. A table fan disturbed the red and yellow flag of the Republic of Vietnam on the wall each time it swept past. Chau Got brought Krech along with him this time, his dark and unpredictable companion.

I was one of a team of six Americans who served as advisors to the district chief and his staff in Tri Ton District, Chau Doc Province, on the Cambodian border a hundred or so miles west of Saigon, where the Mekong River and its brother the Bassac flow into Vietnam. When my orders for Vietnam came I found that I would not command an American rifle platoon as I had hoped, but instead had been assigned as an advisor to a Vietnamese Ranger battalion. I spent two months at Fort Bragg studying Vietnamese language and customs. Later, at the American advisory command headquarters in Saigon, I was summoned to a bare office where a man in civilian clothes with an omniscient air sat behind a small table beneath a captured AK 47. He wore spit-shined low-quarter shoes and a field watch; when he used "negative" for no, I knew he was an army officer working for the CIA. I could tell by his arrogant and secretive air that he was inebriated with his new status and identity: he was covert, undercover, a "spook," and he wanted me to know it right away. He patted my personnel file, which lay on the table between us. He was authorized, he said (by whom he wasn't at liberty to say), to offer me the opportunity to volunteer for the CIA's Phoenix Program, which he explained. I was chosen because I was Ranger-qualified, and so was skilled in small unit tactics, and had had language training. My job would be unconventional "to say the least," he told me in a hushed voice. I asked if I would be in the field, meaning away from men like him and offices of all kinds, and he assured me that I would see all the action I wanted where I was going. I accepted.

I went to the CIA's agent-handling school in Vung Tau where other infantry officers and I learned the standard procedures for targeting and eliminating members of the communist covert government in the villages. I spent the first four months of my tour in Chau Doc, the provincial capital, and there I saw the Phoenix Program at work. Representatives of the various Vietnamese government intelligence agencies such as the National Police, the Military Security Service, and the Police Special Branch worked together in a central office to compile dossiers on the known and suspected communist cadre who for years had covertly controlled the villages and towns. Their physical descriptions, aliases, family ties, and sometimes photos were kept. From agents and informants we collected news of their activities. Nguyen Huong, the liaison chief of village X, was seen in his wife's hamlet on the night of May 5th. The chief of the Finance Committee of village Y visited his home village to collect taxes on the nights of the 10th and 20th. They rarely stayed in one place for more than a day, moving in disguise with falsified papers from hamlet to village to forest. Their real names were almost never known. They assumed the identity created for the papers they carried. Under strict orders not to set patterns, from superiors whose identities they didn't know, they sometimes did nevertheless, their appearance at village Y determined by a schedule that had been created by habit.

Occasionally those who did set patterns or paid frequent visits to their families were surprised and captured or killed by a small team of government militiamen or police. More often they were caught by accident in the widely used cordon-and-search operation. A hamlet in which cadre were known to be actively recruiting or collecting taxes was chosen, and before dawn it was surrounded by local government troops and police. The people were rounded up in the village center, squatting in long frightened rows, and interrogated one by one. Draft dodgers and those with dubious identification papers were arrested and taken away. Sometimes a fearful suspect, threatened with a visit to the district interrogation center, identified a fellow villager as a member of some committee to save his own skin. Sometimes an unfortunate cadre member who was on our target list was caught while visiting his mother. Some were shot and killed while fleeing; their flight was proof of their guilt, and invariably the corpse was identified as a cadre member and our number of reported eliminations increased by one.

Specific targeting of high-ranking cadre was rarely successful because of weak intelligence, communist agents within our own organization, and the incredible skill of the cadre in avoiding capture, learned by long experience. The majority of the lesser cadre, the couriers and committee members, were released because of insufficient evidence or bought their freedom and returned to their covert operations. Many others, including those against whom we'd presented evidence, accepted the terms of the "Open Arms" program, as Chau Got and his men had done. These were drafted into the South Vietnamese army; some would only desert later, but most were happy to change sides, as they had been unwilling servants of the communists and feared reprisal should they return to their villages.

In spite of all our doubts about the effectiveness of the Phoenix Program, most of us involved in it believed that the strategy was the right one. In the first year we thought it could be made to work and that we could weaken the communist infrastructure's hold on the people in the villages. We knew from informants that many of the cadre in Chau Doc province had fled across the border when they learned from hearsay or from our wanted posters that they had been targeted. Captured communist documents railed against the "assassins" and murderous American puppets who were Phoenix operatives; their crude leaflets announced awards for our heads and included a schematic drawing of the inside of our compound, our bunks labeled with our names. Communist propaganda and tax collecting teams came less frequently to our villages, and our agents assured us that the clandestine communist government, especially in the border areas, was weakened because the experienced cadre who were being eliminated were being replaced by less capable and less devoted operatives.

On the district level in Tri Ton we simply did not have the manpower to conduct the same kind of classic cordon-and-search operations that we had at province level. We could not throw such a wide net. Our police and other government bureaucrats involved in the Phoenix Program were assigned to Tri Ton from afar; they were loyal to their own chain of command, and they were Vietnamese, while the majority of the district was Khmer Krom. They were reluctant to share information from within their own agency because they did not trust the Khmer Krom, whose loyalty to the government of South Vietnam they suspected. They knew that there was much crucial information from inside Cambodia and in the border regions that the Khmer Krom were not sharing with them and they resented it. They respected Major Quyen and followed his orders if their own agency found them agreeable. With the exception of Mr. Sanh, the police chief, they listened politely to Major Quyen, Aziz, and me when we exhorted them to cooperate with one another, but they continued to be jealous of their own intelligence information and autonomy. Compiling reliable dossiers was a dubious business at best.

When Chau Got led his men down off Coto Mountain and surrendered, it was decided that he and his men could be best used as an arm of the local Phoenix Program. They had lived and fought in the villages around the mountain all their lives. The CIA chief at province level arranged to keep them at home, paid and equipped them. To be sure that they would not be transferred or gobbled up by the South Vietnamese army when the CIA turned the Phoenix Program over to the Vietnamese, he designated them as "Kit Carson Scouts," which brought them under the auspices of the American program of that name that used former communist soldiers as trained scouts for American infantry units. Working as a team, Chau Got and his men could protect one another while gathering information about the communist leadership, and could work in smaller groups doing the same thing. Individually, unprotected, they would be in jeopardy of reprisal, but if they stayed together, and with us, they would be fairly safe and for us would be an invaluable asset, not just for the Phoenix Program, but for intelligence resources generally. Chau Got and his "Scouts" were ignorant of the details of their status; they put their trust in those of us they worked with, and seemed genuinely eager to kill communists.

Many of our eliminations were surprise arrests in broad daylight. One day, for example, a Scout, or maybe a loyal Khmer Krom soldier, interrupted us with news that Do Mer, the security chief from Nam Qui hamlet, was having lunch at the outdoor restaurant on the Nha Bang road. We scrambled with the Scouts who were in the compound, some police, and whoever else we could roust out. The Scouts were so eager to get into a gunfight that they threw hapless cops and soldiers out of the jeeps and piled on, fingers on their triggers. We pulled over on the road out of sight of the restaurant; the Scouts split up and jogged out into the paddies on either side to block an escape. When we thought they were in place, Mr. Sanh, Aziz, and I, with a couple of retainers, drove in to find the suspect. Mr. Sanh was of Chinese extraction. He was barely five feet tall and smoked fat hand-rolled cigarettes that smelled like smoldering wet trousers. He never wore a hat or a sidearm, but could have a man shot with a flick of his cigarette.

Do Mer looked up from his noodle soup when he heard jeeps approaching. He and his two companions stood up and, trying to look casual about it, headed for the interior of the little thatch restaurant. Aziz unassed the vehicle, waving his .45 in the air, walking as always like a man on stilts. "Put your filthy hands on top of your stinking heads!" Aziz, a Muslim, didn't use foul or carnal language. He told them that our people were waiting out back and they would be happy to shoot them if they saw them, which was very true.

Mr. Sanh never left the jeep. He rolled another cigarette while Aziz bound the prisoners with plastic cuffs, knowing full well that Mr. Do Mer would buy his way out of jail and would be drinking noodle soup in another cafe within a week.

In spite of its flaws the Phoenix Program—using terror and intimidation against the communists as they had against the villagers for so long—was so simple, I thought, so logical, so clear. Beat the communists at their own game. Eradicate their leadership and win control of the villages. Dry up the sea the guerrillas were swimming in. Or better yet, as our name and logo suggested, bring about a rebirth of the people like that of the mythical Phoenix bird, one that would allow them to fly free from the fire and ashes of communist oppression.

"Lieutenant Aziz asks how long it has been since Chau Got has seen his family."

Cop, the interpreter, sat to my left at the end of the table, upright and attentive. He was a native of Tri Ton who had worked for two years as a translator for the CIA at their station in Can Tho, and now had come home, still on the CIA payroll, to work with me and the Scouts. His hair swept back in a pompadour, wearing loafers without socks, Levi's, a sports shirt, and a fat gold wristwatch, Cop was every bit the westernized urban "cowboy," the lover boy on a Vespa, that rural peasants like Chau Got and Krech detested and the communists vilified. Cop was polite, even deferential, with Chau Got, but he did not lower his eyes when Chau Got stared at him.

"He can't even remember how long it was since he saw them," Cop translated for Chau Got. "It was before the planting, the last time, before the women and children ran away to the forest again. His mother and his wife and two small sons, one is nine years old. He misses them too much. His second wife and her children are in Phnom Pi and he misses them more than that."

"The fighting for Coto Mountain is over. The communists are finished there. Erased." Aziz waved a thin hand, brushing the guerrillas aside as he would an insect. "The Mike Force drove them away; you know that."

"Now Aziz is telling them that he hopes the Scouts will send word to their families to come back, like the other villagers are doing," Cop explained. "They will be well protected. Aziz gives him his promise. All the time we are getting stronger. The people can plant rice and no one will bother them."

Chau Got sat rigid, silent. He looked at Aziz, then at me, then back to Aziz. He knew far better than I did what the communists would do to his family to punish him for defecting, for treason. He had not only defected, but he had brought ten men and four weapons with him; he had been an officer. They would make an example of his families as soon as they could, and it would be slow and public and too agonizing to imagine.

I said in Vietnamese that I also promised to do everything I could to protect their families, but Chau Got didn't understand me. When Cop translated for me, Chau Got smiled slightly and thanked me. He believed that I was sincere, and he wanted to believe that I had the power to keep my promise. He sat with his legs crossed, his hands curled together, palms up, in his lap.

"Aziz tells them they should move their families inside this compound. The houses are small. Sometimes there are mortars, but the communists never can get in. He says Chau Got knows that himself very well. Aziz's own family, his wife and little girl, they live here. When the soldiers go to the walls to fight against an attack, they fight so well because their families are behind them in here. Also, Major Quyen is a Khmer Krom and so they will be treated equally with the Vietnamese."

Aziz was a thin, almost bony young man of delicate features and iron disposition. He had been a high school teacher in Chau Doc city before he joined the South Vietnamese army. Trained in intelligence, he spoke French, fair Cambodian, and some English. We were the same age, born in the same month, but even though he had served far longer than I had, he did not expect his captaincy anytime soon because he was a Cham, a Muslim minority descended from the people of the ancient trading kingdom of Champa that was swallowed by the Vietnamese when they conquered the Indochinese peninsula in the fifteenth century. Aziz had been the intelligence officer in Tri Ton for a little more than a year. In Chau Doc I had been told that Aziz and Quyen, with whom Aziz worked closely, were only grudgingly obeyed by the Vietnamese officers and men because they were "outsiders," officers who were untainted by the local system of cronyism and corruption, who were more interested in fighting the communists than in nurturing their own wealth and power—who were racial minorities.

Aziz told Chau Got that he wanted him to take me and his team to Olam village. He wanted him and his Scouts to contact their families, talk to them, decide where they would live, and how we could best protect them. And while in the village, he said, we could assess the mood of the people, learn if there were communists already returning to the mountain as we had heard, learn which of their leaders had escaped and where they had gone.

We also hoped to learn more about the infamous Khmer Krom battalions still hiding in the mountains across the Cambodian border. Like other minority peoples in the border areas of South Vietnam, the Khmer Krom had been driven from their villages in the early sixties by the forces of President Ngo Dinh Diem, who considered their desire for more voice in his government, perhaps even autonomy, an open declaration of resistance. The Army of the Republic of Vietnam crushed the "illegal forces" of the Hoa Hao and Cao Dai religious minorities in the late fifties. In the early sixties, the growing number of Khmer Krom who fled the attempts of Diem to eradicate them and their culture formed into armed units in the mountains. They were considered outlaws because they preyed on both sides, and would serve either for money or advantage. In recent years, however, many of the Khmer Krom had been recruited by American Special Forces and the CIA to provide intelligence, man the Special Forces "fighting camps" along the border, and serve as mercenaries under American command in the Mobile Strike Forces, or as in the case of the three companies of Khmer Krom now in the villages south of Coto Mountain, to serve as Regional Forces to hold their home villages for the Government of Vietnam. We knew that two of the Khmer Krom officers in our villages, Captain Uchs (pronounced Ooks) and Lieutenant Reap, were in frequent contact with the battalions still at large, and we hoped that from Uchs and Reap we could learn the strength and disposition of the battalions, perhaps even induce them to join our side in the struggle to control the border areas.

Aziz did not say, he did not need to, that the degree of accuracy and truth of Chau Got's report from the villages would tell him volumes about the skill and loyalty of the Scouts, and something about my competence.

With the exception of Quyen and Aziz, and me, most of the Americans and Vietnamese in the compound were suspicious and fearful of the Scouts. Some thought their defection was a ruse, that they were a Trojan horse, and that when the time came, during a probe or ground attack on the compound, they would turn on us and butcher us from behind. Others believed that they were spies. No matter how hard they tried, the Americans could not understand how men could fight for the communists for years, and then one day change sides.

Sergeant Putters, the blubbery team medic who distrusted and despised all gooks of all kinds, could not believe that we let the Scouts stay in the compound overnight. He made it clear that he would not stand for it. He would raise holy hell through channels if he had to. If we thought they were going to get medical attention or drugs from him, we were crazy. He had been in Korea; he knew some shit about these kinds of people. Sergeant Burns, the radioman from Connecticut, trusted the Scouts and said he felt even safer with them inside the walls. He had become fast friends with Krech and did not want to see any of them kicked out. He hated Sergeant Putters, "that fat fucking bigot," and threatened to expose him. A couple of nights a week, Putters bribed the guard at the gate of the family housing area of the compound to let him pass, taking a six-pack across with him. He visited the house of a man with a withered hand and his young daughter Co Dep, "Pretty Miss." When the man wasn't looking, Putters would sprinkle some seconal into his beer and leave him snoring, his head on the table, while he and Co Dep made boom boom behind the curtain. Burns told Putters that if he did not shut up about the Scouts he was going to talk to the major about him and his girlfriend, about dispensing drugs, shit like that.

The Vietnamese soldiers in the compound resented the Scouts' higher pay and superior weapons, their special status as mercenaries, and I thought they scorned them because they were sunshine patriots, men who had left their comrades to save their own hides when they saw that the other side was going to win. Nevertheless, Quyen, Aziz, and I believed Chau Got.

"Look at his eyes," Aziz said.

We believed Chau Got's men were loyal to him, and he to us, that he had turned against the communists for the same reason that we fought them. We were eager to give him the chance to prove his loyalty. Only later would we find out that we were wrong about his motives, but not about the man.

Corporal Hai, the staff orderly, pushed backwards through the beaded curtain carrying a large tray. With a nod from Aziz, he set the tray on the table and backed away from Chau Got like a man easing away from a grasping leper. The corporal was a short, light-skinned Vietnamese with a heavy odor of camphor about him and a complexion like a relief map of the moon.

Krech clasped his hands together beneath his chin and made a grateful noise at the sight of the tray. Corporal Hai asked to be dismissed, his voice as heavy with contempt as his clothes were with camphor. Aziz did not answer; instead he asked Chau Got if the tray was satisfactory. Without looking at the corporal, Chau Got nodded approval, and Aziz sent the man away, his point made and appreciated by Chau Got.

"Krech says he loves iced coffee so much!"

Aziz set a tall glass before each of us, then slowly, appreciatively, poured an inch of Eagle Brand condensed milk into each. He placed small aluminum percolators atop our glasses and poured boiling water into each. The aroma filled the room. Krech shut his eyes and breathed deep, still talking. His face was as round as the moon, his skin so dark it was almost black. The other Scouts called him *Kmau*, the dark one. Watching him then I wondered if he was really as old as sixteen, as he claimed to be.

"Krech says when he was on the mountain with the communists he used to be lying down in his cave with hunger and thirst. He forever dreamed about iced coffee like this."

Next came larger glasses filled with sparkling splinters of ice still speckled with the rice hulls they had been packed in. We set the little baskets of grounds aside on saucers, stirred the coffee and thick milk, and poured it over the ice.

Outside the window a female voice exploded in anger. A loud slap, then another and another, each followed by a child's scream of pain. The little girl's crying, like a tiny distant siren, rose and fell in response to the blows to her face and head, each one punctuated by an order to *be quiet!* Suddenly a scuffling noise, an escape, a loud bitter curse from the woman, then silence.

Aziz held his teaspoon to the side of the glass with his forefinger to drink. He told Chau Got that we believed that the communists who had escaped the fighting on Coto Mountain had taken refuge on Cam Mountain, four miles to the north. Was he right?

Chau Got shook his head. He didn't know.

"How many escaped? Where did they go?"

"*Khong Biet.*" He did not know. During the assault on the mountain, he and his team had been in Chau Doc being debriefed by the CIA after their defection, and then they had spent another month in training.

"But you were a company commander. You must have known their plans for retreat and where the leaders would go."

Chau Got shook his head again. He accepted a pack of Marlboros, lit one, squinted in the smoke.

"Chau Got says Aziz should understand that he was only a deputy commander. Even that was not true. The Vietnamese gave all the orders. They didn't tell anything to him or to any Khmer Krom. All the men in charge were Vietnamese, North Vietnamese sent here to replace the guerrillas and regulars killed during their Tet offensive and by the bombing since. They only called him an officer so they could use him as an example to recruit more Khmer Krom. They always lie.

"He knew they were liars for sure after Tet last year. The cadre made the soldiers believe that the people would join them when they attacked the town. It would be the popular uprising that they were waiting for for so long. When his company came into the market place, the people all ran away. The militia shot at them; they didn't join them. It was all a lie."

"The American newspapers called Tet a victory for the communists," I said.

Chau Got sniffed at that idea.

Krech had scootched down, his head almost on the table, to watch the coffee drip into his glass. Chau Got nudged him to sit up straight.

"You looked so angry in that fight," Aziz told Chau Got. "Shooting at us and screaming."

Chau Got grinned, pleased, showing his long yellow teeth. Like his eyes, the skin that creased his face looked far older than thirty.

"Did you see me?" he asked.

"Of course," said Aziz. "I'm the one who shot you in the ass when you ran behind the photo shop. I thought you knew that already."

Krech caught his laughter behind his teeth and swallowed it.

Chau Got nodded. Was it a gesture of admission, or of acceptance? I could see nothing in his eyes and had to look away.

"Was it a bad wound?" Aziz asked.

"He says it was not bad. It went right through him. He could still run. Compared to the others who were caught in the open by the airplanes, it was nothing at all. He says, like Krech's squad was. They all got killed in the rice paddies but him. Roasted like pigs."

Now it was Krech's turn to show nothing.

"I'm sorry," said Aziz.

"He tells Aziz that he has no hard feelings for him. Chau Got was trying to shoot Aziz too. Anyway, now he has five holes where Aziz has only one."

Shirtless Sergeant Burns stuck his head through the bead curtain. "The air strike we requested yesterday is going in in zero two," he said. "We might be able to see it. Come on."

Even though we had exaggerated the number of communists we thought had withdrawn to Cam Mountain in order to get the strike approved, and the Special Forces on Coto had made a concurrent request, we were surprised that the request had been granted because we were such a low priority, and Cam Mountain was so close to the Cambodian border.

We stood squinting in the fierce sunlight. In T-shirts, boxers, and shower clogs, the Vietnamese soldiers who had heard the radio message were standing in the courtyard looking north and talking excitedly. Cop told Chau Got and Krech that the B-52s were coming to bomb the communists who had fled from Coto. At the mention of bombs, little Krech involuntarily drew his head into his shoulders. He knew, as we did, that we would neither hear nor see the B-52s; he could remember, could feel, as we never would, the unspeakable fear at the first cry of "Bombs!"—the complete terror as the whole world exploded above and around them, the soiled pants, shuddering convulsions, and silent screams. Across the compound parade ground, two dark Cambodian boys in sarongs were drawing water from the well. Suddenly they froze, alert, like lemurs at the approach of a tiger. First came the low pulsing sound of distant drumming, then the earth beneath us began to shudder. Krech's eyes grew wider; Chau Got stood rigid, the muscles in his neck twitching.

"There!" said Burns, pointing north. "Look at that smoke! Christ, ain't that the sweetest fucking thing you ever saw? Nuke 'em till they glow!"

Chau Got said something I could not understand.

It was over in minutes, nothing but lazy rising smoke on the distant mountain. If there were survivors, they were stunned out of their wits, bleeding from the nose and ears from the concussions. Chau Got and Krech could only stare.

Cop took my elbow. "Look at Krech," he said quietly. "For him that is the most horrible thing in this life. To him it is magic. He thinks you did it."

"We did," said Aziz.

"Chau Got says tomorrow that forest will stink."

After my radio watch, I joined Cop and two of the Scouts on top of the bunker to drink a beer in the cool of the moonlight. Behind us the rice paddies, covered by perhaps an inch of water, dispersed the moon's reflection like a night sea. The compound was quiet except for the distant voices of radio traffic in the operations room, and the thin sound of a woman singing a child to sleep. While Cop and I talked and smoked, the Scouts slept, Krech's arm draped over Sinh's chest. Before us the largest of the Seven Mountains, Cam and Giai, loomed together like a single dark forested island above the paddies.

Thousands of years ago, Cop said, this place where we were sitting was the coast of the Gulf of Siam, which was now fifty miles to the south. The Mon Khmer people, the Old Ones, came south from the interior looking for land to cultivate for rice, but they found only vast swamps, salt flats, and forests in which no man could walk. They built a small village there at the

foot of a mountain at the water's edge and made their living by fishing. On
the mountain lived a single tree, named *Thlok*, which had been flourishing
for centuries on its top, and the god Naga, the Dragon King, who lived beneath it. The village was called O keo, and they named the mountain *Kauk
Thlok*, the hill of the tree *Thlok*. In Vietnamese, *Kauk Thlok* later became *Coto*.

"That tree," he said, "and also the mountain, were regarded with special
attention by the people."

It was in those early times that the Brahman named Kaundinya sailed
from India in his magnificent ship to find the beautiful Dragon Princess
who lived in the forest beyond O keo with her father, Naga. When the
Dragon Princess beheld Kaundinya's ship, she paddled out in her dugout
to meet him. Naked and erect in the canoe, the Dragon Princess amazed
Kaundinya with her beauty and power. He drew his magic bow, shot an ar-
row into the dugout at her feet and with it subdued her. He clothed her na-
kedness and married her and they lived at O keo. When her father the
Dragon King learned of the marriage, he was pleased; as a gift to his son-in-
law, he drank up all the water that covered Cambodia so the people could
grow rice.

It was not long before O keo became a prosperous port city. In the fifth
century Indian traders from the great Gupta Empire referred to O keo as the
Golden City; there they could find ivory, spices, rhinoceros horns, rare animals to amuse royalty, and especially gold, all transported down the Mekong from the interior. Many traders, especially those from India, settled in
O keo and, like Kaundinya, married the daughters of Khmer chiefs. They
brought with them the religion of Shiva and Vishnu, the laws of Manu, the
Indian legal code, and their alphabet, and the technology to contain and
control the waters so the people could have as many as three rice harvests a
year. The Khmer elite spoke Sanskrit and took Hindu names. Under the
Khmer king Rudravarman, the whole of the southern peninsula, what is
now called the Mekong Delta, was controlled by O keo. The people became
known as the Khmer Krom, or Khmers of the lowlands. As part of the
greater Cambodian empire of Angkor to the north called Chen La, the
Khmer Krom populated and subdued for cultivation 65,000 square kilometers of the Mekong Delta, an area the size of Britain, from the Saigon
River to the tip of the Indochinese peninsula.

Cop lit a cigarette and checked his watch in the light of the Zippo's
flame. Krech sat up, rubbing his eyes, his back to us. The moon was a thin
crescent, a thumbnail, its points toward the earth.

"It's beautiful," I said. "This land."

Cop agreed. "And it's also rich with rice. Don't forget that." His voice seemed weary now, as if fatigue had overtaken him suddenly. "The Vietnamese conquered us two hundred years ago and made us slaves and took our land. Now the North Vietnamese want to conquer them for the same reason. But the land is ours, don't you see? Our gift since the beginning. It's Khmer. The bones of our ancestors buried underneath it connect us to it. The spirits that live here are ours. Only Khmer holy men can talk to them. The Vietnamese tried to cut us off from our Khmer brothers by making a border at the Vinh Te Canal over there, but we don't accept that. They will never give the land back to us; only the spirits can do that, only they will listen and understand." He said that what we could see, the mountains and the twinkling lights of distant hamlets, was beautiful all right. What we could not see, but what was there nevertheless, was not beautiful, not at all.

I imagined he meant the squads of communists in black pajamas moving unseen through the mountain forests, moving toward us, issuing like orderly insects from the tunnels and caves of the dark mounds to forage for food in the villages, or carry weapons and supplies, every one of them fueled by hatred for us and willing to die.

"Fucking communists," I said.

Cop said something in Cambodian, a phrase with the Vietnamese word *Ong*, master, in it, and Krech grunted in agreement.

3

WE HAD FIVE or six bicycles for twelve of us. Krech, Con, and the other smaller ones took turns riding on our handlebars for the first mile or so through the morning paddies. But because the road was so pocked and rutted, the riders so unsteady, it was more a clumsy cursing rodeo of collisions, falls, and tangled, laughing confusion than it was forward progress, so those without bikes gave up riding and shuffled along with us. At Sralong Chey hamlet, the road ahead turned south around Tuk Chup Knoll, the broad foot of Coto Mountain that was called the Million Dollar Knoll for the amount of ordnance that had been dropped daily on its communist defenders in the last year. The once-forested knoll, like the rest of the mountain, had been so heavily shelled, so much gassed and napalmed and bombed, that it was reduced to a charred rock pile of broken granite boulders covering the caves beneath.

Ut Le, upright and bare chested, all bone and sinew, pedaled past Chau Got and me, with Sinh, the even more beautiful bachelor, close behind him. They wore their weapons slung across their backs and their jungle hats pulled down low to hold their hair in place for the arrival. Krech shouted at them to come back; they answered with laughter and obscene gestures and disappeared around the bend. Chau Got did not seem pleased. He waved to the others to close up behind him and we too turned south into the shadow of the mountain.

It was as if we had pedaled across a border or crossed a temperate zone into a new geography and climate. I had flown over the three villages and their spreading hamlets. Beneath the trees I had seen the spires and tiled roofs of the pagodas around which the hamlets were gathered and Major Quyen had pointed out the village centers where the peaked roofs of the long houses were assembled around the largest temples. But I was not prepared for the gentling effect of entering the villages on the ground. We left the harsh sunlight of the open paddies and the scenes of devastation behind and rolled into a softer, older world where the main road and the many branches that spread out from it were shaded by high palms, tamarinds, and long-stemmed mango trees. Like the dwellings of the Vietnamese I had seen,

those of the Khmer peasants were of thatch, but they were not crowded between road and canal, exposed to the unfriendly sun and staring travelers;
they were built back from the road, tending toward their temples, clustered
beneath shade trees with kitchen gardens and fish ponds, surrounded by
hedges of bamboo so delicate that the stalks bent beneath the weight of
tiny birds. The larger houses, only glimpsed as we passed, were not squares
of concrete with barred windows and corrugated tin roofs, but were long,
high structures of teak with thatch or tile roofs and spreading protective
eaves. In the door yards where the elderly watched the children, herbs and
flowers bloomed in large clay pots; smaller pots, decorated with scary hand-
painted faces, were inverted on poles to protect the inhabitants from the unfriendly spirits.

The eager bachelors were waiting for us by the side of the road beyond a
little bridge. As we approached, they waved to us to hurry, come see. In a
bamboo pen littered with rice straw lay a huge albino sow giving suck to her
young. The younger Scouts chattered excitedly, and even Chau Got smiled.

"This is the white sow," Cop told me. "She lived through all the fighting
for the mountain. It's a very good omen that she is still here. Things are going to go well in the village again. Food and peace and large families."

"Do you believe that?" Cop had been to school, studied under the
monks, lived in the city.

"Sure, why not? Do you?"

"Sure," I said.

Just ahead lay An Tuc, the northernmost of the three villages. Chau Got
ordered the Scouts to put on their hats, button and tuck in their fatigue
shirts. We would walk from there, he said. Stay together. Sling your weapons over your right shoulder. Be mindful. Not an easy thing for men and
boys who had been away from their homes and families for so long, but one
that was obeyed.

By all but Krech, who could not resist teasing the children who gathered
to watch us pass, and had to be scolded twice to stop him from calling out
to the old women in their doorways.

Suddenly four Khmer Krom soldiers, naked save for their amulets and
black cotton boxers and armed with old M2 carbines, stepped into the road
ahead of us, their weapons at the ready. They shouted at us to stop where
we were. We didn't. We neither slowed our pace nor touched our weapons.
Three little girls in a door yard to my right scrambled for cover.

Krech called out a name and clapped his hands. A second later, Sinh jingled his bicycle bell and called the same name. The soldier in the middle squinted, then drew himself up showing a pair of golden teeth.

Another of the soldiers, the tallest, lowered his weapon and strode toward Krech.

"*Kmau!*" he laughed. Dark one. Krech's nickname.

Greetings were exchanged, backs patted, hair mussed. A little girl with a naked baby on her hip appeared and quietly took Con's hand.

"Cousins," said Cop.

"All of them?" I asked.

"Probably."

Each of the three Regional Force companies had been assigned to secure and protect one of the villages beneath the mountain. The officers and men of the companies were all Khmer Krom, most from the villages, and all served the Government of Vietnam through Major Quyen in Tri Ton, officially at least. They had been enticed from hiding in the forests three years before with promises that they would have Khmer Krom officers and would be armed and supplied by the Americans. I had heard that Gen. Nguyen Cao Ky, the flamboyant vice president of South Vietnam, had flown to Olam village to welcome the companies. In a garish public ceremony, General Ky had promoted Uchs, their leader, to captain and pinned a medal on him. General Ky and his attendant officers accepted the troops' pledge of allegiance and warned them that "if they ever betray the government of South Vietnam, they will lose their heads and thus have nothing to wear hats with." The men who met us in the road were from Lieutenant Sem Ly's 179 Company, and like those who served under Captain Uchs and Lieutenant Reap, they were poorly armed, barely clothed, and underpaid. The sight of their kinsmen among the Scouts, who were well fed, wore not only new uniforms but new boots as well, carried M16s, and even had their own American who could call for air strikes or a helicopter to carry them away if they were wounded, was a far more hopeful sign to them than the white sow.

We could not pay our respects to Sem Ly, they explained, because he was on a reconnaissance patrol. They would accompany us to Wat Pratheat, the temple and monastery compound in Olam village where Uchs and Reap had their headquarters, and the American captain and his advisory team also stayed. Sem Ly would greet us there later.

The religious complex at Pratheat was a wide, shaded acre of temple, monuments, and buildings that was the oldest and most revered of the many sacred sites in the three villages. It lay several hundred meters south of the village center and twice that distance from Coto Mountain, whose peak seemed a miniature and splendid replica of the spire of the main temple. Once a monastery where dozens of Theravada Buddhist monks studied and maintained the temple environs, providing a thriving religious center for the three hamlets at its edge and the village beyond, Pratheat was now a profusion of monuments and buildings mostly unoccupied and unused. We had seen dozens of huge bomb craters in the paddies nearby, but there was no visible damage to the temple from the recent fighting. The old women sweeping the courtyard, their heads shaved and mouths stained red by betel, ignored us as we entered the shaded grounds. Unsurprised, mindful of their work, accruing merit with each pass of the straw broom, they turned their backs on us.

•

"I hope you don't expect us to feed all of you. I mean you're welcome and everything, but we don't get shit for rations down here."

Capt. John Strait and his counterpart Lieutenant Reap greeted us by a sandbag bunker built against a crumbling monument that housed the bones of some forgotten temple benefactor. Strait was over six feet tall with powerful shoulders and arms from which spread huge hands. The seventh son of a Michigan farmer, he had left high school and the farm to join the Special Forces, where he had served fifteen years, twelve of them as an enlisted man. His cheekbones were high, his nose twice broken, and the sides of his head, which had been shaved in a short Mohawk two weeks before, were growing back in a soft stubble.

I said the Scouts were going to be visiting their families; only Cop and I would stay there and we would pay for our food.

Next to his large American, Lieutenant Reap seemed small, boyish, almost delicate, but his bearing, and the ease with which he accepted the deference of Chau Got and the others, made it clear that he was a man of considerable power. His bodyguard was the biggest Khmer I had ever seen, a scowling slack-jawed creature completely covered with Sanskrit tattoos.

Reap and I bowed slightly to one another and shook hands. "Tonight," Reap said. "We will kill some chickens."

With Reap's permission, and me in tow, Chau Got took the Scouts aside. He told Krech and Sinh, whose families were in two of the hamlets adjacent to the temple, that they would stay there with Cop and me. He made it clear that they were responsible for my safety. I argued, politely, that I did not need protection, but Chau Got insisted, politely, and I demurred. The matter was not so much my personal security as it was a demonstration of my importance, and consequently Chau Got's, and the loyalty of the Scouts.

"Three days?" Chau Got asked me, holding up as many fingers.

"Five," I said.

Chau Got addressed the Scouts formally, slowly, so Cop could translate for me. Chau Got told them to watch and listen, not to draw attention to themselves by showing off their new wealth, causing jealousy. Find out where our enemies are, but no fighting, no shooting. He, Chau Got, would find his first family, get them settled, then spend the rest of the time in Phnom Pi with his second family. Now they could go.

I thought that if he had presumed to give me advice, it would have been much the same, so I resolved to spend the next five days watching and listening, which I was eager to do. Cop and I set out to find a place to stay, with Krech and Sinh and a half dozen curious children following. A young monk, head and eyebrows shaved, saffron robe over one shoulder, said diffidently, more afraid of Krech than of me, that the older monks invited us to use a little house just outside the low temple wall. It was one of three thatch houses set aside for pilgrims and visitors between the wall and the nearest hamlet houses. We accepted hammocks and rolled bamboo mats from the monk, and he accepted a donation to the temple from us. In the distance the village drums called the people home from the rice paddies: two beats repeated in sets of three.

The drums were hollowed trunks of ornately carved dark hardwood with water buffalo hides stretched on both ends. The drum at Wat Pratheat, said to be the finest in the district, was four feet long and two feet in diameter. The same two-beat pattern that called the people home was sounded at dawn to arouse them for work. In an emergency a hard, rapid repetition of three beats was used. The drums called people to prayer on holy days with soft insistent patterns, announced festivals, and sometimes accompanied the sweet song of the stringed *Tror* to provide the rhythm for dancers. Sinh wanted to sit and watch the girls coming home on the path, but Reap said no, first we must pay our respects to Captain Uchs.

•

I had seen Captain Uchs at district headquarters. He was a short, round man with soft skin the color of café au lait and chubby pink fingers. He wore the rank of captain in the South Vietnamese Army, but his uniform of starched khakis and a soft beige beret was of his own design. He packed a coveted Chinese nine-millimeter pistol with a holster and belt befitting a general officer, buffed to a high shine by one of his attendants. It was hard to tell how old he was; he had no scars, no wrinkles, no muscles. I thought he was perhaps thirty. If he was as ruthless and had as little regard for human life as they said, he didn't look the part. Even Major Quyen, his superior officer, treated Captain Uchs with polite caution.

"He thinks you're still with the CIA. If I was you I wouldn't bother to tell him otherwise, if there is an otherwise," Strait said. "And he's impressed that your Scouts are all carrying new M16s and grenade launchers. Nothing impresses Uchs like weapons, unless of course it's money to buy them with here. If you play it right, he'll give you one of his girls tonight."

In the village center, beneath a canopy thatched with palm fronds, eight of us sat at a table with Uchs at the head. Strait and I sat at his left and right with Reap and Sem Ly beside us. Perched on a silken pillow in a large teak chair with arms, Uchs sat a bit above the rest of us with one leg tucked under him, the other dangling in a posture of royal ease. Behind him his bodyguards stood sullenly, one with a hand-axe in his belt, and all around him and the table his servants hustled back and forth with food and drink, always careful to stoop in his presence, not to presume his height. We drank "Beer 33" over shards of ice in glasses kept constantly filled, and picked at dainties with chopsticks. At the far end of the table Sinh watched the serving girl with the magical hips; little Krech watched Captain Uchs in silent awe, averting his gaze only when Uchs looked his way.

The captain had been in council with his agents and couriers from the Khmer Krom battalions and Phnom Penh all morning, he would have us know. He paused after each sentence and as Cop translated it, Uchs watched him with mean little eyes that warned him to choose his words carefully.

"Your B-52 strike on Cam Mountain last week was very successful. It killed more than a dozen communists. The others ran away across the border and they are disheartened. Congratulations." Uchs chewed with his eyes closed, his little lips pursed.

Strait asked if the strike had killed Chau Kem, the man who had been commander of the communist garrison on Coto. The people in the villages believed that Chau Kem was protected by the *kmauit*, the dark spirits, that he was immortal and could disappear and reappear at will.

"Not this time," Uchs said. "But Captain Kem can be killed and we will do it. He is in hiding in Cambodia right now. He is preparing to return to Nui Coto. They will give him new soldiers, *yuons* from Hanoi, and supplies."

While the table was being cleared and another course laid, I asked Cop exactly what *yuon* meant, how it translated. He explained that it was a derogatory word for the Vietnamese, like their word, *tho*, for Khmers. It meant generally savage or uncivilized. "But *exactly*," Cop said with some pleasure, "it means a person with gills. You know, like a fish has."

Captain Uchs signaled to a little girl of about fourteen to come to his side. She was plump, with budding breasts and necklaces and bracelets of dark gold; she held her hands clasped before her and her head bowed. Uchs lifted her chin with his forefinger.

"This is my new wife," he said. "Isn't she beautiful? She loves me too much."

We said yes, she was. Embarrassed for the girl, Strait and I pretended to admire her. Uchs had two other wives in the villages, one an old crone, the other pregnant. No one knew how many wives he had elsewhere.

In bits and pieces, over several courses, Uchs told us what he had learned from his agents. He acted like the information was old hat for me, but I knew he did not believe that it was. He was happy to report that things in Cambodia were going badly for Prince Norodom Sihanouk, which could well be good news for the Khmer Krom and their friends.

He explained, with an air of one familiar with these things, that the new government that had been convened in an emergency session by Sihanouk was all but controlled by the pro-Western factions. Relations with the United States had been resumed. The army, under Gen. Lon Nol, himself a Khmer Krom, had crushed a communist-inspired uprising with remarkable fury and chased the Khmer communists into the hills. There were massive demonstrations in Phnom Penh against the presence of the hated *yuons* in the sanctuaries inside Cambodia, the staging areas being used to wage the war against South Vietnam.

"But that is nothing compared to your bombing." Uchs took a long swallow of his beer, his pinky finger raised and curled.

"The Hanoi *yuons* are getting smashed to pieces everywhere in the border provinces. The Khmers in the villages are running away and many are being killed because there are so many bombs, but so are the communists. It's about time."

Strait, who had begun to drift, perked up at the mention of bombing in Cambodia. I must have looked surprised. Uchs offered a conspiratorial smile that said he knew I was feigning surprise.

I looked at Strait. He said he had heard rumors of B-52 strikes inside Cambodia, but when he reported them through channels he had been told that it was impossible. Communist propaganda?

Uchs's agents said that radar on Soviet trawlers in the South China Sea and agents in Thailand were warning the communists of the approach of the B-52s, telling them their direction of travel and time of arrival so they had plenty of warning and time to move out of the way. But the Khmer people didn't have any warning. All of a sudden in the middle of the night whole villages were blown up, the people wiped out.

Some *yuon* soldiers are killed, but many more villagers. The ones who suffer, blame Sihanouk. They will join the Khmer Krom against him!

I promised myself that I would sit with Strait and Cop that night and try to make sense of what was going on. It was clear that here in the Seven Mountains at least, the war was not a struggle between communism and democracy as I had been taught, nor simply a war between the North and South Vietnamese for control of that country. These people were anti-communists all right, but they served the government of South Vietnam only out of expedience, and, I was beginning to suspect, only temporarily. Self-determination was their primary goal . . . but there was more.

In what seemed a prearranged move, Lieutenant Sem Ly and his bodyguard and Sinh thanked Captain Uchs warmly for the food and drink and excused themselves. His bodyguards motioned to the servers to stay away; the one with the hatchet took over the duty of keeping our glasses filled, mine first, and did a fine job of making me feel uneasy. At Uchs's invitation, Krech moved to a nearer seat, stooping low before Uchs and looking far more solemn than I had ever seen him.

Reap scooted his chair back from the table, crossed his legs, and looked at me. Though his boyish handsome face showed nothing, his eyes seemed to hold mine and something beyond as well. I thought then that he was looking into the future, but later learned that watching Uchs talk with me about the Khmer Krom battalions made him think of other things, and he was "only remembering."

·

In 1952, the year following his father's death, Reap lived with his brother Sok Meas at the monastery in Tri Ton and attended the Khmer school at the temple. That year, their brother Dong was killed in action while fighting for the French, and the Vietnamese known as Viet Minh attacked and burned much of the town. They did very little damage to the French compound, and the temple suffered only scarring of a few monuments. Two years later, Reap learned that his second brother Dom, who had joined the Khmer Krom 43rd Regiment of the French army to avenge his brother's death, had been badly wounded in the leg at the French defeat at Dien Bien Phu and taken prisoner. The French defeat meant little to Reap; he knew only that it was not good for his people. Sok Meas and the monks were anxious about the future, though they taught that one should not be. Before the year was out, his brother Dom was repatriated; a civilian now who walked with great pain, he returned to Coto village to help their mother tend to the rice crops. The fire in Dom's eyes had gone out. He told them with no emotion that President Diem had replaced all Khmer Krom officers in the military: all courses, choice assignments, and access to military schools were closed to them. Khmer Krom officers in armor, artillery, and air force units were transferred to infantry divisions, which could not by law be more than ten percent Khmer Krom.

In the evening, in the heat of the dry season, after his lessons and monastery chores, Reap liked to move his mat outside into the courtyard and lie awake listening to the crickets' music. Often the rustling of animals in the undergrowth moved him closer to the portico where his brother and the older monks sipped tea and talked. In the sharp smell of incense, he usually fell asleep to the low murmuring sound of their voices. When he tried, he understood what they were saying, but not what they meant. The tone of their discussions was very grave. He heard mention of moving the holy books into Cambodia, and of hiding sacred objects. In a deal of some kind, Prince Sihanouk had permitted the French to redraw the border between Cambodia and Vietnam, not at the Saigon River, but at the Vinh Te Canal, effectively abandoning to Vietnamese rule the Khmer Krom who lived there.

The new *yuon* president, this Diem, they said was a Catholic from Hue. Catholics were French, and some Vietnamese. Diem was also a mandarin. Reap had seen caricatures of mandarins: they were little squat yellow men, very yellow, with hideous long, black, dangling mustaches. Sentences his brother read aloud from a paper evoked angry whispers from the other monks: "Society functions through proper relationships among men at the top." And so on.

Then the police from the new Vietnamese government who had replaced the French in the compound across the road came to the temple one morning and on one of the pillars of the *salaa* posted an edict titled "*Ngui Viet goc Mien,*" which meant, he was told, that the Khmer Krom were no longer Khmer people, but now "Vietnamese people of Khmer ancestry." For "the greater good of the people and in a quest for national unity," the teaching of Khmer language, history, and culture were outlawed. His brother and the monks he taught were forced to shed their robes and change their names to Vietnamese. All Khmer Krom men over the age of sixteen were required to register for the draft. The practice of Theravada Buddhism was prohibited. Reap's own school was closed. He and the other students were sent home.

Eager that he continue his education, even in Vietnamese, and avoid the draft, his mother and brothers sent him off to the high school in the provincial capital at Chau Doc. Every three months, he took the bus to Tri Ton and from there walked home to visit his family in Coto village.

"On my way," he said, "I saw my people, young and old, men and women, lying dead by the road, three to five bodies each time. I was terrified and wondered how those deaths happened. Who were the killers, and why did no one seem to care about the tragedies? They died just like animals. I thought there were a lot of secrets involved with the everyday dying of the Khmer Krom people. They might have been killed by robbers, by the Viet Minh, or by government soldiers."

On the corpses, scattered in the road near villages, and pasted on trees, he found propaganda leaflets. They were printed in both Khmer and Vietnamese and exhorted "the two peoples of the south" to unite and form an alliance to liberate the country from the dictatorial government of Diem, who was a puppet of the new imperialists, the Americans. They promised the return of civil rights and even independence for the Khmer Krom people. On one was a photograph of a Khmer Krom monk and a Vietnamese monk holding hands above a caption that promised freedom of religion for all people.

But whose leaflets were they? The Viet Minh had disbanded after the French were driven out in 1954. A very few of them had stayed behind to influence the election that was to have been held that year on the subject of unification of the north and south, but the election was never held, and those few, he thought, had gone away. Impressed by the promises of the leaflets, he was determined to find out, to discover who these *yuons* were who sounded so trustworthy, so interested in the welfare of the Khmer Krom.

He soon learned that they were the Viet Cong, Vietnamese communists who would soon be known as the National Liberation Front. Some of them had once been Viet Minh, but most were new members and all were dedicated to the overthrow of the Diem regime. On a visit with his cousin in the village, Reap saw a Vietnamese man who wore the black pajamas of the peasant, and carried a pistol. When his cousin said yes, the man was a Viet Cong, Reap asked to be introduced to him. His name was Duong, but he would say little else about himself. The three ate their evening meal together at his cousin's house, and afterwards he and his cousin walked Duong back toward the forest at the foot of the mountains, "in the quiet middle of the dark night." Reap was deeply impressed with the sincerity of Duong, his dedication to the cause of equal rights for all peoples of the Mekong Delta, and his assurances that the Viet Cong, who lived among the people, were sworn to protect them from Diem's soldiers who came from afar, lived in their fortresses in the towns, were corrupt, and cared nothing for the Khmer Krom.

Reap began to visit his cousin frequently, talking late into the night about what was happening in the countryside. With help from his American friends, Diem was increasing the strength of his army, and with the new draft, increasing its numbers. The people who had closed his school would destroy his culture and would soon draft him to serve in their army somewhere far away from his village and family. The communists were building an organization that would soon mobilize a guerrilla army like the Viet Minh, which would resist the cruel Diem regime with popular support; they would finally launch a Great Uprising that would overthrow Diem and, more important, restore the Khmer Krom's rights and grant them independence. Unlike the Viet Minh, who had treated his people harshly because they sided with the colonialists, the Viet Cong considered the Khmer Krom their brothers in a common cause, he was told.

From his cousin who often assisted the communists but had not yet committed himself to them, Reap learned that many of his friends and people he respected were doing the same thing. Diem's police and soldiers in the towns knew this and considered the villages around Coto Mountain enemy territory. When they came to the villages in the daytime, they treated the people as communist sympathizers, agents for the Viet Cong. They tortured them for information they did not have, raped the women, took precious food and belongings as taxes. They knew they could not catch the Viet Cong who were hiding in the mountains and never stayed in one place for long, so they took out their anger on the villagers, and doing so, succeeded in pushing them into the arms of the Viet Cong.

Reap sought the advice of the venerable *Kru* Kong. *Kru* means wise or respected one. The word and title come from the Hindu word *guru*, or teacher. But in the case of Kong, and others like him, the title carried solemn spiritual weight. They were holy men, who could not only communicate with the spirits, but control them. It was through them that the Khmer Krom's spiritual ties to the land could be preserved. The old man's followers, who numbered in the hundreds, served both the Viet Cong and the Diem government, but their primary loyalty was to him, and the Khmer heritage he personified. He told Reap that he could not choose a middle path as Buddha taught; he would be drafted and sent away, or must join the many others who had chosen to serve the Viet Cong in their native villages. Reap's body could serve either of the *yuons*, but his soul and heart would remain with the Khmer Krom. He had to obey the *yuons* of the side he chose, and appear to be loyal to them, but he must be ever watchful on behalf of his own people. Be suspicious of *yuon* promises to the Khmer Krom, Kong warned. When the tiger lies down, do not say that the tiger is showing respect. Young Reap pressed his hands together over his head in a sign of devotion, and knelt and touched his face to the floor at the master's feet. *Kru* Kong blessed him, and wished him well.

Reap's cousin took him to Olam village to meet Uchs. Uchs was in his early twenties at the time, but he had hands that had never held a hoe or flail. His cheeks were round, his lips wet and full; beneath their sleepy lids, his dark eyes flitted restlessly, full of suspicion and hostility. He greeted Reap with exaggerated politeness, offering brandy, sweets, and French ciga-rettes. Uchs had only recently joined the Viet Cong, he explained. He was appointed a village official, and was promised that when the time came to bear arms, he would be an officer. It was the least he could expect. Reap was young, Uchs said, but he was from a respected family and he was ed-ucated; he too could expect a position of leadership. Some of the Khmer Krom who had joined the communists were "brainwashed"; they were true believers in the cause, loyal to Hanoi and its ideology. Others, the majority, had joined of necessity, keeping their loyalty to the Khmer Krom in their hearts where it could not be seen by the *yuons*. Uchs didn't tell Reap which category he fit into, and Reap wondered then, as he would many times in the future, if anything but self-interest motivated the man. Uchs said he liked him, and offered to take him to meet Ha Coi on the mountain.

Ha Coi was the commander of the communists in the region. He and his several deputies were Viet Minh who had stayed behind after the armistice. They lived in constant motion, never staying in one place for more than a night, from the caves on Coto Mountain to the mangrove swamps west of the villages, to the forests nearby. Theirs was an ascetic life, gathering wild ginger and firewood with which to buy food, like the poorest peasants. He was a thin, very serious man, a Vietnamese who had lived among the Khmer Krom for years. When Ha Coi visited the villages at night to proselytize, he spoke Khmer, treated the people with respect, and impressed them with his self-discipline and honest convictions. His bodyguard was Ut Le, who even then liked to go without a shirt to show the girls his muscular chest. Ut Le carried a Communist Chinese rifle slung on his shoulder and walked upright with a bearing of confidence that was much admired by the other teenagers in the villages.

On a moonless night in the rainy season of that year, Uchs and Reap took the woodcutters' path to the foot of Coto Mountain. Once in the forest, Uchs blindfolded Reap and led him by the hand up the mountainside, where they met Ha Coi, Ut Le, and two others at the mouth of a small cave. Inside the cave, by the light of a tiny lamp, Ha Coi welcomed Reap. For three hours they sat cross-legged on the damp, rush-covered floor. Ha Coi did most of the talking, but he listened politely to Reap's questions, and with great care eased each of his doubts. No brandy, cigarettes, or girls, no pompous airs; only austerity, dedication, and a will to defeat the Diem government that seemed to Reap insurmountable.

To prove his trust in Reap, and to share "the great news," he told him what no one, even Uchs, had known: that Chau Kem, the Khmer Krom nationalist who had served with the Viet Minh for freedom, had returned from Hanoi and was now there on Coto Mountain, with the rank of first lieutenant in the Viet Cong. Even Reap's father, who had been his enemy, had respected Kem. When the Vietnamese leadership had proposed a heavier tax on the Khmer Krom, Kem had successfully blocked it; he had demanded that Khmer Krom not be used as bearers of supplies unless the *yuons* carried equal loads; thanks to Kem, the Viet Minh had not been permitted to force Khmer Krom girls to dance for them when they entertained their dignitaries. Did Reap need to hear any more? Did he need more time to consider? He did not.

By 1958, the three Khmer Krom villages encircling Coto Mountain were under communist control. A traveler who had last seen the villages ten years before, when Reap's father had been their security chief under the French, would have found little changed. The people of Coto, Olam, and An Tuc villages and their dozens of hamlets and temples went about their business of growing rice, tending livestock and gardens, gathering wood and edible plants just as they had done a decade before. In each village and its hamlets were three to four hundred families, a web of matrilineal clans of the ancient Chau family. In the village centers, the huge raised houses, with steep, thatched roofs and decorated peaks, still clustered near the temple grounds in the cool shade of sugar palms, mangoes, and tamarinds. The village drums still announced the dawn and sounded again at dusk to bring the people home from their labors.

But if the traveler lingered, he would soon notice that in the morning hours there were no troupes of yellow-robed monks carrying their bowls on the roads and footpaths in search of alms. The temple grounds were still swept clean by elderly women with shaved heads, the little gardens still tended by old men, but the brightly painted pagodas and wide porticos were dulled by neglect and stripped of their gold. The *nagas*, the fierce seven-headed serpent statues that guarded the temple grounds against evil-doers, were pale and colorless, some chipped or eroded. The people would still be polite to the traveler, but they would not invite him to stop for something to eat; from their native deference now came a slight but distinct odor of fear. There was no music or chanting within the temple, no spontaneous song from the young women at work in the paddies, little or no laughter to be heard anywhere.

The region of the Seven Mountains, of which the three villages were a subdistrict, was declared "liberated" by the Viet Cong in 1958. The Diem forces had tenuous control of the town and compound in Tri Ton, but the Viet Cong controlled the countryside and the mountains themselves. In two years the Vietnamese communist cadre in hiding in the forests and mountains had increased in number from the few proselytizers like Ha Coi who had remained behind, to several dozen who had returned to the Coto area from Hanoi and sanctuaries in Cambodia. They had returned to create and sustain the National Liberation Front, the clandestine organization that would challenge the Diem regime for power in the south.

To administer the villages from which they drew their manpower and sustenance, the Viet Cong cadre on the mountain appointed a Khmer Krom village chief. Under him was a village policy chief and his committee, who were responsible for the security of the village; this included reporting the comings and goings of Diem soldiers and police in the area, which villagers did or did not pay their taxes, and which were suspected of being disloyal to the communists. The village self-defense chief and his organization provided a village police force. It drafted young men and women to serve as soldiers, to destroy government roads and bridges, and to build "man traps"—deep holes lined with sharpened bamboo *punji* stakes and covered with leaves. For every twelve houses there was a group leader who oversaw the everyday activities of the families in those houses and reported anything suspicious. The Women's Committee leaders monitored the work of the women in the villages, such as providing food and comfort for the soldiers when they came down from the mountains, or entertainment for the guerrillas when they returned from fighting. If an appointed Khmer Krom village administrator failed in his job in any way, he was led into the forest and shot.

Life in the three liberated villages was in most ways typical of life in any of the other thousands of villages throughout South Vietnam at the time that were either under communist control or contested by both sides, an estimated sixty to ninety percent. The Viet Cong infrastructure or cadre lived in hiding, either in the forest or in the vast inaccessible swamps; they were in constant motion to avoid detection by the Diem forces, but they visited the villages often at night. With propaganda that exploited the cruelties and inequities of the Diem government, and simple coercion, they recruited young men like Reap and Chau Got in growing numbers to serve as guerrillas, and the villagers served the guerrilla bands with labor and taxes. Everything was taxed by the Viet Cong: "Food, and even clothes . . . raincoats, hammocks, cash." At night, when the cadre and their bodyguards came, the villagers were assembled either to listen to inspirational speeches, or to be mobilized to dig ditches across government roads, destroy bridges, or lay mines. Those who failed to participate or who were suspected of being less than enthusiastic about the communist cause were led away, never to return. Anyone who protested or questioned the disappearance of a friend or family member was himself led away.

When the Diem forces heard that a road had been cut or a bridge destroyed, they conducted an "operation" in the area during daylight. With superior weapons and numbers, they surrounded the village, herded the people together, and while the "old ones were forced to sit sobbing by the excavated road," those suspected of being communist sympathizers or relatives of guerrillas were interrogated, beaten, and raped, their properties confiscated and whole families arrested. It was a cycle that for the villagers could be broken only by victory by one side or the other.

Soon after he joined the Viet Cong, Reap left Coto village to avoid capture. Along with Uchs, and his friend Sem Ly, he was named a "Secretary of the Armed Forces," a position something like a squad leader or noncommissioned officer in charge of about a dozen Khmer Krom guerrillas. Their unit was called the 512th Battalion; it was composed of about ninety men in three companies of thirty each. Armed with bolt-action Chinese rifles, with very little ammunition, they were commanded by a Vietnamese officer named Sao Dae and six of his Vietnamese lieutenants. While in hiding in the swamps or the mountains, subsisting on rice from the villagers and whatever they could forage, the Khmer Krom foot soldiers and their Vietnamese communist officers lived together during the day, but slept apart at night, each fearful and deeply suspicious of the other. The little action they saw against Diem's forces in the Seven Mountains region was primarily ambushes and raids on isolated outposts.

Sao Dae had learned guerrilla tactics while with the Viet Minh in the war against the French. He had become a master of evasion and escape, with a reputation for iron discipline. He and his infamous relatives Bar and Tu Tap were fierce nationalists who had joined the Viet Cong in its nascent years and later became communists. When the propagandists had recruited enough Khmer Krom men to form a guerrilla unit, Sao Dae was sent to the Seven Mountains to lead them. He was a thin, suspicious man; he killed anyone who got in his way, anyone whom he even suspected was not dedicated to the unification of Vietnam under Ho Chi Minh. "Our lives mean nothing," he liked to say.

Sao Dae didn't speak Khmer, and understood only a little, so he had to rely on two Khmer Krom interpreters, whom he also used as bodyguards. One, Ut Le, had proven himself as Ha Coi's bodyguard and political officer; the other, remembered only as "the small man," was known for his knife-work and the pleasure it gave him. At first Sao Dae, though feared by his Khmer Krom recruits, was respected and even admired because he was strict in his adherence to the egalitarian regulations of the National Liberation Front, which held that all soldiers are equal and must be treated fairly, and he was sincerely committed to the independence of the Khmer Krom.

But soon Sao Dae's suspicious nature and ancient prejudices against the Khmer Krom, savages who had been killing Vietnamese for centuries and had sided with the French, began to taint the way he treated his soldiers and the people in their villages. Among the Khmer Krom who worried aloud about the welfare of their families, minor infractions of the rules were treated as mutinous. Soldiers caught visiting their homes were led away to be killed, their family's taxes doubled. To control the villages, which he believed harbored Diem agents and Khmer nationalists, Sao Dae imposed the same restrictions that President Diem had decreed three years earlier. When Sao Dae visited the villages, his lieutenants and bodyguards took note of those people who welcomed him with too little enthusiasm; when these people were later accused of a minor offense, they disappeared. Those who received him with too much enthusiasm were treated in the same way. In a self-criticism meeting on the mountain one night in October 1959, Sao Dae accused Reap of visiting his family, which Sao Dae took as proof that Reap was an agent for Diem. Uchs and Sem Ly, and finally Ut Le, managed to persuade Sao Dae that Reap was no agent, but from then on, Reap feared for his life under this powerful and suspicious *yuon*.

A high-ranking Viet Cong officer captured in 1968 described the years 1958 to 1959 as the "darkest in their whole lives." Diem's "Communist Denunciation" campaign had eliminated all but the clandestine cadre in most villages in the south. In the north, the communist Lao Dong party was busy with land reform, and though it encouraged its brothers in the south, it offered almost no material support. In fact, it had ordered those like Sao Dae who were organizing in the south not to respond to Diem's violent oppression with armed resistance, but rather to maintain a peaceful coexistence as ordained by Moscow. The struggle in the south, said Hanoi, must be carried out by the "southern people themselves." Loyal Viet Cong officers like Sao Dae beseeched Hanoi to approve and support armed resistance, but Hanoi remained silent.

Sao Dae knew full well that his Khmer Krom soldiers and their people in the villages were chafing under his discipline. He heard from his Khmer Krom spies, whose loyalty he suspected, that the men were murmuring among themselves. Their families were complaining bitterly about the heavy burden of taxation and forced labor. Their meddlesome monks and *krus*, those "mud-eating dream sellers," were filling their heads with ideas about ancient racial superiority, ancestral spirits who would guide and protect them, and even giving them charms that they thought would make them immortal. In their political sessions Sao Dae reminded his Khmer Krom soldiers of the atrocities of Diem's troops. He told them about spontaneous people's uprisings against Diem in other provinces in the south; out of sheer frustration and a desire for revenge, people were digging up weapons caches left by the Viet Minh and defending themselves against the American puppets. The only way you can keep your head on your shoulders, Sao Dae told them, is to carry a gun and use it.

Their occasional ambushes and acts of sabotage were successful only because of the hatred that Diem's reprisals brought. Sao Dae needed a large engagement that would bind his men together. Inactivity was eating away at his control and their morale.

The men who had defended Reap against Sao Dae's accusations that he was visiting the village at night and was a spy for Diem were only lying about the first part. Uchs and Sem Ly were as guilty as Reap was of nocturnal visits to the villages, as were many others. They visited their families. Sao Dae and the Khmer Krom soldiers who were loyal to the communist cause knew this because they saw them returning to the segregated encampment. Those who were sneaking away knew that they had been seen by the spies, the "brainwashed Khmer," and had been reported. But the brainwashed ones did not know that they were also meeting with *Kru* Kong and *Kru* Bin, and under their guidance were formulating a plan to overthrow the *yuon* communists and their Khmer Krom friends.

They called themselves the "Awakened Khmer." "Awakened" because *Kru* Kong and a half dozen other holy men in the three villages had opened their eyes and made them realize that if they were to survive as a people, as a culture, they would have to throw off the yokes of Vietnamese oppression. The heavier yoke, the Viet Cong, would be the first to go. It would have to be a simultaneous uprising of all the people, perfectly planned and perfectly executed. Only a select few, those who had been loyal to the *krus* for years, would be involved in the planning; the many other loyal Khmer Krom soldiers and villagers would know only that there was a covert movement afoot to somehow liberate them "from the sorrow and all kinds of cruelties brought on by the Viet Cong," and restore their freedom and culture.

In the long nocturnal sessions with the chosen leaders such as Reap, Uchs, and Sem Ly, the *krus* made prayer cloths and amulets called *knay tanhs* that were empowered to protect the wearer by "magical incantations" in Pali and the languages of the spirits. The leaders were blessed, alerted, and awakened by the *krus* and the spirits of their ancestors. They carried messages and specific instructions among the holy men of different villages and to others serving under Sao Dae on the mountain. They spread word among the villagers, especially to those who were appointed communist officials, that any hint of the Awakening to the Viet Cong would bring instant death. For months the people were reminded that the more they were persecuted, the stronger they became. No matter what the *yuons* of either side did to them, they must "pretend like nothing was happening to them, and act calmly and meekly." Their time for revenge would come.

Only the *krus* and a few monks knew how many were involved in the plot and who they were. A number of loyal men were sent to join the Diem forces in Tri Ton, there to earn the respect of the government officers and begin secret negotiations with them for protection against Viet Cong reprisals when the uprising was carried out. For months the villagers waited patiently, watching for some sign from their leaders as they prepared for the rice harvest. The crop that year would be an unusually good one; the rains had held off in the final weeks; the rice stalks had changed from deep green to the dusty yellow of mature plants and were laden with grain. As always, the harvest began gradually, with small cooperative family groups starting in the paddies that had been planted first, girls and adult women reaping and the available males threshing.

In late December, at the peak of the harvest, Sao Dae assembled his soldiers on the mountain and told them to prepare to move out that night. In Ba The village, thirty kilometers to the southeast, Diem's soldiers had rounded up the people from scattered villages and remote hamlets and moved them into a central village, which the soldiers fenced and fortified with a well-protected emplacement at each of the four corners. Sao Dae had been ordered to drive the Diem soldiers out of Ba The. Leaving several of his Vietnamese cadre behind in each of the three villages to govern in his absence, Sao Dae led his three companies of Khmer Krom guerrillas south across the paddies and swamps under the cover of night.

They assaulted the Ba The village fortifications every night for five nights and each time were driven back, having done little damage, with few casualties on either side. On the sixth day a convoy of reinforcements for the village defenders arrived from the provincial capital. After one more assault, Sao Dae was forced to withdraw. He divided his three companies and ordered them to regroup and return to the mountains.

In spite of their failure to drive Diem's troops from his territory, Sao Dae praised his soldiers for their courage and discipline against overwhelming odds; he felt confident that in this first major engagement his troops had been blooded, had fought well together under his officers, and in the heat of the battle had been forged into a cohesive fighting unit. So when a ragged old Khmer Krom woman named Yin, with the shaved head of a temple attendant, teeth worn and rust-colored, appeared in his encampment on the evening before their night march back with a message for Reap, Sao Dae thought little of it.

The message came from *Kru* Kong, written by another in Vietnamese. "Dear Son," it said. "The harvest has been brought in. Your commander, companions, and you are invited to have a night of harvesting celebration that is organized by us. You will all be honored and entertained. But on the other hand, your mother is very sick. It is necessary that you come." The mention of his mother's illness was the prearranged authentication. The time had come.

Reap showed the letter to Sao Dae and begged him to honor the villagers with his presence at the festival. When the other soldiers joined him in his plea, asking that they too be allowed to go home for the festival, Sao Dae agreed, saying that he and his three officers would be happy to accept.

They walked all night and arrived at Phlao hamlet south of Coto village an hour after dawn. The hamlet was empty. From the village less than a kilometer away, could be heard "a big noise from thousands of people" who had assembled in the village center to begin their procession through the villages at the base of the mountain. Though they assured him that the commotion was only the beginning of the festival, Sao Dae sent Reap and his friend Sung to the village to be sure. Before they left, Reap nodded to Uchs, who also knew what to do.

The sheer size of the crowd that filled the village and spilled out onto the roads and footpaths as far as he could see filled Reap with a sense of pride and promise he'd never known. He felt dizzy with happiness. They were women and children, boys, old men and monks, all but the monks and the slightest armed with sharpened machetes, hatchets, and curved rice knives. From their midst came the muffled beat of the village drums near the temple grounds sounding the three rapid beats, the call to assembly, over and over again. Two young monks met Reap and Sung at the edge of the village and led them through the crowd to *Kru* Kong, who embraced Reap and blessed him.

"Is it done?" he asked.

Before Reap could reply, the crowd fell silent and parted to make way for Uchs and the other soldiers of Sao Dae's company who approached on the Phlao road behind three men bearing the freshly severed heads of Sao Dae and his two lieutenants aloft on bamboo poles. As planned, they marched through the crowd to the far side of the village to lead the procession on the road to Olam. With no commotion and little noise, the people fell in behind the soldiers and their grisly standards.

At the same time a similar procession marched out of An Tuc village toward Olam, bearing before it the heads of the two Vietnamese cadre Sao Dae had left behind in An Tuc. Before noon the two processions converged on Olam, whose people had gathered at the Pratheat monastery. There they learned that the Viet Cong cadre in Olam had gotten wind of the plot and fled the night before, leaving behind several weapons and a woman named Lang, whose head could be seen affixed to a pole held high above the throng of the people from Olam.

Kru Kong ascended a small platform in front of the monastery and motioned to the crowd to be seated. He told them it was a historic occasion and that that day, 2 January 1960, in the month of *Boh*, would live in Khmer Krom history forever. The people had risen up together, as one, to overthrow their oppressors just as their ancestors had done so many times before. Their plan had worked perfectly, as would their preparations against communist counterattacks. When the beat of the drums called them together as they had today, they would respond with the same speed and unity and would overcome their enemies in the same way. He warned them that they had only killed these tigers; many more still lurked in the forests; this is only the beginning, according to the signs that had been read. They were liberated, he said, but to stay free they must remain strong and united as Khmer Krom.

He paused, waited. The huge crowd became perfectly still. Only the severed heads high on the poles swayed slightly.

"Remember," he said, and paused for effect. "Don't spill the master's tea!"

The crowd thundered its response: "Don't spill the master's tea!"

When the people had dispersed, the men who had led the uprising met briefly. Uchs and Sem Ly agreed that they and their soldiers would flee to the mountains, there to hide and wait to see what would happen. Those like Reap, who chose to stay, should hide their weapons and their identities. What seemed an end to something, they'd soon realize, was only a beginning.

.

Now, almost ten years later, Uchs was telling me that an auspicious time for the Khmer Krom was at hand, thanks to us Americans. Reap listened, but exchanged a look with Strait that I could not read, but Strait certainly could. The Khmer Krom were much encouraged by the boldness of the American bombing. They had been worried by the news that some American troops were being sent home, and that the command of the Civilian Irregular Defense Group in the fighting camps was being turned over to Vietnamese officers, but now they believed that the Americans meant to win. That we would honor our promise to support them.

I accepted a Galloise from Uchs and a look from Strait that said be on your toes.

"As you know," Uchs said, "there are still battalions of Khmer Krom fighters in the mountains. And now they are interested in talking to the Americans." He paused, heavily.

I asked how many battalions there were, and where they were located.

There were two, or three, he said. But he didn't know where they were or how many men they had. He was sorry. And we both knew he was lying.

I offered to talk to my superiors to try to arrange a meeting between our authorities and their representatives. How would I communicate with them? I would have to go to Chau Doc to talk to the Americans there.

"When you have details, you can send Krech with a message." Uchs looked at Krech. "Send him to me or Lieutenant Reap. We will make arrangements.

"This is very good," Uchs said, placing a hand flat on the table. The guard without the axe produced a bottle of Hennessey's. Uchs patted his new wife on the bottom when she appeared with a garnished platter of chicken parts, the feet included.

•

An hour before the morning drum, Strait and I stood in the darkness in our boxers taking turns dousing ourselves with buckets of cold well water. It was the morning the Scouts and I were to return to Tri Ton. A horrible shape, a black flying reptile with a wing span of four feet, swooped by my head causing me to duck and almost fall.

"Goddamn fruit bat," said Strait. "The Khmers like to drink their blood here. They made me drink it once. I puked my guts out. I can't stand eating that blood."

While we dried ourselves and wrapped olive drab towels around our shoulders, I told him about the boy Krech killed the night we went to look for Xuan.

"It's been three weeks since you reported it?" Strait said. "Then nothing's gonna come of it. Just another one killed in action is all. But you can't let them do that here, if you can help it. You got to go along with some things, like drinking that goddamn blood and things, but some things you don't. You got to let them know shit like that's unsat. It's murder to us; to them it's just more of the same old killing here."

I said I had told them that things like that couldn't happen any more, and I thought Chau Got understood. I felt pretty sure.

"He was a Vietnamese, right, that kid? They'll do that if you let them. They'd rid the world of Vietnamese if they had the chance. Same same the other way around, don't forget that.

"Let's see what the ruckus is about there."

A group of men holding lamps aloft had gathered at the bunker around Reap and a ragged, emaciated little man. He was a *hoi chanh*, a defector; he held a leaflet that promised him fair treatment and a reward for his weapon. Some were patting him on the shoulder while he talked with Reap; others examined his ancient weapon, a Dochine Noir, and made jokes about it. When he saw Strait and me, the defector drew back, terrified, and even though the others assured him that we wouldn't eat him or chop off his head, he stayed well out of our reach.

The man was from the communists who had been driven from the mountain, Reap explained. He snuck away three nights ago. There were others who wanted to come too, but they were afraid.

"You know him?"

"Sure," said Reap. "He is Tunh. From Tapor hamlet over there."

Strait shook his head and smiled. He welcomed the man in Khmer, but the man only stared at him.

Reap said that the night before, Tunh had almost walked into their ambush at the canal. He had not seen them, but he had heard them slapping at mosquitoes and he had run away in the darkness.

"God damn it!" Strait exploded. He threw his arms up in the air and his towel fell down. The little group jumped and backed away from the enraged naked white man.

"What the fuck?" It was Sergeant Sirois, rudely awakened from his nap in a nearby crypt.

"What the fuck?" Strait asked. "I'll tell you what the fuck. You know how many times I've requested insect repellent here? I don't know how many. They give us hell for not having enough kills and then they turn around and tell us they can't come up with bug repellent. Not mortars, not a jeep, not machine guns—fucking bug repellent. I'm going to tear somebody a new asshole; I don't care what his rank is."

And all of us, even those who did not understand his words, believed he would do just that. Sirois rolled over and went back to sleep.

4

JOHN STRAIT SERVED his first tour in Vietnam in a Special Forces
fighting camp at An Phu just north of us on the border, between the Bassac
and Mekong Rivers. Like the many other Special Forces camps throughout
the country, An Phu was manned by mercenaries who were paid and commanded by American Special Forces officers and NCOs. Strait's troops at
An Phu had been Hoa Hao, survivors of President Diem's war to suppress the
ethnic minorities in the border regions. Diem's successor, President Nguyen
Van Thieu, had softened Diem's harsh policies against the Hoa Hao, Khmer
Krom, and Montagnard tribes; with promises of restored autonomy and a
greater say in his government, he hoped to win their loyalty and use them
to protect his vulnerable borders with Laos and Cambodia.

Though they did not trust the Vietnamese, the minorities were recruited
by American Special Forces to man the border camps under the authority of
the Civilian Irregular Defense Group, or CIDG. Like the camp at Ba Xoai,
which lay between our villages and the border and was manned by Khmer
Krom, their mission was to gather intelligence on the enemy buildup across
the border, and as fighting camps, to maintain the offensive against the enemy as they crossed the border. Officially, the command of the mercenaries
in the fighting camps was being turned over to the South Vietnamese Special Forces that year, but in practice, in spite of several mutinies of ethnic
troops, and contention and distrust between the Americans and Vietnamese, the mercenary battalions remained intact, loyal to their American officers. Their war was the Green Beret war of the early sixties, a war of counterinsurgency, of small units, of ambush, raid, and counterterror, using the
guerrilla's own tactics against him with great success.

When he signed on for his second tour in 1968, Strait was promised that
he could return to the 5th Special Forces Group, but the changing nature of
the American strategy altered his orders.

"They lied. When we got here they told the whole bunch of us, experienced officers and NCOs, that we were going to be assigned to Mobile Advisory Teams and go to some rinky-dink school for advisors. Only one guy,

a West Pointer, got to stay with Special Forces by knocking that ring some-
wheres. I've had a case of the ass here ever since."

Mobile Advisory Team 105, which Strait commanded in Olam village,
consisted of him and three NCOs. Their job was to advise and support the
local militia units in the rural areas that were "contested." As long as the
militia remained in the area, the South Vietnamese government could claim
that the villages were under its control, "pacified."

"It's bullshit of course and everybody knows it," Strait said. "These villages here, these mountains, aren't any more in our control than all the
others we claim. It's a goddamn Mexican standoff. You watch. The Mike
Force took the mountain and they're up there now, but pretty soon they'll
be gone, all those lives fucking wasted, and the VC will be back in the caves
lobbing shells at us. We can't hold these villages with less than three hundred men, with half-ass weapons, no artillery, no air support, not even a
heavy mortar or recoilless rifle, not even a goddamn fifty-caliber machine
gun here, not even bug repellent."

The Mobile Strike Force, or Mike Force, that had spent so many months
and so much American, Montagnard, and Khmer Krom blood taking the
mountain would be returning to its base camp within the week, or so Strait
had been told. Before they left, Strait and Reap hoped to have at least a
skeletal fortification of the village in place, and with the other two company commanders, Uchs and Sem Ly, a coordinated system of patrols and
ambushes in operation. They rotated their men so that the half who were
not filling sandbags for bunkers and digging defensive trenches could be
working in the rice paddies and helping rebuild the villages.

I went with Strait and Reap on an informal inspection tour of their
meager defensive perimeter. Sinh, who could have been at home, and Cop,
whose interpreting wasn't needed, followed along anyway, lost in their
own conversation. With pomade and perfume as bait, they were trolling for
girls. Everywhere we went, packs of noisy half-naked children followed at
our heels. They had seen me once before but were still shy of me. They
nipped and chattered at the long ambling Strait, vying for his attention, taking his hand, asking for candy, pinching his ass. When Reap shooed them
away, they retreated, then soon scampered back. In the small flooded seed
beds on the edges of the hamlets, the women gathered seedlings for trans-
planting, while the men repaired dikes and rode behind their water buffa-
loes harrowing the larger paddies. Bent over in rows, their sarongs tucked
up between their legs, the young girls in a seed bed near a bunker we had
stopped to inspect sang to one another in impromptu verses that teased and

mimicked. A light-skinned sergeant paused in the placing of a heavy palm trunk on the roof of the bunker to proudly explain to Reap how he had set his aiming stakes and cleared the area to his front for fields of fire. Strait stood listening, one huge hand cradling the neck of the little boy who held on to his pant leg.

Strait and Reap had started out using an interpreter assigned to them by headquarters. Strait could tell that Reap liked him, even trusted him, but every time he had made a suggestion through the interpreter, Reap had responded sullenly, and without saying anything, had ignored or overlooked what Strait had said. Strait asked Staff Sgt. Richard Sirois, the team medic, who had spent his previous tour with a Khmer Krom battalion at the Ba Xoai camp and could speak Khmer fairly well, to sit with him and Reap and their interpreter. Sirois reported that the interpreter, a Vietnamese sergeant, was translating Strait's suggestions as orders, using vocabulary and tone reserved for an inferior. Strait sent the interpreter's ass packing, and with Sirois at first, then alone, he and Reap worked out a patois of English, Vietnamese, and Khmer. Strait learned Khmer quickly and within two months Reap could speak English well enough to call in an air strike on the radio.

First Reap, then Strait, congratulated the beaming sergeant, who saluted them, then bowed in gratitude.

"They couldn't stop a goddamned Girl Scout troop if it wanted to get in here," Strait told me. "Nothing but carbines and a few grenades, no radio to call for mortar fire."

I said they seemed confident enough. I wouldn't want to have to assault that bunker over open ground. Strait smiled and turned to follow Reap.

"Oh, don't listen to me. I bitch all the time here. Right, Reap?"

Reap put his arm around Strait's waist. "Bitch, bitch, bitch," he said.

"You give these Khmers their villages back, give them weapons, no matter how shitty, and their own officers, and they don't want much more. Yeah, they're confident. They'll fight like goddamn wild men here, with their families at their backs. They hate the fucking Vietnamese communists with a passion, worse than I even do; they're happy with a half-ass chance to fight them. I'm not bitching about Reap and these men, I'm bitching about the sorry bureaucrats and high-ups who won't supply them. Right, Reap?"

"They are also happy because there are no *yuons* here," Reap said. "Only Khmer Krom."

•

Reap didn't follow his family home to Coto village when *Kru* Kong had finished his speech after the uprising ten years before. He buried his weapon
in a cache of unhulled rice his cousins had hidden from the tax collectors,
and went to Tri Ton to stay with Sok Meas in his little house not far from
the temple. There he stayed hidden for weeks, listening and waiting. As a
leader of the uprising and a killer of communists, he might expect to be
greeted with some appreciation by the Diem officials in the headquarters
compound, but he was cautious, reluctant to trust anyone until he heard
whether or not the promises of protection for the villages made to *Kru* Kong
and his agents by the Diem government in Tri Ton would be fulfilled.

At that time, Diem had one battalion of troops in the Tri Ton district to
cover the entire region of the Seven Mountains along the border; it consisted of about two hundred men, 70 percent Khmer Krom, 30 percent Vietnamese. The district chief, a Vietnamese major from a far-off province, responded to *Kru* Kong's request for protection for the three villages by
sending Lt. Pham Duc Long to Coto village with a company of about thirty
men. When he did so, he and his commanding officer, the province chief in
Chau Doc, claimed the three villages for the South Vietnamese, a fine
feather for both their caps. Reap and the others in hiding returned to their
villages when Lieutenant Pham had established himself at Wat Triek in Coto
village.

Pham, a North Vietnamese Catholic who had come south with Diem's
other Catholic repatriates in 1954, was described as a fair man, with a fiercely loyal contingent of fellow Vietnamese Catholics serving as his NCOs; he
was a rabid anticommunist who, like the Buddhist monks in the villages,
loathed the Viet Cong for their disdain for religion.

The communists who remained in hiding in the mountains were quiet,
but reports from woodcutters, peasant travelers, and people with relatives
still with the communists made it clear to Pham and the villagers that the
infiltration from Cambodia across the border into the mountains was increasing. Within less than a year, the Viet Cong in the Seven Mountains region were strong enough to resume their attacks on villages and towns
throughout the district. Cam and Giai Mountains, the larger "sisters" to the
north of Coto, were soon serving as staging areas inside Vietnam for communist infiltration. The cave systems in the mountains began to fill up with
supplies carried across the border at night. The immortal Chau Kem, it was
said, was back on Coto Mountain and gaining strength. Pham did not dare
split his company to try to protect all three villages, even though the
people of Olam and An Tuc begged him for protection against reprisal. In

the first month of the first harvest after the uprising, a communist company came to Olam for vengeance. They knew from informants that *Kru* Eo had been instrumental in the uprising. Pricking and stabbing him with bayonets, laughing derisively, they drove the old man to the village well and drowned him there, to show, they said, that the Khmer Krom leaders had polluted their own villages.

The men of the three villages soon realized that Lieutenant Pham was not going to go after the communists, but would concentrate on defending his own outpost. Inspired by *Kru* Kong, the Khmer Krom went after the Viet Cong themselves, raiding their hiding places in the jungles and caves, which they knew so well.

"We chased them and broke them up and destroyed their bases," Reap said. The communists in the Seven Mountains region withdrew across the border to their sanctuaries, and there was "about four months of peace" in the villages. But only four months.

When the communists returned reinforced, "they disturbed us worse than we disturbed them. They surrounded the villages, burned out the defensive fences, the outposts, killed the guards, and caught all men and women that they thought were the leaders of the uprising. The villagers were all suffering again, and Pham Duc Long and his men were not able to help at all."

Neang Ly was nine years old at the time, living with her family in Tapor hamlet. She remembered the months following the uprising as a time of increasing fear. Lieutenant Pham and his men were "fair to the people when they first came, and treated them with kindness." But as the communists increased in strength, and began to come to the villages at night as they had in the past, Lieutenant Pham and his men became more and more afraid, and "their morals changed." They thought the villagers were helping the Viet Cong and would not believe otherwise. Slowly the men who had been involved in the uprising began to slip away to hiding in the forests, followed by the young men of draft age.

Attacks on the government outpost at Wat Triek and the other villages were light at first, but became "louder and louder." When the communists forced the people of Coto and Olam villages to stage a demonstration against Lieutenant Pham's little garrison, Pham's troops panicked and fired on the crowd, killing several. Afterwards most of the women and children fled to Phnom Den across the Cambodian border, joining thousands of other Khmer Krom refugees and abandoning their ancestral homes and their fathers and brothers in the forests with "too much crying."

Armed only with *phkak*, the long machete-like knives they had used to behead Sao Dae, fifteen ancient French weapons with ten rounds each they had been issued by the Diem government, and the weapons they had retrieved from hiding, the little bands of Khmer Krom men and boys from the three villages were once again living in the mountains and vast swamps of the border region. This time they were hiding not only from the government troops, but also from the ever-increasing numbers of Viet Cong who were also using the mountains and swamps as refuge. In tiny bands at first, the Khmer Krom moved by night and holed up in little defensive perimeters at dawn. They lived in constant motion, avoiding contact with the communist guerrilla bands whenever possible, often sharing one of the mountains with them without being detected. From the villages they received their meager supplies of rice and, equally important, news of other Khmer Krom groups. Gradually, thanks to an information network established by four monks and a teacher in widespread hamlets, they made contact with other disparate groups and joined together in larger and larger bands. Outlawed by the government as communist sympathizers and hunted by the Viet Cong as traitors, they slowly formed companies of their own, gathering weapons and ammunition from raids and ambushes against small units of "both *yuons.*"

The largest and best known of the Khmer Krom bands was the *Con Sen Sar*, or White Scarves, led by *Kru* Samouk Seng. Seng was a native of Phnom Pi hamlet of Coto village, a distant relative of Chau Got. Like the nineteenth century Khmer mystic Po Kambo, and Huynh Phu So, the religious leader of the Hoa Hao sect who was disemboweled by the Viet Minh, Seng dwelt as an ascetic at the Pagoda of the Burning Hillside and there practiced acupuncture and ritual magic. His followers were called White Scarves after the white prayer shawls that *Kru* Seng made for them. While he chanted Brahmanic mantras that imbued his action with both the power of the Hindu gods and the strength of the ancestral and forest spirits, *Kru* Seng drew intricate protective designs on the shawls, which would protect the wearer and make him brave in combat. The same was done with tattoos that covered the chests of his followers. The intricate design, which was usually built outward around a central Pali syllable, included images of Buddha, prayers and incantations in Pali, Sanskrit, and Khmer, drawings of spirit creatures, and cabalistic phrases. The shawl or tattoo, or both in many cases, was effective only if it had been prepared for the wearer by *Kru* Seng, and only if the wearer adhered to the code of conduct called *sila* and remained loyal to him. Called suicidal by some, the White Scarves were known for their cold tenacity in combat; as anticommunists, the group, though small, was the best known of the Khmer Krom independent battalions, and was supported by Sihanouk.

By mid-1960 there were an estimated six hundred Khmer Krom soldiers in companies of about sixty each operating in the mountains on both sides of the border in the Seven Mountains region. In other parts of the Mekong Delta—Tay Ninh, Ha Tien, and Loc Ninh—groups of similar size had formed, made up of Khmer Krom refugees from villages, towns, and military units of both sides. Their intelligence and spiritual leadership came from the monks and men like *Kru* Seng and *Kru* Kong; in the forests and mountains they were commanded by men with experience such as Uchs, Reap, and Sem Ly. With little food and inadequate weapons, they could only hide and wait for an opportunity of some kind. They saw no hope for their future with Diem or the communists; from their mountain strongholds, they sent emissaries to Phnom Penh, seeking assistance, or at least assurance, from their Khmer kin.

They learned that the voluble Sihanouk was enjoying a rare period of unopposed power. Earlier in the year the prince had called for a national referendum, and his overwhelming victory was certain. Like the Angkor King Jayavarman VII, with whom his sycophants compared him, Sihanouk was revered by the peasantry. In his long, emotional speeches, he reminded his people that any attack on him was an attack on Cambodia herself. He would protect his people from their enemies, the Thai in the west and the Vietnamese in the east; most importantly, Cambodia would remain neutral in the war between the two Vietnams, and would be a puppet of neither China nor the United States. When elephants fight, he said, the grass gets trampled.

As the ancient Angkor kings well knew, it is one thing to control the peasantry, another to control the educated elite in the cities. By 1960, Sihanouk had endured years and years of plots and counterplots, conspiracies, and attempted coups in Phnom Penh, and had prevailed, at least temporarily. Put simply, he controlled the bureaucracy and the army; he was both monarch, with all the supernatural power that the people associated with the palace, and head of state, with political control of the government in Phnom Penh. The king, Cambodian folklore says, is like the tree and the people are like the vine that grows on it. The tree provides support for the vine, which cannot grow otherwise, and the vine provides protection for the tree.

The leaders of the fledgling Khmer communist movement either had been co-opted by Sihanouk's government or had gone into hiding with the

Vietnamese communists. Sihanouk's old enemy, Son Ngoc Thanh, still led the Khmer Serei, or Free Khmer, opposition, but it was limited to anti-government radio broadcasts from outposts on the Thai and Vietnamese borders. The broadcasts denounced Sihanouk's government as corrupt and soft on communism; they were encouraged by Thai Premier Sarit Thanarat and Diem and financed in part by the CIA. Accused of plots against Sihanouk's life and of fomenting rebellion, Son Ngoc Thanh had to flee once more to the Thai border and was condemned to death in absentia.

Gen. Lon Nol, the minister of defense and commander of the army, was fiercely loyal to Sihanouk and the throne, having for the time set his own political ambitions aside. Like Sihanouk and Thanh, Lon Nol had been educated in Saigon at the Lycée Chasseloup Labat. He was a Khmer Krom from the Cambodian province of Prey Veng on the Vietnamese border. Unlike Thanh and his other educated peers who were also Khmer Krom, Lon Nol still practiced with deep conviction the Buddhist/animist religion he had learned from the *krus* in his native village. His power came from the army, over which he had complete control. Before his peasant soldiers he was proud of his dark complexion, which was proof of his untainted Khmer lineage. They called him "Black Papa," a nickname the intellectual elite in Phnom Penh spoke with disdain. The Khmer *sangha*, or priesthood, revered Lon Nol as their protector.

Initially, some of the Khmer Krom leaders hoped for assistance from the Khmer Serei in the border mountains nearby. Son Ngoc Thanh was a Khmer Krom from Tra Vinh Province and was sympathetic to the plight of the men in the mountains. But at that time Thanh was struggling to keep his own movement alive, and had as yet precious little support from the CIA. More importantly, the Khmer Krom leaders realized, an alliance of any kind with the Khmer Serei would deny them forever any hope of assistance from Sihanouk.

For months Khmer Krom messengers traveled back and forth on the roads and waterways of the Mekong Delta and southern Cambodia carrying memorized instructions and evolving plans to monks in Ha Tien, Rach Gia, and Tra Vinh; to soldiers in the mountains of Chau Doc, Tay Ninh, and Cambodia; to government representatives in Phnom Penh and Takeo; and to clandestine meetings all across the delta region. Unconfirmed reports from agents in Saigon held that the U.S. mission there was exploring plans to arm the Rhade tribe of Montagnards in the central highlands, feeding Khmer Krom dreams of American assistance. Hopes of support from Sihanouk rose, fell, and finally, in early March of 1960, rose again when invitations to a meeting with a "prominent man" in the Phnom Penh government were sent out to the Khmer Krom leadership.

The meetings were held in secret in a hamlet at the foot of Mount Propeal, the Cambodian name for Cam Mountain, the "sister" just north of Tri Ton and the Coto villages. Propeal is the largest of the Seven Mountains, for centuries a home of fearful dark spirits and a refuge for men outside the law. It is the mountain on which the *Aysey*, the messiah made flesh, often appeared. There dozens of Khmer Krom chieftains and spiritual leaders formed the *Front de Lutte du Kampuchea Krom*, the Front for the Struggle of the Khmer Krom, or FLKK. Commissioners were appointed to publicize the plight of the Khmer Krom, recruit members, propagate Khmer Krom art, education, and culture, create an administrative staff, maintain a headquarters, and organize and train the guerrilla bands in hiding. The "prominent man" who had come from Phnom Penh used the nom de guerre Chau Dara, meaning Bright Star. Only a few of the chieftains who met at Propeal knew his true identity, but all the Khmer Krom, following their *krus*, swore allegiance to him. Chau Dara and his assistant Thach Chanh would provide leadership, money, and arms. The monks present, led by the Venerable Chau Ta Hong, chairman of the "Cult Committee," would provide spiritual guidance and blessings. Samouk Seng, of the White Scarves, was appointed treasurer and minister of propaganda. A flag of three horizontal bands was designed: blue for "freedom and democracy," white for the "Khmer Krom nation and its resolve," and red for the commitment to the "struggle to defend their ethnicity."

Their official or national seal later became a depiction of the giant Hindu dragon-god Reahou in the process of devouring the moon. Reahou so loves Buddha-being-Moon that he always wants to swallow him and make him his soul. When he does swallow Buddha-being-Moon, and the moon goes dark in eclipse, the Khmer Krom celebrate the loving union as a sign of good harvests and peace.

·

Sinh and Cop had heard of the FLKK, of course, but that evening in Olam they were far more interested in chasing sarongs in the village. Sinh was eighteen, with strong white teeth and a wave of fine black hair that made the girls' eyes roll when he combed it back. He had given his cousins all his money to care for his mother, but still they pestered him for more, driving him crazy, so he had left them and come to join us. He admired the urbane Cop so much that he not only affected his hairstyle, but tried, not very successfully, to copy the way he rolled his shoulders when he walked. The three of us, he told me, would go to the festival that night to watch, and to pick out girls.

Under the full moon called *Kattick* in the Khmer lunar system, the villagers hold festivals to venerate the moon. In one of his incarnations before attaining enlightenment, the Buddha was born as a rabbit. He was kind and generous to all other living things and would give up anything, even his life, to help others. His selflessness was soon known in all the three worlds of Humans, Heavens, and Brahma. When Indra, the king of Heaven, heard about Buddha's generosity, he took the form of a giant and came to earth to test Buddha-being-Rabbit by asking him for his flesh as food. Hearing this, Buddha-being-Rabbit was greatly pleased and told Indra to build a fire. When he jumped into the fire to offer his flesh to Indra, the earth shook and a huge lotus flower sprouted beneath him, bearing him above the flames. Indra was so surprised and amazed that he created the moon with the image of Buddha upon it, so that all could see him and be reminded of his selflessness.

Chief of the events is *Ook Om Bok*, the ceremony of eating rice flakes, Buddha-being-Rabbit's favorite food. By late afternoon the wide shaded area in front of the temple pavilion was aswarm with people, mostly women and children. The women were thin, some with blackened eyes, others with sunken cheeks; their clothing was patched and tattered at the edges. Around their children, who seemed not so emaciated, the women hovered like wary brood hens. Many people were hanging colored rice-paper lanterns on the pavilion and trees around, but most had gathered around the village center, where an audience of children seated on the ground in rows watched three older women prepare rice flakes. The sight and smell of the sweet flakes and other foods had some of the children in a barely contained nervous ecstasy, while others just stared with mouths wide open like hungry chicks. One of the women roasted sweet rice in a large frying pan and spooned it into the two huge stone mortars, where it was pounded into flakes by the other women. With one hand they pounded the rice with a large pestle, with the other they stirred, between them creating a constant soft rhythm to which they and the seated children swayed. Near the children sat a half dozen grandmothers and grandfathers, before whom lay bowls of the Rabbit's other favorite foods: bananas, potatoes, and coconut. Four elderly monks sat smoking serenely beneath the pavilion; Cop, Sinh, and I watched from our seats on a stone stair.

When the grinding was done, the eldest of the women, with close-cropped hair and a maroon blouse, set a wide bowl with a mound of sweet flakes in the midst of the other food. The noise of the crowd dropped to whispers and giggles as one of the grandfathers called out his grandson's name. With a little push from his mother, a boy of about seven came forward and sat before the food, facing the elders. Another name was called, this time a little girl's by her grandmother, then two others until four kids, giggling nervously but not daring to look away, sat in a row.

Loudly, so everyone could hear, the first boy's grandfather asked him what he wanted to be when he grew up. As soon as the boy answered that he wanted to be a rich farmer the grandfather put a banana coated with rice flakes into his mouth, filling it. Before the boy could chew, his cheeks puffed out like a monkey's, the old man asked him where he wanted to live. When the boy responded with a noise through a mouthful of sweet mush, the crowd laughed and applauded, and the grandfather pushed another piece of banana into his mouth. Next the little girl in the white blouse, with short hair and hoops of gold in her ears—what did she want to be, her grandmother asked? She wanted to be the wife of a teacher. Laughter, applause, and a mouthful of flakes and potato. When she tried to answer the second question, even the old ones laughed at the noise she made; the woman in maroon clasped her hands under her chin and crowed with delight.

Cop turned to Sinh and in the same sing-song voice the grandparents were using, asked him what *he* wanted.

Sinh wanted to fly to America in a helicopter and buy a car there, a Mustang convertible like the blue one we saw on the back of a magazine.

What did Cop want? Cop wanted the girl by the well, the one whose breasts pushed against her blouse, but she saw us looking at her and ducked behind her friends.

5

ONE OF THE conclusions of a study done by the U.S. mission in Saigon in 1961 was that the Diem government should reverse its policy of oppression of ethnic minorities and recruit them for the government side. The ethnic groups such as the Khmer Krom in the border regions of the delta, the Montagnards in the central highlands north of Saigon, and the religious minorities, the Hoa Hao and Cao Dai, in the border region west of Saigon, all previously oppressed and disarmed by Diem, were particularly vulnerable to Viet Cong propaganda for very good reasons. The Montagnards, a collective term used by the French for the many tribes of mountain people in the Annamese Cordillera, were made up principally of the Rhade, Hre, and Jarai tribes and numbered about 800,000. All the minority groups were located in regions crucial to communist infiltration, and President Diem, though he denied it to CIA Station Chief William Colby at the time, knew that the situation in the highlands and border areas of the delta was precarious at best for his troops. He lacked control over regions that could provide springboards for larger operations against his cities and lowland populations, and he was denied valuable intelligence from these staging areas.

The CIA's effort to recruit the ethnic minorities began in Buon Enaoa, a Rhade village near Ban Me Thuot in the central highlands. In weeks of discussion with village leaders, a paramilitary CIA officer and an American Special Forces medic promised the Rhade arms and supplies if they would turn their villages into garrisons against the communists and declare their loyalty to the Diem government. The Rhade agreed: they swore allegiance to the government and declared that no communist would enter their fortified village. A "strike force" was formed and trained by American CIA and Special Forces officers with assistance from an American-trained Vietnamese Special Forces team. First called the Village Defense Program, the experiment at Buon Enaoa was so successful that it soon spread to two hundred other Montagnard villages, and became known as the Civilian Irregular Defense Group. The CIDG forces were led by Vietnamese Special Forces and advised by American Special Forces "A" teams. The villages became heavily armed and well-supplied camps with militia, mountain scouts for surveillance, trail watchers, medical workers, and "strike forces" for offensive operations against the communists along the borders.

The CIDG program grew so large that the CIA turned it over to the Army's Military Advisory Command. The emphasis shifted from armed self-defense of tribal villages to the securing and building of CIDG camps along the entire western border of Vietnam for surveillance and counterinsurgency. Each camp was manned by "indigenous" or ethnic troops and trained and led by American Special Forces teams; its mission: to gather intelligence and interrupt communist infiltration into South Vietnam. Word soon spread among the Khmer Krom that those who joined the CIDG forces were better paid than regular government troops, were armed with superior American weapons and supported by air and firepower, and though under nominal Vietnamese control, were commanded by Americans.

Camps were being built in Khmer Krom territory from north of Saigon to Ha Tien at the southern end of the Vinh Te Canal, manned by Nungs, some Montagnards, and increasingly, ethnic Khmer Krom recruited by Special Forces officers. And as the camps proliferated, Diem's government and its officers in the provinces and districts where the camps were built began to turn a wary eye on the CIDG program, which was training and arming groups of ethnic soldiers whose loyalty to the South Vietnamese government was suspect, who might one day, under certain conditions, become independent armies.

They had good reason for their concern. The Khmer Krom were watching the CIDG program with great interest. Under the FLKK, the Khmer Krom forces maintained the integrity of their units in the mountains and hinterlands, but sent many of their number to join the CIDG. The temptations of better weapons, generous pay, and the chance to serve in Khmer Krom units in their homeland were great; but for the time being they were offset by the fact that Vietnamese officers were in nominal control of the CIDG units and the government might at any time disperse the minorities in the camps. The Vietnamese officers of the CIDG and the ethnic recruits they called *moi*, or primitives, were hostile allies, barely held together by their American advisors and the common threat of the communists.

In September 1961, after months of secret negotiations, leaders of seventeen "nations," including all the ethnic minority groups and highland tribes in South Vietnam, met in Phnom Penh with Sihanouk and delegates from Hanoi and the Viet Cong. The Diem government was invited to attend, but declined. Les Kasem, the leader of the Cham independence movement, and Y Baham of the Montagnard peoples were the prime movers. The FLKK was represented by Sang Sar Iam. In three days of meetings, attended by Sihanouk and Vietnamese communist delegates, the leaders of the minority groups laid the groundwork for the formation of the *Front Unifié de Lutte des Races Opprimées*, the Unified Fighting Front of the Oppressed Races, or FULRO. At the close of the conference, the delegates signed a document that guaranteed that the ethnic minorities could pursue their united struggle for self-determination, equal rights, and cultural identity without interference from Cambodia or the Vietnamese communists. Their names, languages, religious practices, and unique cultures would not only be honored by the two powers present, but would be protected whenever possible. In an atmosphere of promise and possibility for their various peoples and their united front, the representatives chose delegates to travel to Washington and present the FULRO case to President Kennedy some time before the end of the year.

After the conference, the Khmer Krom units in the Seven Mountains and other provinces, notably Tay Ninh, consolidated as four battalions of five hundred to six hundred men each. Under the leadership of Chau Dara, who was increasingly generous with arms and supplies, the officers and men of the small army flew the flag of the FLKK in their mountain strongholds. The followers of *Kru* Kong and *Kru* Seng, among others, formed the 106th Battalion of the FLKK in the Seven Mountains region.

Reap and Uchs, leaders of the Coto village uprising three years before, now commanded companies of the 106th Battalion on Coto and Giai Mountains under Sang Sar Iam, the FLKK delegate to the FULRO conference. The families of the men from the three villages at Coto Mountain returned from exile in Cambodia, given safe passage and transportation by Lon Nol's army.

In 1962 Reap was ordered by Sang to make contact with the team of American "advisors" stationed at Wat Krang. He did so by sending messages to his cousin, Sing, who was an interpreter for the American advisory team in Tri Ton. They chose a neutral site, a knoll on the south slope of Nui Cam. There the American explained to Reap that his mission was not to arm or supply the Khmer Krom, but to train them to "protect themselves and their villages." He could, however, recruit them as American mercenaries to fight the communists who were coming across the border. Hopeful but cautious, Sang Sar Iam sent four men to join the Americans "for the purpose of finding out the truth of what the American said." But the four were soon under investigation by the South Vietnamese secret police and had to return to the 106th Battalion before they were compromised.

The hopes the Khmer Krom had placed in the FULRO agreement faded fast. The raids on their villages and encampments by the Viet Cong did not cease as the communist delegates had promised; if anything, they increased. "The signature the North Vietnamese signed on the paper was useless," Reap said. "They never practiced what they agreed upon. Instead the NVA ordered their troops to search and destroy us in any place or anywhere we appeared." The Americans at Wat Krang were driven back to Tri Ton and the 106th Khmer Krom Battalion waited and watched from the mountains.

At the same time, the flagging Diem government launched its Chieu Hoi or Open Arms program. Leaflets dropped on the mountains promised to welcome any defector to the South Vietnamese government with open arms, amnesty, and financial rewards for weapons brought in. A typical leaflet, written in Vietnamese, extolled the democratic and economic promises of the South Vietnamese, berated the communists as oppressors and enemies of Buddhism, and offered 17,500 piastres for an AK 47, 20,000 for a B-40 rocket launcher. Officially the Chieu Hoi Program targeted individuals: communists who had been drafted or recruited and taken from their home villages, and were suffering doubt and extreme physical hardship, especially lack of medical care. Many leaflets bore photographs of "returnees" receiving medical care or employed in civilian jobs. Further rewards were offered to returnees who could persuade their former comrades to change sides: so much money paid for a heavy weapons expert, so much more for a village security chief.

Officials of the Diem government in Chau Doc and other Khmer Krom provinces sent emissaries to the FLKK leaders of the battalions in the mountains with assurance that they and their soldiers, though not communists, were eligible for all the benefits of the Chieu Hoi Program should they surrender individually with their weapons and join the Army of the Republic of Vietnam. The opportunity to serve under one enemy to fight against another was politely refused by the FLKK. Instead, they "continued to fight both *yuons*."

•

On 1 November 1963 President Diem was overthrown in a coup and assassinated by American military clients in the South Vietnamese army. Though perhaps not sponsored by the CIA, the coup was encouraged and abetted by the agency. In Phnom Penh, Prince Sihanouk greeted the news of the death of President Diem, who had been supporting his enemy Son Ngoc Thanh, with both satisfaction and apprehension: satisfied because he could now attack Thanh's forces in South Vietnam without fear of retaliation from the Diem government; apprehensive because his misgivings about the quality of

American loyalty to its clients in Indochina had become a frightening reality.

Since the Geneva Conference nine years before, Sihanouk had been receiving American economic and military aid amounting to about 25 million dollars a year, or approximately 14 percent of his country's revenue. But with the aid came conditions and consequences that Sihanouk found increasingly intolerable. American diplomats and Foreign Service officers in Cambodia, reflecting the single-minded Cold War anticommunist climate in Washington, considered Sihanouk's efforts to keep his country neutral dangerously "soft on communism"—even hostile to the efforts of the Free World to stop the Soviets, supporting the North Vietnamese, and the Chinese, supporting the Viet Cong, from devouring first Vietnam, then all of Indochina. Sihanouk was said to be "cozy" with both Moscow and Peking. Though he denied it publicly to his own countrymen and the rest of the world, he knew that the North Vietnamese were using neutral Cambodia to transport supplies and men from north to south, and were establishing safe base areas in his border provinces in direct support of the insurgency in South Vietnam.

Sihanouk found the American diplomats condescending and duplicitous. He believed them incapable of understanding him and his country, much less the situation in Southeast Asia. Restrictions on American military aid he found insulting, and he believed that the anti-American de Gaulle government in France, which was secretly supplying him with economic aid at the time, and the Chinese would together make good the loss of American aid, both happy to "de-Americanize" Indochina. Cutting off relations with America would weaken the pro-Western right wing of military leaders and capitalist elite in his own country led by Lon Nol and Sirik Matak, and cooperation with Hanoi and Peking, he hoped, would silence his enemies on the left, the fledgling Khmer communists whom he derisively called the "Khmer Rouges."

That week Sihanouk's congress agreed overwhelmingly to support his renunciation of American aid and to nationalize Cambodian foreign trade and banks in an effort to overcome severe economic problems and wrest financial power from the Sino-Khmer merchants and the urban elite so loathed by the rural poor, his children. This "socialization" would also appeal to his allies, who could provide aid in lieu of American dollars.

On 20 November, when President Kennedy learned of Sihanouk's denunciation, he was puzzled. How could Sihanouk break off relations with the U.S. because of radio broadcasts by Son Ngoc Thanh's Khmer Serei, whom he had never heard of? He learned that the CIA and State Department had indeed been supporting the Khmer Serei, and he made plans to send Dean Acheson to Phnom Penh to talk with Sihanouk. The matter was set aside for a few days while Kennedy traveled to Dallas.

Two weeks after the Kennedy assassination, Sihanouk's old enemy Field Marshal Sarit Thanarat, the premier of Thailand, died. Sihanouk announced a period of celebration, with public entertainment at the royal palace. "At two-week intervals our enemies have departed one after the other. At first the one in the south, Diem, then the great boss Kennedy, and now the one in the west, Sarit. All three have always sought to violate our neutrality and make trouble for us, to seek our misfortune. Now they are all going to meet in hell, where they will be able to build military bases for SEATO. Our other enemies will join them. The gods punish all the enemies of neutral and peaceful Cambodia. The spirits of our former kings protect us."

The American ambassador to the United Nations called the speech "barbaric." Sihanouk responded to this "gratuitous insult" by recalling the Cambodian diplomatic mission.

"Americans are shit," he announced.

Soon after the institution of the prince's economic initiatives, the Bank of Phnom Penh failed and its director sought political asylum in Saigon. The nationalization of the bank and other enterprises was a blow to the wealthy elite and hence a source of satisfaction for the masses and amusement for Sihanouk. The loyal government servants he appointed to take control of the new state enterprises were without experience and as corrupt as the capitalists they replaced. With no evident improvement in the economy, Sihanouk's initiatives served only to further alienate the pro-Western businessmen in his cities.

His military and its leadership suffered even worse. American aid had provided not only salaries for its soldiers, but crucial arms and equipment. As the hardware deteriorated and was not replaced, and soldiers went unpaid, the army degenerated. The weapons and equipment supplied by communist countries were of poor quality, few in number, and not interchangeable with the American arms. Resentment among the military leadership increased dramatically. When Sihanouk made a secret agreement with Hanoi to use his army to transport Chinese weapons and ammunition from the port at Sihanoukville to the Vietnamese communist staging areas on the border inside Cambodia, he and his officers were given 10 percent of the military goods in payment. Many Cambodian officers made their fortunes from this 10 percent, but in doing so, they would later admit, they undermined their own morale. They'd been long used to many forms of corruption in Cambodian life, but they had never before lined their own pockets with money from *yuons* or communists.

Sihanouk's break with the Americans, and the consequences for his military, was a double blow to Lon Nol, the commander-in-chief. He and Sihanouk's pro-Western cousin, Prince Sirik Matak, remained ostensibly loyal to Sihanouk, even while he drifted to the left. Privately, they struggled to keep the Cambodian army as healthy as possible under the new conditions and kept a suspicious eye on the Vietnamese communist sanctuaries that were growing and proliferating in their border regions, including Lon Nol's home province of Prey Vieng.

•

While the Khmer Krom battalions were still independent, arms, ammunition, and supplies being smuggled to them from Chau Dara inside Cambodia increased in quantity, but were still sparse. The Khmer Serei under Son Ngoc Thanh were better equipped, receiving their support from Thanh's "American friends," presumably the CIA through the 5th Special Forces Group. Khmer Serei delegates visited the FLKK in the mountains and invited them to join the Khmer Serei, but the FLKK remained loyal to Chau Dara, their leaders, and their declared goals. Thanh, they believed, was eager for power for himself, whereas Chau Dara sought only the restoration of Khmer Krom land and freedom. Son Ngoc Thanh lived in Saigon and had a Vietnamese wife. Chau Dara was a holy man, a godlike warrior, a pure Khmer in flesh and in spirit, perhaps even *Aysey* himself, incarnate.

Split into companies of several hundred men each, the Khmer Krom in the border region lived a meager existence in the forest. They slept in hammocks beneath tarps. Like the Vietnamese communists moving into their staging areas on the Cambodian side of the border, they depended on the Khmer Krom villages for rice for which they could not pay. They foraged for food in the forest, eating grubs and snakes, roots and leaves; without medicines of any kind, they were frequently ill and were often infested with debilitating intestinal worms.

They raided communist encampments or ambushed carrying parties for weapons and supplies. They often hired out to the American Special Forces in the CIDG camps, earning the title "gunmen" and a reputation as bandits. The Green Berets who dealt with the Khmer Krom in the early sixties generally mistrusted them and scorned them for lack of military discipline and ignorance of tactics. The Green Berets thought that anyone anywhere who was not anticommunist was an enemy and that a man who fought for money rather than ideals was less than honorable. They made a point of referring to the Khmer Krom as the KKK and relished the negative connotation.

One of the stories often told in Special Forces clubs and billets at the time, which Robin Moore included as a chapter in his book *The Green Berets* with some name changes, was about Capt. Larry Thorne. In it Captain Thorne outsmarts a villainous fictional version of Captain Uchs, who is described as the "KKK chief."

When the old French border outpost they had rebuilt and fortified proved to be an easy target for the Viet Cong mortarmen in the mountains around it, Captain Thorne moved his "A" team of two officers and three enlisted men to a new site. The South Vietnamese authorities, fearing another uprising, took away his 250 trained Hoa Hao mercenaries and dispersed them in Vietnamese main force units. Captain Thorne found himself and his team building a new camp, and recruiting and training new troops at the same time. He had about a hundred Vietnamese Mike Force soldiers and an equal number of Khmer Krom recruits. The new camp, called "Phan Chau" in the story, was a mile from the Cambodian border and four miles south of a communist-controlled Vietnamese village called "Chau Lu." Across the border, safe from attack, was a large communist encampment complete with bunker systems, hospitals, and an airfield.

Agent reports said that the Viet Cong were preparing an attack on the unfinished camp to destroy it before it could become too strong. The communists were making ladders to lie over the barbed wire and minefields, and to be used as stretchers for removal of the dead. They were also making wooden coffins. If for some reason they failed to take the camp in the first assault, or Captain Thorne and his troops managed to mount a counterattack, the Viet Cong could flee across the border or be reinforced from their main camp inside Cambodia. Since Sihanouk had severed relations with South Vietnam and the U.S., "hot pursuit" across the border would cause a political uproar that Captain Thorne's superiors could not afford. Something bold and unorthodox had to be done, and Larry Thorne was the man to do it.

His many admirers in the Special Forces referred to him by his given name, Sven, or called him "The Viking." He was forty-four years old, twenty years older than his peers in the rank of captain. He was a Finn. As a young man, he had fought the Soviets when they invaded his homeland. He joined Hitler's Wehrmacht and served two years fighting the Russians on the Eastern Front. After the war he joined the American army in Europe, hoping to serve the required five years that would earn him his U.S. citizenship. In 1955 the "blue-eyed Nordic giant" and some friends got into a barroom fight with some Special Forces soldiers. When the fight was over, the major that Thorne had thrown over the bar invited him to join the then-secret 10th Special Forces Group at Bad Tolz. In the years that followed, Thorne graduated from Officer Candidate School and operated overtly as a Special Forces officer and covertly for the CIA. He was tried and acquitted of murder for killing a German citizen he believed to be a Russian agent with his fists. Robin Moore says, and many Green Berets believe, that Thorne was the "ideal Special Forces officer": he was unmarried and attached to nothing but Special Forces; he was not interested in a career as a staff officer; he was a genius at unconventional warfare; and since the Soviet invasion of Finland, he had devoted his life to killing communists.

At "Phan Chau" not all of those he considered his enemies were communists. Four miles north of the Viet Cong village at "Chau Lu" was an encampment of fifty Khmer Krom led by a short, stocky man who wore a khaki uniform, a "thoroughly mean—and suspicious—looking bandit," whose name Captain Thorne never learned. He and his executive officer Lieutenant Schmelzer blamed the company of "KKK bandits" for several ambushes of their own troops and believed they were allied with the communists. A week earlier four Khmer Krom monks had passed through Phan Chau on their way into Cambodia to buy gold leaf for their temple, the money for the purchase contributed by the people of their villages. Thorne and Schmelzer warned the monks not to cross the border, but they went anyway. On patrol in the "KKK area" three days later Thorne found the bodies of the monks lying on a trail; their severed heads were tucked under their left arms and their money was gone. He blamed the Khmer Krom company, assuming for reasons unknown that they would rob and murder their own holy men.

The morning before the expected Viet Cong assault on Phan Chau, Lieutenant Schmelzer took his platoon of Vietnamese soldiers and walked north to talk to the Khmer Krom "chief." He explained to Uchs that they wanted to reconnoiter the area across the border from their camp, but could not legally do so. He offered Uchs ten dollars per man and five rifles and five automatic weapons to cross the border that night, patrol south past Phan Chau, and reenter Vietnam at a rally point six miles beyond. Half the money and weapons would be up front; the other half would be paid at the rally point where they would meet for debriefing. Uchs accepted.

That night two of Captain Thorne's American sergeants took a hundred of their troops across the border and set up a blocking position. With a river between them and the main communist encampment at their back, they faced the border and the Viet Cong village to their front. When the blocking force was in place and the Khmer Krom were moving south, Captain Thorne and his Vietnamese troops attacked the village from the east, driving more than one hundred communist guerrillas across the border directly into Uchs and his men and the blocking force beyond. When the firefight erupted, the Khmer Krom found themselves taking fire from both front and rear. They could not see the blocking force behind them, so they took cover and engaged the men coming at them from the village. In a few minutes twenty of the fifty Khmer Krom who had gone out were dead and twenty more wounded. But what mattered to Captain Thorne was that more than sixty of the communists who were to have taken part in the assault on his camp were killed, and very few of his own men were lost.

Before dawn Thorne withdrew his blocking force from inside Cambodia and went to meet Uchs at the rally point. He took Lieutenant Schmelzer and his company of Vietnamese with him for protection. Uchs and a dozen of his men were waiting for him, talking among themselves in the hazy morning light. Uchs's khaki uniform was spattered with mud and torn at the hip; his men, all of them fouled with mud and blood, were shaky and apprehensive as they faced the well-armed Vietnamese. When Lieutenant Schmelzer confronted him and solemnly began to peel piastre notes from a soiled wad of money, Uchs demanded that he be told who it was that they had fought in the darkness. Schmelzer answered with exaggerated innocence bordering on open ridicule that it had to have been Viet Cong he had fought; who else could possibly be on that side of the border?

Uchs's anger and frustration were palpable. The Vietnamese who now surrounded him were amused; his own men watched his wrathful eyes, then turned with apparent relief to assist the rest of his broken company as they began to limp in. Those lightly wounded carried their more seriously wounded brothers to a stand of mango trees where they propped some up against the tree trunks and laid others on the ground. Last came those bringing in their mangled dead, slung on bamboo poles like so many freshly killed pigs.

The communists were running from fighting in Chau Lu village, Uchs said. He demanded to know why he had not been told about the attack on the village and who was firing at him from behind. Schmelzer's interpreter, embarrassed and a little afraid, said that he, Schmelzer, thought that Uchs understood that they were going to attack the village, and that the heavy fire from their rear had to have been communists from the main camp. The

Americans felt sorry that he had lost so many men; they would have their medics tend to his wounded.

Uchs now knew very well what had happened and knew that he and his crippled survivors could do nothing about it; they were out of ammunition, outnumbered and outgunned by the smirking Vietnamese. He glared and ground his teeth as Schmelzer counted out the second half of his payment.

His men had killed as many as a hundred communists, Uchs said, and now the ones who had survived would hunt him and his men down for revenge.

Captain Thorne stepped forward and stared down at the "sinister little brown bandit." He said he would pay an additional five hundred piastres each for twenty-five Viet Cong killed, and one thousand piastres for each of Uchs's men who was killed. No more. He ordered his interpreter to get a signed receipt for the money and to take photos of the payoff. He "grinned good-naturedly at the scowling KKK chief" and walked away satisfied that if the fighting across the border was reported and the Cambodian government complained, he could explain, and prove, that he had paid Cambodian outlaws to engage the communists and hence bought precious time to complete his camp's defenses. A little unorthodox maybe, but a damn nice mess of dead communists.

•

In early 1965 Uchs, along with his diminished band, appeared to a Khmer Krom sentry on the western slope of Cam, still wearing his khaki uniform and carrying two M2 carbines. His men were few but healthy and well armed with a variety of weapons; each of them bore a sack of rice over his shoulder or a number of ducks and chickens tied together. To Reap and Sem Ly, who greeted him cautiously, not having seen a Khmer Krom with so much flesh on his bones in years, Uchs explained rather haughtily that he had received direct orders from Chau Dara himself to join the battalions and together with Sang Sar Iam, Reap, and Sem Ly, to find a way to open negotiations with the Americans. Within a month, Sang was called to Cambodia, and orders came from Chau Dara making Uchs commander of the 3rd Company of the 106th Battalion. Reap and Sem Ly were surprised, a little suspicious, but "not feeling alarmed."

Through Sing, the interpreter who had acted as go-between for Reap in his earlier attempt to negotiate with the Americans, a meeting was arranged at Wat Chi Eng, "more quickly than we thought." There the South Vietnamese province chief Lt. Col. Le Ba Pham and "an American consultant" named High met with Uchs, Reap, and Sem Ly in a formal but friendly session. The

Khmer Krom explained the position of the FLKK and its goals. They hoped for official recognition from the South Vietnamese government and for friendly relations with them and especially their American allies, whose efforts against the communists they supported. Nothing was signed, nothing promised, but the meeting ended in a positive tone and was followed by a party, the dancing girls supplied by Uchs.

Three months later the same men met at the Special Forces camp at Chi Lang. This time Uchs, as directed by Chau Dara, proposed that the 106th Battalion join the CIDG. They would be supplied, paid, and commanded by Americans while retaining their own chain of command, and would have their own camps along the border. Like the Rhade and Hoa Hao in other camps, they would provide a loyal fighting force for border interdiction; with their established network in Khmer Krom territory on both sides of the border they could provide first-rate intelligence. Mr. High seemed pleased. He said he would return to Chau Doc and talk to his superiors, and would have a reply very soon. If the response was positive, Uchs promised, he would bring five hundred men to the Ba Xoai camp within a month, the rest to come per further agreement. A ripple of hope spread through the mountain camps of the 106th Battalion. Reap had just married Kim Chorn, his high school classmate, in a humble, well-guarded ceremony in her village; he dreamed now of having money for her and of visiting her often from Ba Xoai.

But Le Ba Pham had no intention of letting the Americans create and supply a private army of Khmer Krom in his province. He did not believe the Americans' promise that the Khmer Krom would be turned over to his control eventually; even if that did occur, he had no illusions about where their loyalty would lie.

Late at night a week later, an unlighted helicopter made a low pass over the district headquarters in Tri Ton. A jeep was dispatched to the helipad and returned with Lieutenant Colonel Pham in civilian clothes. In the district chief's office Pham met privately with Uchs, who the night before had moved his company to Nui Coto, for what he called security reasons, leaving the other two companies on Cam Mountain. Neither Reap nor Sem Ly knew of the meeting.

At dawn, Sem Ly's sentries woke him to report that the knoll on which they were encamped was surrounded by a regiment of the South Vietnamese 9th Division who demanded his immediate surrender. If he accepted, he and his men would enjoy the terms of the Chieu Hoi program. Uchs had already accepted the offer, he was told, which included a commission in the

South Vietnamese army for him and good salaries for his men. If he refused, he would be annihilated by artillery, air strikes, and ground attack. He accepted.

On the northern slope of Cam Mountain, Reap's company was not surrounded but was faced with a blocking force of the 9th Division that included a squadron of armored personnel carriers and an artillery battery. Reap ordered his men to spread out as far as they could without losing contact with one another and start up the mountain under the cover of the forest. Above them, only barely glimpsed through the trees, a helicopter bristling with machine guns and rockets made a slow pass. From it came the magnified voice of Uchs, calling Reap's name almost plaintively. Reap sat down in a cleft of rock, his carbine across his knees, his eyes closed.

"You can no longer run or hide," Uchs's voice said. "You don't have to wait for the Americans to accept your terms. Sem Ly and I have already accepted the terms of the province chief and they are the same."

Reap thought that he should acquiesce, but could not bring himself to disobey Chau Dara's orders, to betray the FLKK. He did not believe that the terms would be the same as those Chau Dara had insisted on, or honored if they were. He ordered his men to continue the ascent of the mountain, then to swing south when they reached the crest, hoping to avoid contact during the day and slip away at night. At noon he decided to let his people rest and cook some rice. The forest erupted. Everywhere in their midst artillery rounds exploded, some detonating in the trees and spraying shrapnel, some landing in the boulders amongst them, adding granite shards to steel. Pieces of his men were "flying everywhere." Vietnamese Air Force T-28s strafed the mountain with 20-mm cannons and dropped their bombs.

Within an hour more than two hundred of Reap's three hundred men were dead or dying. Stunned, weeping, and shaking with fear and anger, he ordered the survivors to disperse, "to go their own way for their survival." Most went down off the mountain and surrendered to the Vietnamese. Reap made his own way home to his mother's house to lie down and wait. One by one every hope he had had for his people and himself took leave of him, so that it was "only an empty body" that the American major named Johnson found the next morning when he came by jeep to Coto village to find Reap. Major Johnson was "very kind"; he explained that he'd been sent to pursue the negotiations begun by Mr. High, but now that Uchs and Sem Ly had surrendered to the province chief and Reap's company was destroyed, there was nothing left for him to do but join Uchs and the Vietnamese, which he did.

"Despite that I lost the battle and accepted that loss, my bitterness remained. I always waited for one day to continue the struggle for Khmer Krom independence. What I felt then was beyond anger against Uchs and the Vietnamese, but if I have shown my anger I would be killed. I would die with great suffering. How couldn't I be so angry when my soldiers were killed and died and their bodies were scattered through the forest? These soldiers have left their wives and children to die here. But I must not show my anger then.

"As for my soldiers, they were all very angry against Uchs, who they saw selling them out to the Vietnamese enemy like selling his own children. Some refused to accept the surrender and escaped to be killed later at the border. The Vietnamese paid Uchs a king's fortune of 700,000 piastres for bringing the Khmer Krom to them."

6

"**WE'RE TAKING** small arms fire from that slope, there, at three o'clock." The American pilot banked the helicopter sharply so that his door gunner could get some shooting in, but Major Quyen barked into the headset telling him to get back on course and take us down. Chau Got and Krech sat together in the outboard seats across from me and Aziz. It was their first time in the air over Coto Mountain and the knoll. I wondered what it must be like for them to be inside one of the helicopters that once terrified them while they cowered in the caves below like the few communist survivors were doing now. Though he was buckled in, Chau Got gripped the edge of the seat with both hands and bent, rigid, away from the open door. Krech, leaning over in Chau Got's lap, pointed at a spot in the jumble of boulders on the southern slope, shouting excitedly above the prop noise. Chau Got squinted, nodded, then abruptly slammed the squirming Krech back into his seat.

"More fire from the same area. They call this fucking mountain secure. I'm taking you straight in, Major; hang on to your seats."

But the mountain *was* secure, at least as secure as it would ever prove to be. During the past few years the Mike Force had launched a number of assaults against the mountain to try to destroy the communist units and their headquarters in the deep caves once and for all. The Mike Force was made up of specially trained battalions of Khmer Krom and other ethnic CIDG mercenaries, commanded by Americans, whose mission was to provide quick reinforcement for CIDG fighting camps under attack or conduct sudden assaults against enemy strongholds. Units of the 4th Mike Force had assaulted Nui Coto and the knoll the year before, and though they had taken heavy losses, had gained the summit. But they had had little support; they were outnumbered by the communists still in the caves and on the slopes, and soon had to withdraw. No blocking force had been provided to seal the approaches to the mountain after the Mike Force left and it soon returned to Viet Cong control.

The incessant bombing had denuded most of the mountain and all of the knoll, creating a heap of granite boulders, some the size of houses, all sharp and lying askew, which covered the caves beneath and obscured the entrances. From among the rocks, snipers armed with Soviet scope-mounted rifles and famous for their high percentage of head shots, could fight unseen. Guerrillas hiding in the mouths of the caves could fire straight up into the groins of the attackers as they stepped over them. Among the uneven boulders, ricochets turned every single round into a burst of shrapnel. Deep in the mountain in the labyrinth of larger natural caves, which were unfazed by the bombing, were the headquarters of three communist battalions, a hospital with more than forty beds, and subterranean barracks that housed more than three hundred male and female fighters.

Coto Mountain was the anchor at the end of a chain of mountain strongholds used as secure resting places for the communist main force units infiltrating the Mekong Delta area from Cambodia. Since 1950, when they were Viet Minh fighting against the French, Chau Kem and his troops had held Coto and from its impregnable headquarters within had controlled the surrounding villages. For the communist propaganda teams that recruited in the villages at night the communist possession of the revered mountain was a symbol of their power and invincibility. The more it was bombed, assaulted, gassed, and napalmed, seemingly without effect on the strength and morale of the defenders, the more the people in the villages believed Chau Kem and his guerrillas to be immortal.

In March 1969, the month before, in what was to be the largest American Special Forces–led operation of the war, the entire 5th Mike Force from Nha Trang and three fighting camps in the north—three battalions of Montagnards of the Rhade and Koho tribes and their Special Forces leaders—were ordered to take the mountain. An American artillery battery, a specially formed troop of jeep-mounted recoilless rifles and heavy machine guns, and a South Vietnamese battalion formed a blocking force between the three villages and the mountain. The few Khmer Krom still in the villages were herded together in an attempt to identify those who had kin among the communists. Their rice supplies were confiscated, their every movement watched.

At dawn on 4 March, the Mike Force assault troops stepped across the assault line at the foot of the mountain. The defenders waited until the lead units got onto the mountain before they opened up. The lead company took 20 percent casualties in the first two minutes. Among the boulders it was impossible for the attackers to see where the fire was coming from. It took four hours of fierce fighting and heavy casualties to gain the summit of the knoll. From there the Montagnards and Khmer Krom formed an assault line on the western slope and began to sweep south along the mountain to clear the caves. It took three weeks. It took flame throwers, satchel charges lowered into caves, and hand-to-hand fighting in close quarters.

A team of Sgt. Albert Belisle's Montagnards, armed only with fighting knives and grenades, was lowered into one of the main passageways. While scouting the cave complexes for access, they found caches of AK 47s with which they armed themselves. Near a cistern that gathered rainwater from above, the team ran into a patrol of women who asked if they needed assistance, thinking, because of their weapons, that they were Viet Cong. The team killed seven of the women and escaped the caves with a Soviet battle flag and enough information to get their comrades into the caves. The assault took forty-three Montagnard and two American lives. It cost the communists at least a hundred lives, tons of supplies, huge stockpiles of weapons, and 95,000 pages of sensitive documents. Two of Chau Kem's lieutenants were taken, but Chau Kem, with untold others, managed to escape.

Our pilot wanted us to disembark from a hover a few feet above the rocky clearing on top of Hill 614, the crest of Coto Mountain, but Major Quyen shook his head and told the pilot to touch down. When he did, muttering into the headset something about taking orders from a fucking gook, we alighted from both doors and hunkered down, eyes squinted shut, while he lifted off. Quyen brushed his starched sleeves, blew the dust from his sunglasses, and snapped them into the case on his belt. The Mike Force company that held 614 was spread out around us in a crude encampment, their defensive perimeter barely visible among the boulders. A dozen or so of the strikers were lounging and napping in a little grove of blasted trees near a square of empty ammo boxes covered by a tarp and bristling with antennae. Over the entrance a cardboard sign read, "Welcome to the Sniper Hilton V.N.C.B. Chieu Hoi!" In its shade a black American was washing his feet in his helmet.

The American who greeted us was a lean and exhausted Special Forces captain with a Greek-sounding name. Uncovered, unshaved, in torn fatigues and boots that looked like they had been worked over with a bastard file, he saluted casually and looked us over . . . another unwanted deputation of rear echelon motherfuckers. It was his thirtieth day on the mountain and he was in no mood for giving tours.

It was Major Quyen's nineteenth year of war, ten of them spent commanding main force units in combat, and he was in no mood for listening to a captain's description of a simple company perimeter defense. He told the captain, in halting but clear English, that we had not come to interfere or be entertained. He was making final plans for the positioning of his local forces around the foot of the mountain and wanted to look again from the top. He had brought his intelligence officer—Aziz rendered an impeccable salute—and also two men who had been officers with the Viet Cong C-805 Company on the mountain for many years. The captain's people could learn more about the caves from them, if they wished.

The night before I had had dinner with Aziz and his wife in their little thatched house inside the compound. We ate on a wooden ammunition crate that covered the entrance to the family bunker dug in the dirt beneath the house. Afterward, while his wife tended to their infant daughter, Aziz told me how much he admired Major Quyen. In the mid-fifties, when Aziz and I were still in grade school, Quyen, then a platoon commander, was wounded fighting the outlaw Binh Xuyen army in Saigon and decorated with the *Chevalier Ordre Nationale*. Whenever his men went into the attack, even here in Tri Ton where they were not well trained, Quyen was up front, his pistol drawn, "always up front." Nothing surprised Quyen. Aziz had never seen him strike a lazy or incompetent subordinate, as many other officers often did; rather, Quyen would correct the man in such a way that he would wish Quyen had hit him. He had been a battalion commander in the 21st Division and the chief of staff. He took no bribes, no payments from anyone. He was the kind of officer that Aziz wanted to be.

Cop stepped forward with a green bundle and handed it to Quyen. "Ah, yes," Quyen said, and presented the captain with a bottle wrapped in a sand bag.

"I hope you like cognac," he said. "There is more always for you when you visit Tri Ton. It shows only humbly our gratitude for what you have done. Also, if you care to send two men to Wat Luong at the bottom of the south slope, they can escort my men who are carrying a nice pig for your soldiers."

A much friendlier captain invited the major to join him in a drink, but Quyen declined politely, explaining that we had only limited time.

I watched Aziz as he watched Major Quyen and wondered what this ragged little perimeter would look like if he, Quyen, were in command. No open shirt fronts, no hang-dog looks, no sleepers in the listening posts. In the American army, front-line troops took pride in their relaxed discipline and appearance in combat—a kind of tattered badge of courage that set them apart from the rear echelon troops. In Major Quyen's and Lieutenant Aziz's army, spit and polish and discipline under *any* conditions, especially the worst, was a matter of pride.

A Khmer Krom sergeant named Son Ha, who commanded the reconnaissance platoon, introduced himself to us in fair English. He had been very
sick, he said, because during the assault he had been so thirsty that he had
drunk gasoline thinking it was water and almost died. While Aziz and the
Scouts pored over a map of the mountain with the black American and Sergeant Ha, I found a high boulder and climbed up to sit in the sun and have a
look around. I had spent two weeks, which seemed like two months, con-
fined to the Tri Ton compound by the seemingly hopeless task of creating
an intelligence coordinating center of several government agencies in the
district, urging them in polite but futile meetings to cooperate and institute
a system of dossiers on the Viet Cong infrastructure in the district to chart
their movements and collect evidence against them. All in order to cripple
the local communist cadre and thereby to satisfy the increasing demands
that came from our superiors in the Phoenix Program for numbers of cadre
eliminated.

A month before, thanks to the Mike Force who had scattered and scared
them, we were able to claim almost two dozen communist cadre "neutralized" by capture or surrender, among them Chanh Chau, the VC chief of An
Tuc village, and the notorious Chanh Puth, chief of the Propaganda Entertainment Section. That made us look good, but served to increase the appe-
tites of our superiors so that they now expected that many or more each
month, condemning us to frustration and failure by declaring us a model
district Phoenix Program. Now, in May, with the Khmer Krom companies
holding the villages and the majority of the communists having fled across
the border, we had had only one neutralization so far: the pathetic little
Tunh who had surrendered to Reap at Olam while Strait and I bathed at the
well.

The sun was hot overhead, but atop my perch I was above the humid
paddies and could relish the light breeze that ran ahead of the afternoon
rains soon to come from the southwest. Beneath me lay the villages and
their scattered hamlets, in the center the trees and roofs of Olam and Wat
Pratheat beyond. I thought of the Scouts' decision to keep their families in
the villages rather than move them into the compound, and I believed that
it was a good sign, as Aziz had said. Several of them were visiting their families that afternoon, and I wished I was in the hammock in the shade in Tapor listening to Con play his stringed *Tror* and to the teasing songs of the
girls in the rice paddies.

"Do you miss your family very much?" Major Quyen had climbed onto a
boulder to my left without me seeing him. I thought he must have been

standing there for a while; he was not looking at me but at the distant mountains across the border. He had just learned that his brother, who had been with the Viet Cong for years, had been executed by his superiors for unknown reasons.

"Yes, sir, I do. But I was thinking about the villages. And how close we are to Cambodia. Is that the Vinh Te Canal, the border, that we can see there?"

"Yes," he said. "The Vinh Te Canal, but it is the border for only twenty years. Exactly. Since 1949." He peeled a glob of hardened napalm jelly from the rock and standing alone in the bright sun, his eyes on the horizon, picked off one small piece at a time and flicked it down the mountainside.

That canal, he said, had been dug 150 years ago by Khmer Krom from the villages who had been enslaved by their Vietnamese conquerors. Working in labor gangs under Vietnamese taskmasters, the Khmer Krom died by the thousands of disease, abuse, and starvation. To inspire their exhausted slaves, the overseers devised a gruesome skit, a morality play for those who would disobey their superiors. Before an audience, three slaves were ordered to dig a great hole, five feet deep and about two in diameter. They were then bound and forced into the hole, standing upright, their faces outward, shoulders barely touching. The hole was filled in until only three heads showed in a small triangle, a hideous mockery of the Khmer Krom hearths formed by three large round stones supporting a metal plate, which the Vietnamese scorned as primitive. A fire was ordered lighted in the center of the triangle of heads, and a plate with a pot of water balanced on top of them to boil for the overseers' afternoon tea. As the fire was stoked and burned, the heads began to jerk and twitch; because the mouths were packed with dirt, the screams of the heads sounded like the distant cries of the dark ones in the forest. In a pall of burning wood and flesh, the overseers taunted the heads: "Don't spill the master's tea!" they scolded.

When the fifty-kilometer ditch was finished, the surviving gangs of Khmer Krom slaves were secured together with crude wooden pillories "to keep them from mobilizing," and led into the empty canal. With much ceremony, the dam at the western end of the canal at the Gulf of Siam was opened and as many as two thousand laborers were drowned by the flood . . . "no one left alive."

"Had you known about that?" Quyen asked.

I said I had not.

"Then did you know about the granaries?" When I said no, he sat down next to me and wrapped his arms around his knees.

Quyen was raised in the coastal province of Vinh Binh, to which he had returned from high school in Saigon to help his father manage the family's rice fields. His village and the province surrounding it were at the time populated entirely by Khmer Krom and under French control, though its borders were "contested" by the Viet Minh.

During the celebration of the Khmer New Year, word reached the village that a Regional Mobile Battalion of the Viet Minh had surrounded the district, announcing that it had come to rid the area of the "undesirable elements" of Khmer Krom who were spies, informers, and criminals who fought alongside the French. The Khmer Krom armed themselves with "knives and hammers," but could do little against the Viet Minh. In Quyen's hamlet, eight men and boys were killed, among them his uncle; more than fifty men and boys were captured and led away. Three of the captives were released and returned to the hamlet, only to die of the wounds they had incurred while being tortured. The people packed up their belongings and fled to a district thirty kilometers away where the French provincial forces were strong enough to protect them. In their absence, the Viet Minh moved into the abandoned villages, burned the houses, and claimed the rich rice fields for the Vietnamese revolution.

The fifty prisoners from Quyen's village were marched across the delta to Rach Gia province, another Khmer Krom enclave that had suffered the same fate as their village, for the same reasons. Thousands of other Khmer Krom, men and boys between the ages of sixteen and sixty, were brought from all over the delta to Rach Gia as prisoners. There they were held in the large rice granaries built by the Japanese. When the granaries were full of people, the Viet Minh set them on fire; those who tried to break out were shot or hacked to pieces; those who could not were roasted alive. When word of the massacre spread among the Khmer Krom, the families of the victims swore to seek revenge, *kum*.

Later that month, Quyen's father predicted that for the next twenty-five years the people of Cochinchina would see nothing but racial and civil war. He sent Quyen to Saigon, where he joined the French 5th Cavalry Regiment to serve as a driver and translator for VIPs. On the night of 21 May 1949, the French National Assembly voted to connect Cochinchina, its former colony, not to Cambodia as had been promised, but to Vietnam. The Vinh Te Canal, whose muddy bed covered the bones of the thousands of Khmer

Krom slaves who had dug it, was now a wide watery grave that separated them from their Khmer kin.

I had heard about the Khmer obsession with revenge. Another Khmer Krom had told me that if vengeance is not exacted sevenfold for a wrong against the family, clan, or race, then there can be no integrity, personal or familial pride, and no possibility of harmony with man, god, or nature. "If I hit you with my fist," he explained, "and you wait five years and shoot me in the back one dark night, that is *kum*. It is the infection that grows on our national soul."

In the pagoda in Tri Ton I had seen a rubbing from a frieze on the wall of the ancient Angkor palace that depicts *kum* in its purest form. A princess who has been somehow insulted is in the process of disposing of the body of the person who had wounded her pride. Her enemy's head already impaled on a stake behind her, the princess kneels over his corpse, her right arm deep in his chest cavity. Assisting her are seven fierce attendants; to the nearest she passes a handful of entrails, which he in turn passes on to others who are busy mincing the organs and intestines on a platter. The last attendant sprinkles the tiny pieces on the ground beneath the feet of her pike men who grind the remains into the dirt with their bare feet beneath a banner bearing the symbol of Angkor. Perched on a limb behind the busy princess, a grateful raven feasts on a liverish lump of viscera.

"I want to show you something before the helicopter returns," Major Quyen said. "It's on the other side."

We were looking south now, over a vast emptiness of flat swampland toward the coastal town of Rach Gia and the Gulf of Siam. But Quyen was not interested in the horizon. He moved us from one spot to another until he had the light at a certain angle. He put an arm in mine and pointed into the paddies below us just past Coto village and its hamlets.

"You can hardly see them," he said. "But look there. And there."

Barely visible on the wide marsh in the near distance was a large area of darker, slightly higher ground, and from it radiated at odd angles a pattern of irrigation ditches and dikes that had nearly disappeared.

"That is O keo. An old man showed me. He is seventy. That is from the first century when O keo was a great city and this was the coastline of the empire of Chen La."

He explained that French archaeologists claimed O keo was farther to the south, but the Khmer Krom disagreed. This was the mountain with the tree that the original people revered.

"And this came from here."

He opened a little white cloth bag and shook an ancient coin into my palm. It was a heavy bronze coin, so worn at the edges that it had almost lost its shape. On one side was a horse, on the other the head of a Roman emperor, only his silhouette and curls still distinguishable.

"Caesar?"

I said I did not know.

7

CHAU GOT, Aziz, and I were eager to test the intelligence system we had been nurturing for more than a month. The information the Scouts had brought back from their visits to the villages had all been verified by local and provincial sources, and some of it had been exploited. We wanted to mount a small operation against a specific target, using only the Scouts and thereby not only testing the district Phoenix Program's system but also proving to their detractors that the Scouts were loyal.

A report from the Police Special Branch at Province said that a woman named Neang, head of the Women's Liberation Committee in Tanop Tasor hamlet, would be attending a committee meeting in the hamlet that night. I knew Paul D., a former Chicago detective who was the advisor to the Police Special Branch in Chau Doc, and knew that he would only send me information that he believed accurate. The report had come directly to Aziz in the daily packet, so it couldn't have been compromised. I was sure that this was the one.

At the kitchen table in the advisors' team house, Aziz read the report to me and Chau Got. Krech and Ut Le were eating French bread heaped with peanut butter and jelly. We had a dossier on Neang, including a photograph from a prior arrest. She was a light-skinned Khmer Krom, perhaps twenty years old, with delicate features, almond eyes, and a thin horizontal scar on the tip of her chin. I showed Chau Got her photograph; he nodded solemnly and passed it to Krech and Ut Le.

Did they know her?

"Yes, certainly." Chau Got did the talking; Krech stared at the photo.

Was she likely to be armed, have bodyguards?

"No, neither."

Did the report about the meeting sound true to him?

"Yes."

Then we will make a plan, and go tonight to capture her.

Silence.

"What's wrong?" Among us we had come a long way in creating our own patois of English, Vietnamese, and Khmer like Reap and Strait had done, but now I wished that Cop was here to translate. Chau Got held my eyes with his and spoke in Khmer, pausing to let Aziz translate each sentence as well as he could.

"This woman is Sinh's niece. She is also a cousin to Con. They will go after her, even kill her, if you order it. But it will break Chau Got's face among the Khmer Krom."

She did look like Sinh: the same high cheekbones, the same wistful eyes. I thought I understood. Political affiliations were only of secondary importance, at best. The Scouts were loyal to Chau Got and through him to me. We armed them and provided for their families. I had fought to preserve their integrity as a group, kept them from being drafted and sent away. They trusted me. They could fight with us against their former comrades in arms, but loyalty to their primary kin group was their first virtue, or so it seemed to me at the time.

"Then we won't go after her," I told them.

Aziz nodded approval. He handed the police report to Chau Got for disposal. I prayed that I was doing the right thing.

·

Chau Got had a ceremonious air about him the next day as he stood at the desk in the team office with Cop at his side. They had both just bathed, and oiled and combed their hair. Chau Got wore a clean, pressed uniform; Cop was dressed in his big-city best: silk shirt and black slacks with an Ivy League buckle above the buttocks. Normally Chau Got would have invited me to the restaurant himself in our clumsy dialect, but today he spoke Khmer and let Cop translate.

"He has a surprise for you. We do. But it's a secret and it's serious so you must not ask about it. Okay?"

Sinh and Con met us at the restaurant. They wore their best and very new civilian clothes. Sinh had come from the dentist's, where he had had his gold tooth buffed. Con sported the new Seiko watch I had bought for him in Can Tho. Among the Scouts I felt closest to Con, and he to me. We had been teaching each other our languages, he learning mine much faster than I was his. Educated as a monk for four years and much respected as a scholar and musician, he was kidnapped by the Viet Cong when he was sixteen. His dream was to go to the university in Can Tho, and I was encouraging him. I gave him a quizzical look hoping for some clue about the surprise, but he only smiled. The owner of the restaurant, famous for his noodle soup and spring rolls, waited on us with a white towel on his arm;

his sons assisted him but maintained a respectful distance. We had the table in the front, which could not be seen from the street. At Chau Got's request, none of us was armed.

We ate and talked for hours, until the lowering sunlight slanted into our corner. We talked about girls, of course. Con teased Ut Le about a recent escape from the wrath of some girl's father in Nam Qui and predicted that he would be killed by an angry husband before the communists killed him. Sinh said he would take his chances; he would rather do that than live like a monk as Con did. Cop said that whorehouses were safer, though he had no personal experience with them, certainly not in Can Tho. Con wondered how he could not, as the whole city was a whorehouse. We ate from dozens of bowls of meats and fresh vegetables. Chau Got held each porcelain spoonful of noodle soup aloft for what seemed like a full minute to achieve just the right temperature.

"We are going to meet Chau Thi," he said. "He is going to give you his blessing." We were walking in the middle of the busy main road through Tri Ton.

I said I felt very honored, and a little scared, no, anxious. Chau Got took my hand and held it as we walked toward the temple complex beneath the palms.

"We must not tell anyone he is here, even the monks."

Chau Thi was one of the *krus* who lived in the forest. It was said that he spent most of his time on the east side of Coto Mountain and had lived there undisturbed by either side during the fighting. In the early sixties the Viet Cong had decided to execute him. In the village square, an officer shot him twice in the chest with a French pistol and ordered that no one should touch the body upon pain of death. When the Viet Cong had gone, Chau Thi sat up and then helped himself to his feet. There were two holes in his chest but no exit holes in his back, and "almost no blood to be seen." He was weak but refused help from the frightened villagers. He simply walked away to the forest. Now he was in his sixties and though he had trouble breathing, a whistling wheeze, he seemed in good health.

In what must have been a monk's sleeping chamber, the old man waited with legs crossed on a bamboo mat against the far wall. Small oil lamps burned on either side of him, and spread out before him on a second ornate mat were a prayer shawl and several white rice bowls with a single item in each. He had long white chin whiskers and huge ears with double ear lobes, and he smelled of garlic. I glanced down at his chest, looking for the bullet holes, but much to my disappointment, he wore his faded shirt buttoned to the top. Sinh knelt and touched his palms and forehead on the floor before the *kru*. The rest of us bowed low. Con sat in the corner by the door, as far away from the old man as possible. Con was a Buddhist; he had no patience for what he called magical incantations. Chau Thi was an animist, a man who claimed control of the spirit world; he practiced arcane Hindu rites and the asceticism that Buddha had disavowed.

Chau Thi's chanting was barely audible, at first more sounds than words, his mouth barely open, but slowly his voice rose and became more musical in a language I thought must be Pali. He did not look at us, but at the array on the mat before him and a little blue amulet bag with a long drawstring. Each of the objects would go into the bag to make a *knay tanh*, an amulet that had a spiritual power of its own, which could only be released by his especially powerful blessing.

A solid boar's tooth whose point and root had been removed, placated the *kmauit*, the dark ones of the forest, who live on dirt and feces and appear in hideous forms like the tall starved demons with mouths "no bigger than the eye of a needle"; who can cause panic in men and wild animals or cause a knife or scissors to enter a woman's body and swell up inside her. The tooth was for courage; because boars with solid tusks are almost impossible to kill, the tooth will make it equally difficult to kill the wearer. He set it carefully on its side on the mat.

A blade of grass represented the *neak ta*, the ancestral spirits who were usually friendly but if ignored could do one terrible harm. With great care he balanced the blade of grass on the tooth and tapped it lightly with his long fingernail until it had made a complete rotation on the tooth without falling. The blade of grass was for life, this life.

On a sheet of Khmer newsprint saturated with sweetly scented pomade, he arranged the tusk and blade of grass, then into the curve of the tusk nestled a little ivory Buddha the size of a thumbnail. The Buddha had a face on either side so he could watch this life and the other life at the same time. The Buddha was for one's soul, here and in the kingdom to come.

He rolled all three up in the scented paper, put them in the bag, and drew it shut, drawing his chanting to a close as well. He handed the amulet to Chau Got, who placed it around my neck.

They believed that the *knay tanh* protected its wearer from gunshots and made him brave when going to war, but it was effective only if the wearer practiced *sila*, ethical behavior. If the wearer should be killed with the *knay tanh* in his mouth and Buddha close to his soul, he would pass directly into the other world without fear or pain.

"Like the silver cross that the Catholics wear," Cop explained when we had taken our leave. "If you believe it and behave in the right way, it will save you from death and fear.

"But it is stronger than that because it includes *all* the spirits and is blessed by the *kru* in the language of Brahma. This one, yours, is made even stronger because of Chau Thi's power."

"I wanted to see if he really has bullet holes in his chest."

"He does."

"Have you seen them?"

"No, but I know he does. He is very powerful." Cop's voice fell to a whisper. "He has seen *Aysey*. He has actually met him."

"Who is *Aysey?*"

"Not who is he. What is he. *Aysey* appears as an old man who wears white clothes and has white hair and a long white beard. He appears on Propeal, Cam Mountain, at night—any night he wants, out of nowhere. The old man in white is not him, but only a form he uses. *Aysey* can bring dead people back to life and he can't be killed either. He can appear as a normal man. Some say he has come already. And when he is in the form of a man, he will be a warrior king who is like a god in battle. He will appear to lead the Khmer Krom people in the great war against the *yuons*. He will restore all Khmers to the Empire of Chen-La. The people who say that he is already here say we will know by a sign when he is ready for us to rise up with him. This will happen soon."

8

WE THOUGHT we had a fifty-fifty chance of ambushing the tax-collecting team that our informants told us would be coming into Nam Qui hamlet some night soon. They had so many aliases and we knew so little about them that we called them "Hare Lip and his woman," just as the villagers did. They would have a few enforcers with them, and if they were true to their pattern, would leave with a few of the villagers drafted to serve as bearers of food taken in tax. Hare Lip was a Vietnamese communist, originally from Tri Ton, an aged man remembered by a few as one of the old believers among the Viet Minh. His woman—whether she was his sister or his wife no one knew—did all the talking and had no problem at all ordering people beaten or even shot. The local soldiers claimed that they had tried many times to catch them in an ambush but had yet to succeed. Many people believed this was because Hare Lip and his woman were invincible; Chau Got believed it was because information about the ambush plans had been leaked.

We told no one but Aziz, and of course Major Quyen. With a hand-drawn map, which he destroyed after each session, Chau Got briefed us over and over. It would be a conventional L-shaped ambush along the trail north of the hamlet. In the longer arm of the L, running parallel to the path, eight of us would be spread out hidden in the grass with Con, our gentle mortarman, as the anchor with his 60-millimeter tube. On the short arm, crossing the trail, would be Ut Le with the M60 machine gun and four others behind two claymore mines. There would be no radio, as there was no possibility of air or artillery support. The surprise would have to be complete and our fire-power overwhelming, especially in the first few seconds.

From the way he thumped the diagram of Ut Le's field of fire, it was clear that Chau Got was as worried about Ut Le getting carried away with the machine gun as he was about anything else. I suggested that he set up stakes on either side of the barrel to contain Ut Le's sweep in the excitement and dark, but Chau Got said that that would insult Ut Le. There had been palpable tension between the two recently because Ut Le had been challenging Chau Got's authority, citing his higher standing with the communists as bodyguard to three commanders including Chau Kem, and his reputation among the villagers. I was authorized to pay one of them about ten dollars a month more than the others, as a leadership slot, and Ut Le had suggested that I split that money between him and Chau Got. The machine gun we had requested earlier arrived in the middle of the quiet face-off, and we made a big deal of presenting it to Ut Le as the man most capable of dealing out death with it. He took to wearing crossed belts of ammo on his bare chest and made frequent public displays of cleaning the gun and practicing positions with it in the compound parade ground. He had yet to fire it in anger, but was itching to do so.

After the Mike Force withdrew from Coto, its positions on the top of the mountain and knoll were manned by elements from the three companies in the villages. This further thinned the blocking force at the base of the mountain, stretching Uchs's and Reap's resources dangerously. With the Mike Force went the air and artillery support, and soon the communists were filtering back to those caves not guarded by the three companies. Among the communists who were infiltrating the area and returning to the mountain strongholds on Coto, Giai, and Cam were some survivors of the fighting, but many were fresh troops from the border sanctuaries. All of the enemy coming across the border were well armed and well fed. We had reason to believe that some of them were lead elements of the North Vietnamese 18b Regiment, but when we reported this, we were told it could not be so.

"If it is their 18b Regiment," Strait said, "they'll be headed down into the U Minh Forest where nobody can get their asses. When the time comes, they'll go after the whole Mekong Delta here—Saigon, too. Hell, our 9th Division down there is sending people home. Our people know it's North Vietnamese regulars coming down here, but they just won't admit it. They don't dare to. Chicken shits."

So in our rehearsals for the ambush we included the possibility that we might surprise a large band of hardened northern regulars rather than a raggedy-ass little committee of tax collectors. The prospect made my palms go damp and cold. It was our job to wage war on the infrastructure, to go after specific targets such as Hare Lip, but if we ran into regulars we would give them a good fight. Chau Got and the others didn't really care what kind of communists they killed, but their favorite targets were *yuons* from the north.

We had been on several ambushes since our first operation when Krech killed the boy with his grenade launcher, but we had not made contact on any of them. Since then Aziz and I had emphasized to Chau Got the importance of specific targeting and positive identification of those we captured or neutralized. We needed papers or documents of some kind if it was a kill. They had insisted that the killing of the boy had been necessary, that Krech had acted in self-defense; nevertheless, we didn't want it to happen again, or if it did we wanted proof that any killed were communists. Chau Got said he understood, as did the others, but we did not think that they agreed that identification was of any real use. They would prefer to kill them all and let Buddha sort them out afterwards, as the saying goes.

The militia ambushes I had been on while in Chau Doc had been company-size operations planned at headquarters by South Vietnamese staff officers and their American advisors. There were dozens of overlays or mapped operation plans, artillery and air support and briefings attended by anyone who might be interested. We were ferried or driven into position in the evening and set up along the Vinh Te Canal. None of the militiamen or officers expected to make contact, and we never did. Most of the troops slept; some even listened to little portable radios. They knew that communist agents at headquarters had passed the ambush plans, even at times the overlays themselves, to the enemy and that they would avoid the ambush. But at Tri Ton, where only a few knew we were going on ambush and only we knew where, our target—or the enemy, for no one else would be out at night in the area—would walk into the ambush unaware if they were there; if they weren't, we would withdraw at dawn to appear elsewhere.

Half of us went to Olam by jeep, while the other half walked to Luong Phi village, where they would wait until midnight, then meet us at the predesignated rally point. We left our mines and heavy weapons under a tarp in the jeep, with Con watching over them, and made noises about having come to meet with Uchs, but everyone seemed to know that we were there to go out on ambush and no one seemed too concerned about it, except perhaps Sergeant Sirois.

"Why don't you let me go with them?" he asked Strait.

Ut Le stood at Sirois's side. Shoulder to shoulder they were of equal height, both so thin that their ribs showed, both wearing amulets—a *knay tanh* and a St. Christopher—both of broad smiling fearless countenance, one light-skinned, the other dark.

"Fuck that," said Strait. "That last time you went with them you complained about the mosquitoes for two days afterwards here. Pain in the ass." Strait ran his hand back over his short Mohawk to stand it up, a gesture Sirois took as a good sign.

We all knew the story of the strange bond between Sirois and Ut Le. We had heard it several times. A month before, Ut Le had accompanied a group of Strait's men, including Sirois, on an ambush near the border. No contact was made. In the morning, while waiting for a truck to pick them up, Sirois and Ut Le had shared a breakfast of "leaves and confiscated fish" on the canal bank. Ut Le told Sirois that while he was with the communists operating around the Special Forces camp at Ba Xoai he had been decorated for killing an American lieutenant in an ambush in the same open plain that they could see in the distance. A helicopter was also shot down. Sirois was slack-jawed. The ambush Ut Le described, and further verified with every detailed question he was asked, was one in which Sirois himself had almost been killed.

"I nearly shat! He described to me exactly what had happened! Imagine two years after he was decorated for killing my lieutenant, I was on the same side as him! Fucking Vietnam."

Strait turned as if to walk away from the conversation.

"Aw, come on, Captain. I want to see my boy here work that M60. Hot shit, eh, Ut Le?" Sirois made John Wayne machine gunning gestures and Ut Le responded with a wide grin.

"Number fucking one!" he said.

Strait smiled. He could not help it. He told me that if I was going to take his medic, I was going to take a radio too. We would be out of range of his new 4.2-inch mortar, but he could scramble a reaction team and get it out in the jeep if he had to. I was happy to have Sirois go with us; he was not only a good medic, but an experienced and incredibly energetic fighter, much respected by the Khmer Krom for both. Strait would hate to lose him and he let me know it.

Strait was old-school. He'd been with Special Forces since the beginning, first as an enlisted man, then as an officer. He was devoted to the Special Forces mission of helping oppressed peoples in their fight for freedom. He could fight with his fists—he often did—and he could fight with any kind of weapon in anyone's arsenal, from a bolt-action rifle to an artillery piece. He led by example, taught with patient repetition, rarely slept more than a few hours at a time. First and foremost were his men, his people. His covenant with them was sacred. If they would trust and follow him, he would provide for them, he would risk his life for them, he would never abandon them. Better death than betrayal.

Which was not the way the politicians and his superiors were seeing things in 1969. Expedience was outrunning principle. To slip out of the war and their commitment to the Khmer Krom, among others, the Americans were turning command and control of ethnic troops over to the Vietnamese. Many Americans in the field were willing to look the other way, but men like Strait were not and would do battle for their people, would risk career and personal welfare to honor their covenant.

"I would have failed if it hadn't been for that asshole questionnaire. With them and me too out of Special Forces, we weren't supplied by Americans any more, but by the Vietnamese. All this bullshit about Vietnamization is just a way of saying we're going to look the other way while these bastards skim off supplies meant for our troops in the field. I raised hell all the way through channels but couldn't get shit, not even toilet paper here. Ammo twenty years old. Or they send fresh rations that go bad in two days because we got no place to keep them.

"So when this questionnaire from that candy-ass advisors school I went to came down here, I told them the God's truth. I called them liars and cowards and every other goddamned name I could think of for somebody who'd make a promise to fight, then break his own promise to even provide for the fighters when the shit hit the fan.

"First comes this gimpy colonel. He flies in here and the first thing he asks me is if I'm Regular Army. I say no, and he starts giving me shit because my boots are unbloused. I told him it's the only way we can keep our feet half-assed dry here, but he didn't hear me. He said what I wrote on that questionnaire was causing a to-do and my ass was going to get handed to me. I said okay you can have my ass, but get my people those supplies. Get them medicine here. Weapons. A fucking antenna. I got one Prick Twenty-Five radio but no antenna and no second set. What good's it do to have one radio when you got people out on patrol or ambush? Jesus fucking Christ.

"After him comes a letter of reprimand saying that what I said was okay but the way I said it wasn't. All right, but let's have those supplies. Then comes General Deane. He's down here to see the mountain and talk to the Mike Force people, and he stops in to see me here. He remembered me from 10th Group in Germany, which surprised the hell out of me. He said he heard I was raising a stink and he'd look into it if I wanted. That's what did it. He kicked ass and took names. We got our jeep, our mortar, decent small arms and ammo, even C-rations, all from Special Forces channels of course. No goddamned generator yet, though. The bad guys had one on the mountain there, but we can't get one. Or a damn claymore. It's a sorry-ass joke here is what it is. I'd laugh, if I could, I swear it."

I said I could leave two claymores with him if we did not use them that night. He said he would love to have them, but he hoped we had a good reason to detonate them, to blow some Viet Cong asses back across the border. Kill some commies for Christ.

A few hours later I was kneeling in high wet grass watching the vague figures I knew to be Sinh and Chau Got as they set up the claymores on the path and ran the charge wires back into the brush. Each mine, six inches high and twelve wide, was loaded with over six hundred ball bearings, packed with plastic explosive in a convex mold that would spray a wide area. The Scouts had been taught how to use the claymore and had detonated several in practice, but had yet to see them work against troops in the open and were eager to.

We lay in three inches of water about ten feet apart, hidden from one another by the thin grass and some ugly long-stemmed succulent plant. I could see only the dim shape of the trail in front of me and assumed that the others, those in the short arm of the L, could see well enough. The soggy ground and my own sweat soon did away with what was left of the insect repellent and the mosquitoes settled in a humming swarm on my head and neck and hands, flying up my nostrils, stinging my eyelids. I thought of the centipede that had bitten and almost killed Sinh on the last ambush: as thick as my thumb and over a foot long. My outer thighs, rubbed raw by the fins of the mortar rounds I had carried, burned and felt like they were still bleeding, which I was certain would attract leeches. I was afraid the Viet Cong would detect us somehow and circle around behind us. I worried about Ut Le's field of fire and that Con, who was watching our flank, would fall asleep. I swear I could hear a man snoring to my right.

Someone screamed "Hi!" and opened up with an M16 on full automatic. Both claymores went at once in a dull orange flash whose noise broke the night open and sent a shock of fear through me that almost made me faint. The volume of fire from the machine gun and small arms, punctuated by exploding grenades and mortar rounds, was so heavy that it created a roaring, an "aaarr" sound, a long, loud metallic groan. I couldn't see anything to my front but dutifully fired two or maybe three shotgun rounds at the path. There couldn't be anything alive in our field of fire, but the Scouts kept it up, loading and emptying clips, lobbing grenades. I could hear Sirois yelling, "Three! Bursts of three!" at Ut Le, but the machine gun kept up a steady fire, its tracers riding high, poorly aimed. I screamed, "Cease fire!" but no one obeyed. They were firing every round we had with us.

When they finally quit, Sirois was still swearing at Ut Le. We let our eyes adjust to the dark again, then stood up cautiously.

"Let's get the fuck outta here, Captain. There's more of them, maybe lots." I could barely see Sirois. "Somebody over here got trigger-happy. I could see more of them. If they regroup, we're fucked."

"Let's go!" We started off to the northeast for the abandoned temple that was to be our rendezvous. I slipped and fell into a ditch, and someone right behind me did the same, cursing in Khmer. I felt like I was running through deep water. From behind came a single pistol shot, followed by the rapid emptying of the entire clip into something or someone. It had to be Chau Got, as he had the only other .45, or one of the enemy. Ahead, in the darkness, Sirois laughed and someone else giggled.

I squatted against an ancient *stupa*, smoking and scratching the backs of my hands. My eyelids and lips were swollen from mosquito bites and I was still shaking slightly, but I felt elated. A couple of the younger Scouts were re-enacting the detonation of the claymores, mocking another who had covered his head with his arms when they went off. I had worried aloud at our arrival that we were missing three, but Sinh assured me that Chau Got, Krech, and another were right behind, that they had stayed to examine the ones we'd killed or find traces of those who'd escaped. Our plan was to return at first light for a careful inspection of the site, but Ut Le and Sirois's conviction that there were more of them made me eager to get away.

Chau Got seemed to appear from nowhere. He squatted next to me and lit a cigarette. Resting a hand on my wet knee, he drew deeply and exhaled. He said we did very good. We killed two of them for sure, maybe more. One was a regular soldier and had an AK 47. The other was a tax collector. No papers, but we know him. He was the tax collector Xuan. Not Hare Lip this time. Did I remember Xuan? From before, when I "washed" in the canal? We killed him this time.

"Are you sure it's him? Did he have papers?" I asked.

"Krech, come here!" he called.

Little Krech appeared before us and lit his Zippo. He was beaming with pride. Chau Got made an appreciative noise and Sirois gasped.

"You see?" said Chau Got. "No papers? No problem. Xuan!"

Krech was holding a human head by a lock of hair entwined around two fingers. The head's eyes were wide open, the mouth frozen in a terrible smile. I tried to pull away, but felt Chau Got's hand tighten on my knee and only averted my eyes.

"Xuan the *yuon!*" he said with delight.

"Get that goddamn thing out of here!" Sirois was not pleased. "Go on, get rid of it. Fuck!"

Krech understood. His face fell, shoulders drooped. He closed his lighter and disappeared in the darkness.

Chau Got's hand fell from my knee. He flicked his cigarette in a long red arc. It landed among the shadow figures of the other Scouts and one of them stepped on it.

9

KRECH WANTED to drive. He pestered me about it for days, promising me a girl at the wedding celebration, anything, if only he could be the one who drove the jeep. He made me watch him as he drove around the assembly area in the compound, sitting on a folded flak jacket, wearing sunglasses and his .45 in a shoulder holster like the bodyguards in Saigon. When the Scouts teased him about needing the flak jacket to make him tall enough, he spat back that it would save his ass from shrapnel when we hit a mine. He had to sit forward in the seat to reach the pedals, but though he lurched and struck his chest on the steering wheel every time he shifted gears, he managed it pretty well and I finally relented.

Ut Le and two others had been squatting in the shade of the bunker watching the driving demonstration. When Krech strutted up to them and announced that he would be driving to the wedding, Ut Le made a noise of disgust, spat into the puddle at Krech's feet, and walked away. The others did the same, but looked over their shoulders and smiled back at the triumphant Krech. Ut Le was angry and embarrassed that he had not been invited to the wedding. He insisted that he was not included only because he was of another clan, but privately it galled him to think that Chau Got would be treated like a chieftain by Uchs, so publicly, at such a prestigious affair, while he had been snubbed. That little *Kmau* would be driving, which he, Ut Le, could have done handsomely, made it all the worse.

But Krech did not drive. He rode in the back with Sinh and Cop. I drove, and Chau Got rode shotgun. Earlier, while Krech washed and polished the jeep, Chau Got had taken me aside with Cop and politely explained Ut Le's embarrassment, and how it would be made worse if Krech drove the jeep. I apologized for being so stupid, and Chau Got, now himself embarrassed that I should have to apologize, suggested that in the future he be the one to make these "little decisions" about the Scouts. I promised him that he would be.

The wedding ceremony itself, between Reap's niece and one of Uchs's many lieutenants, had already taken place before family and close friends. The celebration we were going to was to be a much larger affair: a reception and feasting that would not only celebrate the marriage but would be a proud, conspicuous festival to celebrate the increasing power of Uchs and the Khmer Krom companies. That Chau Got had been invited to the festival was a public recognition of his new status since he and his men had defected, a way for Uchs to welcome him to our side and rub a little shit in the faces of the local communists. That he was invited to bring his American and two bodyguards and to sit with Uchs and the other Khmer Krom chieftains, was a great honor for Chau Got and one which he meant to enjoy.

He sat stiffly in the front seat as we drove out of the compound and through the noisy crowd of people who had gathered to see us off. He wore starched American tiger fatigues and on his hip, his .45 in a polished holster. With his well-armed retainers and an American to drive him, he was every inch a Khmer Krom warrior chief on his way to a high council. There was no sign in his bearing or appearance of the starved and stinking guerrilla defector he had been only months before. Unlike Krech and Sinh in the back seat, who waved and laughed and exchanged greetings with the people we passed on the road leading out of town, Chau Got did not smile or speak, but his normally fearful visage was softened and the eyes that usually threatened now looked fondly on those who waved from their doorways. When we slowed to pass the guard post at the bridge, the Vietnamese militiamen stood at attention, but Chau Got pretended not to see them.

It was the month of *Asat*, when rice seedlings are transplanted and weddings are held. The road was busy with men in sarongs leading cattle to plowing, children carrying thatch, and groups of women walking single file. Outside the town, driving west through the paddies, the air was cool and fresh, washed clean by the afternoon rain. When I slowed for a muddy pothole or to pass women and girls arranging bundles of seedlings on the roadside, the sweet scent of pomade rolled forward from the back seat, anointing us all. Ahead, between us and the celebration in Olam, Coto Mountain rose up out of the flat paddies like a barren and blasted island rising out of a calm sea. As the road approached the mountain and its shadow, the back seat fell silent. Some parts of the mountain were now occupied by friendly forces, but we all knew that the number of North Vietnamese replacements was increasing in the caves deep inside the knoll and that they were probably watching us as we drove along within pistol range of the tumbled and burned boulders that hid their entrances. In the shade, the air was still and close and stank of napalm, burnt vegetation, disturbed soil, and charred flesh. The Scouts rode quietly, their M16s in their laps, their eyes on the caves where they too once hid.

As we rounded the mountain and the road pulled away from it toward the sunlight, we approached a middle-aged couple who were hurrying along on foot, dressed in their best silks and bearing a gift wrapped in pink cellophane. When I stopped beside them, they held their hands pressed together over their heads and bowed in reverent *sompeah* to Chau Got, who returned the gesture with hands held lower, as a prince would. They may not have recognized him as the man who had been decorated by the Americans and Vietnamese for his part in the fighting on the mountain, but they clearly saw a Khmer Krom chieftain and responded with bows and whispered thanks when he invited them to ride with us. They climbed onto the back in silence, as fearful of the machine as they were of the dark mountain, and we drove out of the shadow into the sun.

The road became increasingly crowded as we approached the village. Families dressed in colorful sarongs and bright silk shirts carried gifts wrapped in crepe paper. The music from the loudspeakers increased as we neared the friendly shade of the village. I recognized "Love Potion Number Nine," which was cut short with the shriek of a sliding needle and replaced by a traditional Khmer love song. Krech and Sinh and the couple we had picked up chatted with people as we crept past them, and the jeep increased in size and weight, like a magnet pulling through metal filings, as children climbed onto the rear bumper, then the front and sides, crowding everyone but Chau Got. The air was rich with the sticky sweet smell of roasting bananas.

"One mortar round in this crowd . . . ," I said.

"No," Cop assured me, "there won't be problems. They canceled it two times already because the *kru* said the signs were bad. Now the signs are good."

"Did anything happen on the days they said would be bad?" I asked.

He looked at me like I might be teasing him.

"I don't know. It doesn't matter. If they had the wedding on those days, something bad would have happened, but since they didn't, nothing happened. Do you understand?"

I said I did.

Just as it seemed we were about to be swallowed by the crowd, Chau Got told me to stop the jeep. He stepped out, and Krech and Sinh dispersed our riders with a few words and a laughing kick at the ass-end of a teenage boy. With his men ahead of him to part the crowd, and Cop and I beside him, Chau Got walked slowly to the altar in front of the pagoda. Spread out before a small stone statue of the Serene One were low tables heaped with offerings of fruit and sweets and little bundles of cigarettes. While several young monks in saffron robes watched, Chau Got bowed at the altar, put burning joss sticks in a condensed milk can filled with uncooked rice, and set our gift, a small silver cup, in the center of the table. Those watching murmured and the oldest of the monks nodded his approval. When we turned to leave, I saw Strait approaching us in washed and pressed jungle fatigues, the trousers bloused over shined boots.

"Where are we supposed to go?" I asked. I had hoped he would be there.

"To the big house," he said. "We're supposed to sit with Uchs and his boys here. Come on." He deferred to Reap, who led the way with Chau Got.

"You the only American that came?" Strait asked, raising his voice above the music and the noise of the crowd.

"Major Fields had to go to a meeting at Province," I said. "He's worried that Uchs will be slighted because he didn't come. He wants me to explain that he had orders to go to this meeting."

"Uchs can take a flying fuck. He's been gone for a month and now here all he does is preen and slouch around like the king of fucking Siam. Reap's sick of him too, but he isn't saying anything about it. Don't that roasting pork smell good?"

I thought it did, and so did the spices and perfumes and incense. Though we walked in the wake of Chau Got and Reap, people reached out to touch Strait, women and kids to take his hand, men to pat him on the arm and back, as though he was the provider of all this food—which he was, in a way.

"There's a hell of a lot of new faces here today. Christ, I love those skimpy silk blouses; look at that one there."

"I wonder how many of the new faces are VC," I said.

Strait laughed. "There's some, all right. Fuckers will do anything for a free meal. Uchs's men know who they are. There won't be any trouble here; they wouldn't dare."

The cleared center of Tapeang Truol hamlet was dominated by the huge chief's house, whose tiled roof peak flared up toward heaven on both ends. Like its smaller neighbors that faced the open village center, it was draped with paper lanterns, red and blue bunting, and little FLKK flags. The ground floor of the big house was an open kitchen, a confusion of women and girls busy over tables of food, open fires, and clay ovens. The guards at the foot of the stairs to the second floor were dressed in new uniforms, Special Forces issue, and as we passed between them, they snapped to "present arms" with new M16s.

Uchs and four of his lieutenants greeted us on the second floor with salutes, handshakes, bows, and gracious smiles. High above the rest of the village the second floor was open on three sides, and on the floor at the end toward the village, on freshly woven bamboo mats, places were set for twelve. Uchs invited us to sit, and when we had, he sat at the head, his lieutenants on either side of him. He spoke Khmer, with a smattering of French and English phrases; there would be no Vietnamese spoken in this house, Cop had warned me, so I had to rely entirely on him and Strait to understand.

At Uchs's invitation, we dipped our glasses in large bowls of beer cooled by floating chunks of ice, and while we drank, women served sweet ansom cakes on banana leaves and bowls of nuts. Uchs seemed completely unaware of the deference, even reverence, with which he was treated by the people around him. On either side of him, his lieutenants leaned forward to hear him so he wouldn't have to raise his voice above the music. He drank with a ringed finger extended. Behind him, a boy with a wide board fanned away the smoke and flies that rose from the kitchen fires below. With a motion of his hand to the two girls tending the phonograph behind us, he lowered the volume of a heartsick song.

I watched with wonder the confusion of people and colors that crowded the hamlet below us. At least a dozen separate feasts were being held in as many houses; among them wove laughing groups of boys, clusters of girls in white and gold, gangs of children with fists full of sweet cakes, and beneath it all a commotion of chickens pecking at termites and bits of food.

Sinh said that the two girls tending the phonograph were dancers from Takeo who would perform later.

"Krech wants the one in white, but she loves me very much. Watch her look at me."

The first course was rice paddy crabs ground with tamarind and peppers and served on beds of *sdao* leaves in wooden trenchers. When the servers withdrew, Uchs insisted that the lieutenant on his right be the first to eat. He said the man was as lean as a monk's belly from his long trip.

"He's been snooping around inside Cambodia," Strait said. "He's been gone ten days here; he don't look lean to me."

"What'd he find out?" I asked.

"I haven't talked to him; he only got back this afternoon. Ask him."

Uchs answered for the thin man. He spoke slowly so that Cop could translate for me and Strait. Fifty kilometers to our north in the mountains across the border, the first full-strength elements of the North Vietnamese

18b Regiment were consolidating. They were encamped in several areas and being resupplied by Soviet freighters unloading at Kompong Som on the Cambodian coast. He said the North Vietnamese had completed filling the ranks of the local Viet Cong 273rd Battalion. Eighty percent of it was now North Vietnamese regulars; he estimated that there were thirteen hundred of them. It did not take long, he said, for the North Vietnamese to gain complete control of the Viet Cong. Their plan was to move an entire division through our district to the U Minh Forest in the heart of the Mekong Delta and have it in place when the Paris Peace Talks resumed. Nothing new, only confirmation, no mention of the Khmer Krom units still in the mountains.

Chau Got did not seem to be listening; he was watching the bride and groom as they passed from feast to feast in the houses below, bringing cigarettes and treats to their guests. I wondered if Chau Got cared at all about these frightful reports; he didn't seem to, nor did the others.

"Just when we thought we had this place secured, somebody pisses on the party," said Strait. "According to these guys, we're bombing the hell out of them in Cambodia, but I wonder if they'll use the B-52s on them inside Vietnam."

I could not imagine any way that we could stand up to North Vietnamese regulars. Our dozen or so understrength, poorly armed little militia companies were strung along the border without artillery or air support. The North Vietnamese would completely retake Coto Mountain and the six other mountains and from them overwhelm us one at a time. The Mike Force battalions might have held them off if they had stayed, but they were long gone, and only Captain Uchs's several hundred men were left. Strait was right: We'd won the guerrilla war in the villages and had thought that that meant we were winning the war. But now it was plain that the guerrilla war did not matter any more; the North Vietnamese had taken it over. No more running gunfights with guerrillas; now it would be massed assaults of disciplined regulars on our outposts, villages, and towns.

Uchs said nothing about the Khmer Krom battalions still at large across the border. I had relayed his invitation to talk to our authorities about bringing them over to our side, but had heard nothing in response. As he did not mention them, I kept quiet.

"We don't have to worry," Uchs said. "Soon the B-52s will wipe them out." He smiled at the thought. "Annihilate them."

"*Asukop!*" said a lieutenant, and the others agreed.

"What's that?" I asked Cop.

"He means the Vietnamese communists. They are monsters, and betrayers. Pig people."

Several courses followed, with women constantly going up and down the stairs to the kitchen below, assisted by obeisant boys with bowls of fruit—mangoes, durian, papayas—and tall bottles of beer to wash down the *satay* chicken, lemon beef, and *prahoc*, a rancid fish sauce. The girl in white took the microphone and sang a soft, bird-like song that made Sinh's eyes water and Krech's gold-capped teeth glisten in the fading sunlight. Beneath us, in the open village center, the crowd moved about slowly now, some sitting on the ground to listen to the singing, others chatting in groups, still others lighting the paper lanterns that hung on the trees and houses all around us.

The little boys who had scaled up into the sugar palms to watch us eat giggled and made rude hand gestures to Krech and Sinh. Uchs barked at them, and they shimmied down the trunks like gibbons in flight.

With the catfish and *loofah* stew came the rice wine, the infamous *ba si day*. Uchs removed the leaf stopper from the first bottle of the oily, fermented liquid and ate it to show that this bottle would be emptied on the first toast. The music was stopped and Uchs offered a formal welcome to his friends, toasting Strait, Chau Got, and me.

Calls for help from the women below were answered by two of Uchs's lieutenants, who disappeared down the stairs at his bidding. They returned carrying between them a large platter, which they set before Uchs. On a bed of leaves, on its back, lay a turtle the size of a small child. His stomach plate had been removed, with no apparent damage; he lay boiled, naked, and exposed, his feet and head drooping over the edges of his shell.

"It'll be the choicest parts for you," Strait said.

When Uchs began to dismember the pale figure on the tray, I looked away. The first effects of the rice wine were pleasant, a vague numbness in the limbs and a general softening of things. The gay lanterns that hung in the rafters of the house and the treetops around us glowed brighter as the darkness increased. As the girl in red began to sing meekly, the village grew quiet and watched her. She was far more beautiful in the golden light than I had noticed before. But the one in white was prettier, and Sinh had been right, she was looking at us. I was certain it was me she was looking at, not him. When I told him so, he laughed and nibbled at the webbed foot pinched between his chopsticks.

When the girls took their leave to prepare for the dancing, Sinh and Krech both rose to follow but were stopped by a word from Chau Got, who reminded them that he would not have his men make fools of themselves in Uchs's house.

Imperious, swaying slightly, one hand on his polished holster and the other holding the microphone, Uchs waited on the edge of the second floor until his people had seen him, hushed one another, and raised their faces to hear. He began softly, with words of thanks and praise for his honored guests. His was a father's voice, one of quiet certainty. He bade them look around, at the food, the families, the old ceremonies, the color of gold, all protected by the spirits of their ancestors and the resolve of their fighting men. This, he assured them, is how it will be when their enemies are destroyed. And they will be destroyed! he shouted. The time is coming soon! His voice carried above the village and beyond to the mountainside and the dark swampland where the enemy lurked. Before the child born from this marriage was born, Uchs promised, the corpses of the *yuons* would feed the wild boars in the mountains and fertilize the rice paddies.

"We will pay no more tributes. We will have our fatherland and our freedom, and peace for our children, just as our forefathers had. We'll have revenge. And tonight, in the present time," he waved his hand, "we'll have dancing!"

Sinh held my hand as we made our way through the churning crowd toward the lighted house where the dancing would be. We were both a little uncertain on our feet, made even more so by the packs of curious kids who bumped our legs and fell over one another in flight when Sinh made a feint at them. The boldest touched or pinched me, then strutted for the others as though they had counted coup on the white man.

The matron in charge of the ceremonies seated us in a row of baby blue folding chairs on the edge of the dance floor. Behind us, the other guests sat on stools and mats, and behind them hundreds of the curious created human walls, sealing us in on all sides. While the stringed instruments and drums of the orchestra warmed up, guests came one at a time to the center of our row to offer their respects to Uchs and lay pieces of colored string on the wrists of the bride and groom for good luck—the last ceremonial act of the three-day wedding. The bride and groom sat with their hands on their knees. She wore as much gold as any princess, from crown to 14-karat gold anklets. He, all in silk, smiled sheepishly, his eyes on the mirrored pagoda in the center of the dance floor, the same pagoda that I tried to use as a focal point to steady my vision.

"I'm going to puke," I told Strait.

"I wouldn't recommend it, not here," he said. "You think you feel shitty now, wait till you drink some of that fucking pig blood that's coming around in a beer bowl later."

The dancers appeared one by one. They danced toward the pagoda with sweeps and bows and turns as graceful as any kind spirit's. Their hands were splayed, fingers and painted nails bent in backward arcs; no angles, no sudden movements, but all a circular, sinuous motion of girl and gold. Sinh was motionless, his arms at his sides, his neck outstretched, as still as a crane stalking fish in a paddy. He was watching the tallest of the dancers, the one who had been wearing white at the phonograph, and she was watching us.

When the tempo increased, one of the dancers approached our chairs and danced for the bride and groom. She stopped before Uchs and bowed low in *sompeah*, her hands pressed together, then invited him to join her in the *Romvong*, the circular dance for couples. Uchs laughed and declined. She approached Sinh in the same way, and when he followed her onto the floor, the crowd broke into applause. Another invited Krech to dance, and he leapt to his feet in a pirouette and bowing sweep. The young men laughed and applauded him; even the dancers grinned. The third begged Reap to join her, and the last, the girl who had worn white, stopped before me.

"Oh, no, thank you very much," I said. Cheers and jeers rose from behind me; fingers poked my ribs and hands pushed at my shoulders. She watched my eyes through the temple formed by her clasped hands. She was a goddess. I looked to Chau Got for help, but instead got a look that said, "You must," so I joined her, delighting the audience.

I watched the other men, and dipped and turned and waved my hands slowly, trying to dance like they did. Laughter and applause. Krech was singing, softly at first, then louder as others joined in. Seven graceful Khmers and Ichabod Crane in tiger fatigues. Strait and Chau Got held their thighs and shook with laughter. Encouragement from Sinh brought a sense that I was not doing too badly at all, until I saw my reflection in one of the mirrors on the pagoda, ghostly white and glistening with sweat.

The tempo increased, and with it the speed of our turns on the same slow orbit around the pagoda. Figures and reflections became confused, the air heavy as warm steam; I lost the music and went down on one knee, slowly, as before a king. The other dancers thought I was clowning and laughed, and began to pass around me, but I was being pulled to the ground; I put a hand out for more support, to stop the swaying, and would have gone down in a heap if Krech and Sinh had not come to help.

Sinh took me under the arm and held me steady. Krech, at my right side, told the dancers to keep on playing.

"Outside," I said to Sinh. "Outside please."

The people who parted to let us through were quiet; they stepped back as if from a passing corpse. As I drew in the cool evening air, the nausea subsided but still the torches and lanterns swelled and shrank, swelled and shrank.

"I have to lie down," I told them. "I'm sorry. I'm very sorry."

"Don't worry," said Krech. "It's no problem."

They laid me down on a mat on the cool ground in a dark house. Before I could escape into sleep, they sat me up again, removed my pistol belt and shirt, wiped me dry, and made me a pillow. I lay on my side, sick with wine and shame, and curled into the fetal position. I felt a hand on my bare chest, rubbing softly, then on my shoulders.

"Feel this hair," said Krech.

Sinh declined. "Let's go back," he said.

"You go. The one in white is yours now. I'll come soon."

•

"Stop the jeep! Stop here! Stop!" Krech shouted. When I finally did, he rolled out of the vehicle and started toward the foot of the mountain, not fifty meters from the road. He lifted one leg at a time and brought it down hugely, as he did when he played *Reahou*, the moon-eating dragon, for the children.

"What the fuck's he doing?"

"He's still drunk from last night," said Cop. "He's insulting the communists up there."

Chau Got just sat and stared at him as he approached the boulders at the foot of the knoll. He'd chosen a grassy clearing where there were no trees between him and the mountain.

Sinh's eyes closed, fluttered open, then closed again as he sank back into sleep. We were within pistol range of the caves above, parked in the sunlight as though to facilitate sighting. When Krech reached the foot of the hill, he climbed up onto one of the tumbled boulders, put his hands on his hips, and hallooed the mountain.

"Up there, half way, you can't see it—the lookout cave," Cop explained. "It's used for spying and sniping on the road here. It's where the communists put people who are in bad odor with the cadres. Krech spent plenty of time in there."

I understood only a few of Krech's words, a phrase or two. The others in the jeep shook their heads at such foolish behavior. Cop did not bother to translate as Krech went on and on about iced coffee, *satay* chicken, girls dressed in gold, eating in restaurants, new boots. He waved his arms like he was directing an orchestra.

"They could shoot him, for Christ's sake," I said. My head throbbed; my tongue was still slick from the rice wine.

"They might," Cop said. "He's inviting them to try."

"Krech!" I stood up in the jeep. "Get your ass back here. Come here! Now!"

He turned, called my name, and with a cackle began to dance the *Rom-vong* on the boulder: bowing, waving his arms, spinning slowly. Then he went down on one knee, then a knee and a hand, and groaned like a man who was about to be very sick. Cop grinned; he shook Sinh's knee to wake him and they both laughed.

I let out the clutch and drove away in first gear, slow enough that he could intersect us at the end of the clearing ahead. Krech hesitated, gave the mountain one last shout of defiance, then broke into a run. When he caught up with us and rolled into the back seat over Sinh, I cussed him for making fun of me, and I cussed the rice wine.

He laughed and hugged me from behind. "Don't kill me," he said. "Don't kill me."

Chau Got told him to go to sleep.

I drove slowly on the road across the paddies away from the dark mountain. The sun was hot and heavy, the damp paddies steaming. Sinh and Krech slept, and Chau Got, though upright, was beginning to nod.

By the time I stopped at the empty roadside cafe outside Salon hamlet, Cop had joined the others in sleep. Chau Got and I left them curled up in the back seat like puppies and took a table in the shade of the corrugated tin awning of the cafe. Chau Got ordered two large iced coffees, which we drank eagerly, then ordered a second round for the taste. We said little. Chau Got looked tired; he asked for a cigarette and smoked quietly while the timid proprietor and his son watched us from the cafe door.

"I'm sorry I fell down," I said. "That was very bad."

Chau Got smiled weakly.

"No problem," he said. "All of us were drunk." He pointed to the sleepers.

"But I acted like a fool. I embarrassed you in front of Uchs."

"It was all right. You don't understand that wine, how strong. It's okay." He held my eyes with his. "You can believe me. And anyway, the spirits will get revenge for it, you know."

It was early afternoon, and soon the rain would come. The air was growing heavy, oppressive; in the south and west the sky loomed huge and black, threatening. The proprietor moved the thatch walls into place. A piglet dropped his melon rind in the gutter between us and the jeep and sought cover under one of the tables, and across the way a boy led his water buffalo into a grove of palms.

"We should put the cover up on the jeep," I said, and began to rise.

He pulled me back. "They can do it. The rain will wake them up. We can have something to eat while it is still peaceful."

TWO · KINGDOM COME

In the radiant night sky the moon smiles
Tendering light for the earth.
All Nature shivers, delighted by his beauty.
But soon Darkmoon comes.
Lightmoon has taken his turn,
Fulfilled his duty.
Now the darkness serves in turn
And all Nature becomes silent,
No smile in the dark heavens.
Slowly and lonely, we hear the sound
Of Nature breathing along with the windblow.

CAMBODIAN SONG,
translated by Thach Prum Sira

10

WHILE HIS FOUR exhausted companions slept in the undergrowth behind him, the youngest of the group crouched in the boulders, keeping the daylight watch. They were North Vietnamese regulars, half of a machine gun squad on their way to Coto Mountain. Only five months before, in February 1969, they had been recruited from their farms and jobs in North Vietnam, trained for three short weeks, and been sent south to help liberate their Vietnamese brothers. For four months they had walked the torturous Ho Chi Minh Trail from northern Laos to southern Cambodia. In the mountains their bruised and lacerated feet had become infected, making each step a little agony; at night, cold and soaked by the ever-present mist, they had shivered themselves to sleep while insects crawled in their clothing. In the lowland jungles they had endured swarms of mosquitoes, malaria, and sucking leeches as fat as their thumbs. Of their group of thirty that began the trek, three had been killed by bombs from the B-52s, two by napalm, and five from disease. Their only food had been rice and there had been little of that. On each day's march a new guide had led them through the labyrinth of trails to the next way station; they had never known where they were. Fear, homesickness, hunger, and debilitating fever had weighed them down.

At a well-hidden base camp in the Cambodian mountains between Takeo and Coto Mountain, they had rested for three days before they crossed the border into South Vietnam. There the cadre who manned the camp, healthy men in fresh uniforms, had replenished their supplies and filled their lean backpacks with medicines, ammunition, and food for the regiment on the other side of the border. They had reminded them that once they were in South Vietnam they would be greeted with open arms by their oppressed cousins, who would fight at their sides to drive out the American aggressors and their puppet soldiers.

In the darkness in the open rice paddies, they had waited at the Vinh Te Canal while a lone sampan ferried them across a few at a time. When the last five had crossed, they had hurried over the five hundred meters of open ground to the rally point in the trees just south of the nearby hamlet. But their comrades had gone on without them, or they had missed the rally point. Skirting hamlets, fearful of enemy patrols, they worked their way east toward the dark hulk of the nearest mountain. At dawn they found themselves not on the mountain proper, but on the lonely little knoll that nudged into an intersection of two well-traveled dirt roads. The people they saw on the roads were Cambodians, not Vietnamese; they decided to wait until darkness to move onto the mountain.

I do not remember what we were doing that day, why we were out on the road. Chau Got, Krech, six other Scouts, and I had been in Kvao village on some business and were on our way back to Tri Ton. It was the hottest part of the day, when everyone but us was resting in the shade. Chau Got was walking alone, as usual; ahead of him three Scouts walked abreast, while the rest of us strolled along together a few meters behind him. At the place where the road brushes the foot of the knoll, Sinh parted from the other two up front and headed up the hill for a thicket of trees and vines where he could squat in private.

Before he reached the trees, an AK 47 opened up on him from the top of the knoll. He came scampering back, and before we could react, the whole hillside erupted in small arms and machine gun fire. When we spread out and took cover behind the paddy dike, kneeling in the mud, we realized that the fire was going well over our heads; it was wild, uncontrolled, and all seemed to be coming from the same place. It was not a well-laid ambush, but Chau Got was outraged anyway, making that sucking noise with his teeth, to be caught by surprise in daylight and worse to have cowered behind the paddy dike.

He signaled Con and Sinh to take the flanks with the grenade launchers, then popped his *knay tanh* into his mouth and stepped out onto the road, waving to the rest of us to do the same. None of this fire-and-maneuver shit; no crouching and running from tree to tree like the Americans and Vietnamese; no calling for artillery or air strikes or surrounding the knoll to wait for reinforcements. Not this time, at least. Chau Got drew his pistol. We spread out five to ten meters apart on either side of him and walked up the hill, firing as we went.

Then the machine gunner got himself together, lowered his barrel, and began firing at us in bursts. On my left, Krech broke into a run, tumbled, and disappeared. I dove behind a huge ant mound, and as I did, a burst of several rounds tore into the other side of it. Krech shouted something, my name, and I started to get up, but suddenly it felt as if the whole lower half of my body had burst into flames. I screamed and rolled and tore at my clothes, and as I did, rolled into even more ants. Crying out like a kid being spanked, I got away from the nest, got my shirt off, and pulled my pants down to my boots. They moved so fast. They stung and held onto my skin with their mandibles when I tried to brush them off. Stark naked in the bright sunlight, I stomped and slapped and shook, dancing like a wild man to the sporadic popping of rifles and the steady bass of exploding grenade rounds. Only when I had killed the last of the ants did I realize that the firing on the hill had stopped.

They were stripping the sprawled dead when I caught up with them. I saw Krech, counted seven others, and was relieved. Sinh and Chom were arguing over an AK 47; Sinh was offering a North Vietnamese belt with star buckle and a wad of Hanoi money, but Chom wanted the weapon. The machine gunner had taken a round right through his eye, and Krech was taking his leather belt when he saw me and laughed.

"It looked like the spirits were trying to teach you how to dance," he said.

Somebody passed smokes around while they prodded and discussed the dead bodies, arguing over the souvenirs. The dead were nothing but little emaciated boys, none of them over a hundred pounds. On the smooth gray chest of the smallest, Con found a crude tattoo, awkward black letters done with a needle and ink: *Sinh Bac Tu Nam*, Born in the North, Die in the South. Con said that that was true and turned away.

Sinh said it was his grenade round that killed the one whose weapon they were arguing over; he told Chom to look at the body, there were no big holes, only little ones.

The shouts from the hillside below us turned out to be from an old man and a boy, breathless, holding hands and pointing to the paddies.

"Come quickly! One more *yuon*, out there!"

The fifth North Vietnamese soldier had fled down the north side of the knoll, and there in an open paddy, just plowed, he had run into three local militiamen who had cut him off and were holding him at bay in the open. He held his weapon at chest level and glared at us as we joined the militiamen in a wide half-circle. He was pale and shivering, but there was no fear in his eyes, only hatred. Chom said that this one would die well.

"Put your weapon down," Chau Got raised his pistol, "or we will kill you, too."

The boy was motionless. He stared at me—his first white man, an unnaturally tall creature naked to the waist, pale and covered with little pink spots—then turned quickly to his right to see Krech, who had just arrived carrying a head in each hand.

"Surrender and you won't be hurt!"

The boy's eyes were on the heads.

Krech held his trophies out for the boy to see better. One was the machine gunner, with a blue hole for an eye, already infested with flies.

"Look at your friends, *yuon!*" He made the heads kiss, squishing their lips together. Someone giggled.

The soldier make a quick motion, and everyone shot him at once. His body did a back flip, landed on its hands and knees, then hopped straight up off the ground like a frog before it finally fell flat.

I only wanted to sit down, to get out of the sun. The inside of my mouth felt like it was coated with dust; my crotch and legs were on fire, and I felt faint. I found a wide grassy puddle in the shade at the edge of the knoll and sat in it. My brain felt swollen, carbonated—from the ants' poison, I thought. Con came and squatted beside me; he soaked his hat in the puddle, then filled it and put it on. We had nothing to say. . . until Krech approached us with half of a human liver on a blood-soaked cloth in one hand and his bayonet in the other.

"Eat some." He sliced off a piece. "Get his courage."

Con raised his hand and hid behind it.

"No! Take that away," he said. Krech shrugged and left.

I rinsed my mouth and spat back into the puddle, rinsed and spat again, then washed my face. Con was trying to get a wet cigarette lit.

"How do we stop them?" I asked. "More and more come across the border every month. They have the mountains and they're moving into the delta."

"We keep killing them. Like these. They send them, we kill them, like his tattoo said."

"But this is only five," I said. "For every one of these, I'll bet ten got through. It seems like I'm the only one who's worried. The Americans tell us they're not here. . . ."

"They also say they aren't bombing them in Cambodia."

"And the Khmer Krom know they are, but they don't seem to care one bit."

"They're not afraid because they believe another army is coming that will wipe them out."

"What's this other army, anyway?"

"I don't know," he said.

But he did know, and he believed it. I thought it must have something to do with Chau Dara, or the *Aysey,* or both. And it had to be something more than a mystical dream because Con had little faith in the spirit world.

Destruction of the main caves on Tuk Chup Knoll, Coto
Mountain, by U.S. Special Forces demolition team, 1969
Author's collection

Chau Got (*third from left*) and his team, the day after their
defection, Chau Doc, 1968   *Courtesy Herbert Martin*

Left to right, front: Captain Uchs, Lieutenant Aziz, author, Lt. William Adams, 1969
Author's collection

Krech, 1969   *Author's collection*

Lieutenant Reap   *Author's collection*

Capt. John Strait, 1966   *Courtesy John Strait*

Sinh and the author, Olam village, 1969   *Author's collection*

Sgt. Son Ha (*front center*) and his Mike Force reconnaissance platoon preparing to board aircraft for the Pochentong airfield, 13 March 1970   *Courtesy Son Ha*

The Scouts and their American advisors, Lt. William Tucker (*left*) and Capt. Richard Vela (*center*), Tri Ton, 1971   *Courtesy William Tucker*

Con playing the
Tror, Tri Ton, 1971
Courtesy William Tucker

Chau Got and the author, Olam village, 1969   *Author's collection*

Chau Got, 1969
Author's collection

Left to right: Sinh, Chau Got, Chom; Tri Ton, 1968   *Author's collection*

Left to right: Chau Got, Krech, Cop (*in white*) with captured weapon, Coto, 1969
Author's collection

The road to Olam village, looking north, 1968   *Author's collection*

Maj. Thach Quyen, Tri Ton, 1969   *Author's collection*

Captain Reap, Tacoma, Washington, 1994
Author's collection

Col. Thach Quyen, San Francisco, 1995
Author's collection

11

"YOU CAN'T SEE his mother tonight because they are still roasting her." Krech leaned back and sniffed the air, his nose uplifted like a water buffalo's.

"I smell tamarind, too, and sweet potatoes," said Ut Le. He had brought along his new portable radio, a little Sony with a shoulder strap.

Chau Got, his voice almost a snarl, said he was surprised that Ut Le could smell anything under all that pomade and bath water. The day before, Chau Got had had to break up a fight between his two wives in the compound and he was still smoldering from the shame of it. I had not seen it, but had heard that he had pistol-whipped one of them with his .45. The other Scouts, determined to enjoy themselves on this outing, stayed out of his reach.

We left our bicycles at the sandbagged checkpoint on the road leading into the villages. The sentries were Reap's men; they wore new uniforms, helmets, and flak jackets, even unit insignia, and were armed with new M16s. Two claymores were cemented into the ground amidst the concertina wire in front of their emplacement, little watch dogs poised to tear someone's legs off. The soldiers saluted me and Chau Got as we passed, then exchanged grinning obscenities with Krech. One said something about Ut Le's radio and pinched his nose at "the whorehouse smell."

Con and his little entourage of cousins and monks had come out to greet us at the bridge and escort us into the hamlet. We had granted Con the husband three days leave to come home to witness the birth; now Con the father, in white silk shirt and black silk trousers, greeted us with *sompeah* and said that he was honored that we had come. When I returned the gesture and said in clumsy Khmer that I was the one who was honored, an old monk holding a black umbrella that shielded no one from the sun smiled and bowed to me. The only woman in the group, a determined elderly creature with flashing black eyes, arranged us for the procession into the hamlet. Con and I walked ahead, with the monks behind us, their parasol held aloft; behind them, Chau Got came alone, with his men following. The old woman walked among the noisy cousins to keep order and keep the Scouts from falling back to leer at the girl with the tender eyes. Ut Le propped his radio on his shoulder like the boys he had seen in the city and took up a swaying, walking dance to a sweet love song from Radio Phnom Penh. The girls pulling seedlings in the paddies called out to one another to come see and gathered at a shy distance from the road, giving Ut Le the opportunity to let them see that he did not notice them.

In the hamlet center, in the shade of sugar palms and two high-prowed teak houses, Con and I parted from the others and went to drink beer at his brother's house. Reap and Strait, we were told, would join us there later.

"When the villagers have plenty to eat and feel safe and happy like this," Con said, "then Reap and Strait get very strict with the men."

There had been a lull in the fighting throughout Vietnam during the month of July. Some said that the communists were responding to the announcement of the first American troop withdrawal; others warned that a buildup for another "popular uprising" was under way. The optimists believed that the B-52 strikes on their base areas in Cambodia, still officially denied by Washington, were devastating them. The patrols from the village companies and the CIDG camps were reporting ever-increasing North Vietnamese border traffic into the Seven Mountains and increasing contact with smaller communist units. But in Tri Ton, the South Vietnamese, who were not sending out patrols, were reporting that there were no signs of any North Vietnamese activity in the district.

Captain Uchs had gone back to talk with the Khmer Krom battalions in the mountains. Reap, a captain now, was in command, and with Strait at his shoulder, was busy day and night checking perimeter defenses, monitoring patrols, scolding his troops against complacency. For that reason and others, there was a well-fed familial sense of security in the shaded hamlet.

At Con's brother's house we sat on bamboo mats, drank beer, and ate the traditional dish of crabs ground up with tamarind, peppers, and rice. In cupped hands, Con presented his brother with four packs of Marlboros tied together with red ribbon. His brother replied by calling for his family and presenting them one at a time. Con wanted me to notice how big and strong his two young nephews were for their age; he praised his beaming sister-in-law as a "perfect mother." I had seen them a year ago, with swollen bellies and blackened eyes; I could appreciate how healthy they were now.

Con translated the news that his brother "felt honored to announce" to me.

His brother had rehearsed. "That guy" Sihanouk, he explained, thought he could keep his power and his communist friends if he let Gen. Lon Nol form a new cabinet to govern the country. He thought Lon Nol would stay loyal to the throne and that he and his right wing, whom Sihanouk called the "Blue Khmers," would make a mess of things and then the people would beg him to come back and that this would satisfy the other side, the "Red Khmers." But!—he poked a finger in the air—Lon Nol is smart—the finger tapped his temple—because he invited Son Ngoc Thanh to join him in the government, and already three battalions of Thanh's Khmer Serei were on their way across the border to join Lon Nol's army. He also made a law to devalue the *riel*, so now it is impossible for the North Vietnamese to buy rice in Cambodia for their troops. Lon Nol promises to drive all the Vietnamese, all the communists, from Cambodia. The Americans are his friends; all of the Cambodian army follows him; all of the monks and holy men give him their blessing; all of his Khmer Krom brothers love him and will fight for him, for their country.

As we were about to take our leave, Krech and Sinh arrived with the poor tender-eyed girl in tow. With some ceremony, Sinh placed a covered pot of soup in the center of the mat; he said it was prepared especially for me and he begged the host to serve it. Krech nudged the girl and she set a bowl of what looked like tapioca pudding next to me.

"It's like caviar," Con said.

I thanked the girl and she slipped away between the grinning Scouts. Con's brother ladled the soup into bowls and passed them around. It was an orange, fishy-smelling soup; as it settled in my bowl, beads of grease rose to the surface and with them the bodies of dozens of boiled red ants. I looked at Con. He smiled seraphically.

"To make it crunchy," he said.

"Before, they ate you," Sinh slurped a spoonful. "Now you can eat them!"

Krech gobbed a little pile of the pus-colored "caviar" onto a dish next to my knee. "And this is their eggs. Very good. Eat them before they are born to eat you."

•

I drifted into a half-sleep in my hammock, accompanied in and out of dreams by tiny yellow points of lamplight and the muffled sounds of children. I dreamed, or heard, a quick exchange of small arms fire near the base of the mountain; dreamed, or saw, chickens take flight when a night hawk swooped down from a banyan tree.

Krech shook me awake, babbling, almost shouting at me in Cambodian. A terrified boy in blue pajamas ran past. I could not understand Krech, but

I knew he was frightened and that was something I had never seen. He took my hand and pulled me out of the hammock; off balance, barefoot and blinking, I struggled to awake on the run as Krech nearly dragged me across the village center.

"My pistol!" I said.

"No. No. No time!"

The people who had not already gathered beneath the big house near the pagoda were scurrying toward it from all directions. Krech knocked into an old man, who would have hit the ground if his wife had not caught him. The people on the fringes of the crowd were looking up at the moon, a waxing crescent, gesturing at it, pointing. A woman called out something to me I did not understand. As we got closer and the crowd got thicker, Krech dropped my hand and shouldered a path through the people; I followed in his wake. At the center of the shifting crowd was an inner circle of about twenty men in all manner of undress squatting on their heels around Ut Le's radio, which sat on a bench in a dark golden light.

It was Radio Phnom Penh. The voice was American. It was Neil Armstrong, and he was walking around on the moon talking to us about it.

One of the squatting soldiers shook his head and his beer bottle back and forth. "It's not true," he said loudly. "It's a trick."

"Fuck that," said Sirois in English and Khmer. "Shut up and listen."

A man standing at my elbow asked if this was true. I said it was.

"It can't be true," someone said. "Human beings can't walk on Buddha-being-Moon. *Reahou*, the dragon, would devour them!"

"The *krus* didn't predict this. Someone run to the temple and bring the monks."

"If they are up there, then Buddha willed them to be."

An old man holding a lantern said no one could win against the Americans now. "They can see the communists from there. They can't be on the dark side because that's inside *Reahou*'s mouth."

"They can see *us!*" One child, then another, began to cry.

"How can they see us? We can't see them."

"If they can get there, they can see us," a woman claimed.

Two boys pushed and pulled a smaller one away from the house and crowd into the moonlit hamlet center. The boy wailed and ran back under cover; the ones who had dragged him out hesitated a second, then ducked back into the shadow.

Strait made his way over to me with a bottle of beer for each of us. "They can put a damn rocket ship on the moon," he said. "But they can't get me a half-assed radio here. Flash Fucking Gordon."

.

The little old lady with the ground-down teeth and stubby fingers who had arranged our entry procession turned out to be the midwife. Only she could decide when Con's wife, Chanthi, was done roasting. After the child was born, Con moved out of his house to make room for the roasting and leave things to the women. On a raised bed of bamboo slats built in their little house for the occasion, Chanthi lay roasting over six small smokeless fires built in clay pots beneath the bed. The midwife and Chanthi's sister took care of the house and the fires and the baby.

"If she is cold she could get sick," Con told me. "The heat from the fires helps her relax and heal. She's not hot from them, only warm."

It was a boy child, their first, and they had named him Chau Scott for me. I was married, but had no children of my own. In one of our language learning sessions, Con told me that if it was a son, they were going to name him for me because of my "kindness." He said he felt sorry for me and my wife, married three years and still no children.

Chanthi sat upright in a little chair in the doorway of their house. She and the child were covered with a red striped silk shawl so that only their faces showed. The monks who had walked in with us sat cross-legged on a mat near her feet. They took turns chanting blessings in a low sleepy humming that seemed to put the older monk to sleep. Chanthi made a little speech to the midwife; she asked her forgiveness for all the trouble she had caused her. Con took two bundles of sweets wrapped in pink cellophane from Ut Le and presented them to the midwife. Attached to one was a roll of American money as fat as a cigar, which quickly disappeared into her blouse pocket. Con took the boy, bundled in a yellow cloth, and held him against his chest while the older monk chanted a blessing and Chanthi watched.

The midwife made me sit cross-legged facing away from the monks, then gave me the baby to hold, adjusting my forearm, a little impatiently, so that it supported his head. Krech laughed and made a cooing noise, but she stared him quiet. Reciting a poem or psalm in Khmer I could not understand, the old woman tied white strings around the child's wrists for good luck. His skin was golden brown, his hand barely big enough to close around my little finger. She daubed a thumbprint of rice flour onto the soft spot on his head to make the skull close up, and with a pat on his tummy, pronounced his name: "Chau Sa-cot."

Ut Le said something solemn. Con explained.

"He says when my boy grows up it will be good for him to have an American name. The Americans will save us and our villages."

"*Aysey* will save us," Krech said.

"The Americans will help him."

12

HO CHI MINH was dead, but it didn't matter to us, not to the South Vietnamese and Americans at least. When the Khmer Krom heard that Sihanouk had attended Ho's funeral in Hanoi, the only chief of state who did, they said that here was final proof, if any proof was needed, that Sihanouk would betray his country to the *yuons* any day now if nothing was done to stop him. Ut Le listened to Radio Phnom Penh and every word of gossip about Cambodia nightly; he was full of predictions and plans for Lon Nol's Cambodian army. His favorite scenario, usually punctuated with kicks and stabs, was that of a massive offensive from the west by the Cambodian army against the North Vietnamese in Cambodia that would drive them headlong into the Khmer Krom in the CIDG camps along the Vietnam border, where they would be blown up by bombs and ground into the dirt by the Khmer Krom. The prisoners—he jabbed them with his bayonet—they would drown in the Vinh Te Canal. Don't spill the master's tea!

In the communications bunker, where several of the Scouts and I sat talking in the evenings, Ut Le raged to the choir. The South Vietnamese artillery battery by the landing pad was firing intermittent rounds over our heads at the mountain, each round another brass casing for the platoon leader to sell on the black market. Krech sat in the dark corner, naked except for black boxer shorts, visible only when he dragged on his cigarette.

"I want to see Sinhanouk's gambling houses. They are golden palaces."

"The communists will take them."

"He gave Kompong Som to the Chinese to bring weapons to the North Vietnamese in ships. He'll give the gambling houses to the *yuons*. He'll give them Phnom Penh. The whole kingdom forever. Slaves!"

Ut Le spat. "Not me."

Our own radio was quiet, but on the South Vietnamese net in the far room, a frightened voice was reporting incoming mortar rounds on his lonely outpost. To the militiaman calling in from the darkness, it was the end of the world; to us it was yet another group of northerners lobbing a few mortar rounds on an outpost to keep the defenders' heads down as they crossed the border.

Sinh shook Con awake. Con had taken to wearing a flak jacket all the time, even while he slept in the bunker. Sinh thought it was an insult to the *knay tanh* he wore around his neck; Con said it was just "insurance," using the English word to confound Sinh.

"Go get your *Tror*," Sinh said, "and play us a love song."

.

The bad news came in two packets on one helicopter. The American packet was delivered by a round-faced young second lieutenant wearing brand-new jungle fatigues and Military Intelligence brass. He saluted and introduced himself as Lieutenant Horan, then handed me the mail pouch.

"Your orders are inside, sir."

"What orders?"

"I thought you already knew. Sorry 'bout that. I'm your replacement."

I was ordered to report to the province senior advisor in Chuong Thien Province, there to serve as advisor to the Province Phoenix Program. I thought there must have been some mistake; it had to be a mistake. I found Chuong Thien on the map, a hundred miles south, deep in the flooded delta, right on the edge of the nefarious U Minh Forest where the North Vietnamese who were passing through our mountains were headed to regroup.

"It won't be much different down there," Major Fields told me. "No main force American units now, with the 9th Division leaving, North Vietnamese crawling all over the place. Flatter, maybe. Hot too, in more ways than one, if what I hear is true. Flatter'n a tortilla."

I found Cop and together we found Chau Got and Ut Le lounging in a jeep. I asked Cop to explain.

I watched Chau Got's face while he did: at first surprise, then that blank look.

"Vi Thanh?" Chau Got said the name of the province capital where I was to report. "No, I never heard of that."

"Don't go," said Ut Le. "That's wrong. *Buku* communists in Chuong Thien."

Cop said that the Khmer Krom down there were very poor, powerless, almost not even citizens. It was all Vietnamese.

How could they replace me, take me away from the Scouts? We worked so well together. How could a round-faced butter bar with a nervous laugh and no infantry training . . . ? How would I tell Con? What about the child?

"I only have three months left. They won't make me go. I'll fight this."

The bad news in the other packet, which came down through the South

Vietnamese chain of command, was explained to Major Fields and me by Major Quyen. Due to the American withdrawal, the government in Saigon had passed the Mobilization Law, which extended the draft age for the regular army to thirty-eight; seventeen-year-olds and men from thirty-nine to forty-three would be drafted in the regional and popular forces. He showed us a list of the many professions and special assignments that would no longer provide exemption from the draft. He underlined "Kit Carson Scout" with his thumbnail.

If they were drafted, they would be split up and sent to regular South Vietnamese units. They would be mocked and mistreated. They would be sent ahead on point to trigger ambushes or step on mines, wasted. They would be taken from their families and if they were paid at all, it would be a pittance. And I would not be there to help them.

"We promised them we'd take care of them. I promised them. I don't believe this shit!"

Aziz moved to my side and squeezed my elbow to warn me to watch my manners, be calm.

Major Quyen was amused. He told me not to worry.

"I'm not leaving until I'm sure they're going to be taken care of," I said.

"Like hell you aren't, Captain." Major Fields was not amused.

"Those were *orders* you got this morning, not a fucking suggestion. You been hanging out in the villages too long. Your orders say Chuong Thien tomorrow and that's where you'll be. The Scouts aren't your problem any more; they're Lieutenant Horan's, and ours."

"Why can't they join Captain Reap's company? Then they could stay here and. . . ."

Major Quyen held up his hand. "Don't worry, Captain. We'll take care of this. We can change the name of their status if we have to. They won't have to go to another place."

"Don't tell the Scouts about this," Major Fields said. "They might do something rash."

"Like split and join the Khmer Krom in the mountains? I wouldn't blame them."

"Which is exactly why you're not going to say anything to them. Instead, you're going to start getting your shit together so you're ready when that chopper comes in in the morning."

I turned to go.

"And while you're getting your shit together, you can do some work on your attitude. You're an officer."

"Yes, sir," I said.

Aziz followed me out. "I'm a man, too," I told him.

"Yes, so are we."

Chau Got sent word to the Scouts who were not in the compound that evening, and they came in, all but two, to say goodbye. They knew I was angry and frustrated. Krech and Ut Le tried to cheer me up with sumptuous descriptions of the Vietnamese whores in Chuong Thien.

Sinh promised that he would come visit and introduce me to his cousin who lived in a village near Vi Thanh. With Cop interpreting, and the others agreeing, Chau Got assured me that they did not feel betrayed that I was leaving them. They knew I wanted to stay and could not; it was not my fault and I should not think it was. They would be fine with the new lieutenant and they would teach him like they had taught me.

After a short meal and many bottles of beer at the restaurant, where Sinh gave me his red-and-gold scarf and Con presented me with a Zippo engraved with "Chau Scott" to remember his son, and him too, seven of us went to the photographer's shop and sat for a group portrait before a mural of mountains and waving palm trees. In it, Aziz is frowning in disapproval at Ut Le and Krech, who stand next to him laughing. Con and I sit together in the front row, with his hand on my knee, mine covering his. Chau Got sits rigid, clamped upright, at the front center. His jaw is locked tight; his black eyes are fixed on something approaching, slowly and relentlessly, in the distance.

13

THE PHOENIX PROGRAM in Chuong Thien Province was nothing more than an elaborate and tedious little bureaucracy created to generate a steady stream of paperwork for higher headquarters, in triplicate, documenting the elimination of the members of the Viet Cong infrastructure—the VCI—in the five districts. We reported weekly and monthly, and in each successive report the number of neutralized VCI increased. A staff of eight Vietnamese civilians, most of them educated young men who were avoiding the draft, typed and retyped and mimeographed reports from the districts to send up through channels to Saigon. They made elaborate briefing charts and acetate overlays with colored columns: red for killed, blue for captured. In an adjoining office three American enlisted men, a first lieutenant and I did the same thing in English.

We had no way of knowing whether the reports were valid or not; there was no way to check. We Americans believed that the numbers were inflated. Chuong Thien ranked as the third least "pacified" province in South Vietnam, meaning that it was almost completely controlled by the communists. We controlled the province and district towns and in daylight the main roads, but the rest of the outlying hamlets, the U Minh Forest to the east, and the vast open rice paddies and canals were controlled by main force communist units and the North Vietnamese. Daylight ambushes of small units and their American advisors were common, as were large-scale ambushes of South Vietnamese heliborne operations. They seemed to know our every move before we made it; indeed, as it turned out, they did. We responded with B-52s, artillery, and helicopter gunship attacks on their fortified positions and troops caught in the open. Entire companies on both sides were ground up on a single operation.

There were certainly enough communist corpses that could be "identified" as communist cadre by the local Phoenix personnel. Questioning the validity of the identification of the dead and captured as part of the infrastructure would have been an insult to the district chief. Worse, it would have offended the dignity of Colonel Trung, the province chief of police. A fat, sweaty man with oiled curls and inch-long pinkie nails, Trung controlled the Phoenix Program and the Police Special Branch. He resented the Americans who presumed to advise him—me, a lowly captain, in particular; he tolerated us only because we had the money and materiel to increase his own power. I rarely saw him; when I did, he spoke, one eyebrow uplifted, and I listened. It was said that he stripped female prisoners and taped their legs and thighs to the cell bars so he could have them from behind at his leisure.

The American compound was on the opposite side of the town from Trung's prison and headquarters. It was well guarded, recently built, spacious, and comfortable. Many of the officers' quarters were air-conditioned, as were the offices. The tennis courts were clay. After dark, when the native help had gone home, it was a well-contained American camp with movies in the evenings, the smell of grilling steaks in the air, and music by Sergeant Pepper's Lonely Hearts Club Band.

In my room I read books, wrote letters home and to Tri Ton, and crossed off the days. I thought of offering to extend for a second tour if I could be guaranteed that it would be in Tri Ton, but news from home made it clear that my marriage was in peril; another tour would destroy it. Cop wrote letters to me for the Scouts who Major Quyen had managed to keep in Tri Ton in their same status. He said that Lieutenant Horan was having a special room built for them in the compound, and the Scouts liked and trusted him. As if he sensed that I was jealous of Horan, he added that the Scouts missed me too much and wanted me to come back. They were going on many more ambushes. Con took a tiny piece of shrapnel in his left eye and had to go to the hospital in Can Tho. Captain Strait had "found" a jeep-mounted recoilless rifle, and he and Reap and Sinh were shooting it into the caves on Coto. Reap's wife had another baby, "also a girl."

Cop's last letter came a few days before I left Chuong Thien for Saigon and home. It was typewritten, single-spaced, on two blue sheets of paper so thin that the *e*'s were punched through. I read it a dozen times. The first sentence said, "I am sorry to write you that your friend Sinh is already dead." He knew I would want to know all the details.

Lieutenant Horan and seven of the Scouts were walking on a paddy dike east of Krang Don hamlet, looking for a group of four communists that had been seen out there earlier. They saw the four men moving toward the mountain about three hundred meters away. Instead of waiting for orders, Sinh and two others got in a hurry and jumped down into the paddies to give chase. Sinh stepped on a mine. His foot was blown off and most of the flesh below the knee peeled back. They put a tourniquet on it, but he was bleeding badly and screaming. Lieutenant Horan sent two Scouts to run to the outpost at Krang Don, where there was an American advisory team and a medic, and a radio to call for a helicopter. He made sure that they understood to tell the Americans that the wounded man was to be described as an American. One of the most important things they had been promised when they were recruited as Scouts was that they would be treated the same as Americans, "*Yim yao my*," when it came to medical evacuation priorities.

When they came back, the medic, Sergeant Rosario, put on a better tourniquet. Lieutenant Horan told him to hurry up and slam Sinh with a morphine syringe, but the sergeant said he had not brought any morphine because they had said it was a Scout and his captain told him the morphine was for Americans only. Lieutenant Horan swore at him and sent him away.

They waited and waited for the helicopter. Sinh screamed and dug with one foot in the paddy mud. Lieutenant Horan held him in his lap. Sinh cried out for the helicopter. The other Scouts told him do not worry, we get treated the same as the Americans. Sinh got delirious, crying, "*Yim yao my!*" over and over and over again. It was more than thirty minutes before the helicopter came. By then all of Sinh's blood had drained out into the paddy and he was gone with it.

Lieutenant Horan screamed at the helicopter pilot asking what had taken him so long to respond for an American wounded. The pilot said the request he got was for a Vietnamese wounded. Lieutenant Horan cursed the man and told him to go away. They wrapped Sinh in his poncho and slung it beneath a length of rebar to carry him home. Lieutenant Horan wouldn't let anyone spell him on his end, even though his shoulder was gouged raw by the iron bar.

After they took him home to be buried, they found out that when the American radioman at District called in the request, he was asked which American was wounded and had replied that it was one of the Scouts. The request was downgraded. Then they learned that the month's pay that was promised a Scout's family after his death, with a year's pay to follow, would not come for months or more. This meant that Sinh's family could not afford a proper funeral. Lieutenant Horan drove to Can Tho and waved his .45 at a frightened clerk until he got the money. Cop said it was a beautiful funeral, with monks and music.

In a handwritten postscript, he apologized for so much bad news at once, but said I should also know that Con's little son Chau Scott had died. Dr. Brown said to tell me "causes unknown." No one knew where Con was or whether he knew about his son.

14

CHAU DOC, the capital city of the province, sits on the Cambodian border at the confluence of the two main branches of the Bassac River, the brother of the wider Mekong with which it intermingles and will soon join downstream. For fifteen centuries Chau Doc was the Khmer temple city of Moat Chruok, the Eastern, or Glorious, Gate of the great Khmer Kingdom of Angkor. Long before the building of roads and canals, traders on vessels from India and China that had labored upstream from the South China Sea with silk and spices met beneath its temple spires with others who had come downstream from Cambodia and Laos with gold, ivory, and exotic animals. In the last years of the eighteenth century, the Vietnamese took control of the city and renamed it Chau Doc.

Under the French it became the provincial capital, a commercial and administrative center between Phnom Penh and the rice rich delta of Cochinchina. Along the river bank the French built a stone retaining wall, and atop it, a wide, paved promenade with a stone balustrade, an avenue shaded by palms and mangoes and cooled by the soft evening breeze off the wide river. With taxes taken from the river trade and the rubber and rice harvests, the colonial masters built imposing administrative buildings of cement and stucco, with tile roofs, marble floors, and high ceilings; with them, also fronting the promenade, they built private mansions with courtyards, fountains, and gardens. Chau Doc's elegant French and Vietnamese restaurants, notably the Cuu Long, attracted European visitors from as far away as Saigon. Twelve years later, the administrative offices were occupied by military and civilian officers of the government of South Vietnam, and most of the grand stucco buildings and mansions, air-conditioned now, were headquarters and homes for the province's American military advisory team.

When Strait, Reap, and Sem Ly landed at the helipad behind the American compound, they were told that it would be three hours before the swing ship, the helicopter carrying mail and supplies to the districts, would be leaving for Tri Ton.

Strait didn't mind the layover, quite the contrary; it was the fat sweaty sergeant behind the desk that riled him. Porky Pig with sideburns.

"You know where the bar is," he told Strait. "I mean you. I don't know about them." He had that way of talking about Vietnamese—to him all Asians were Vietnamese—as though they could not understand him; he pointed at Reap and Sem Ly like they were pets.

"What's wrong with that one, anyway?"

He meant Reap, who held a limp, skinny hand over his mouth.

Strait started over the desk, airborne in an instant, but Sem Ly caught him by the shirt tail and pulled him back in a flurry of papers.

"That one is a captain, you sorry-ass excuse for a soldier! Can't you read rank? That one's recovering from a serious wound he got defending fucking fat boys. You get up off your ass and salute him or I'll. . . ."

The sergeant complied.

"Now tuck in your shirt. If you can."

When their backs were turned, the sergeant saluted them with his middle finger.

Strait suggested a cold beer in the bar in the Seabee compound next door, but Sem Ly said that Reap should get a little exercise and maybe a bowl of soup. They would walk to the market and meet him back at the helipad in two hours. He did not say, did not need to, that after three months in an American hospital, a stroll among the sounds and smells of his own people would be far more restorative than an American barroom.

They walked slowly along the promenade toward the market. Sem Ly measured his pace by Reap's weaker one, and held one hand discreetly behind his back in case he stumbled. The air was sweet with the smell of roasting bananas; here and there along the balustrade people were gathering in small groups, chatting excitedly among themselves and calling out to passing friends.

A young mother, her child propped on the railing, beckoned to a friend. "The bodies are coming," she said. "They were in Bai Mia this morning. Come watch with us."

Sem Ly left Reap for a second to go to the balustrade and have a look at the river. He saw nothing unusual, only sampans crossing and passing upstream, fishermen throwing nets from their bows, a boy on the bank drowning a caged rat for his breakfast. As Sem Ly caught up with Reap, he wondered if Reap was telling the truth when he said there was no pain; he moved so slowly, seemed so old, so frail, and even timid, the perfect opposite of what he had been on that night back in December only a few months before.

·

It was at the peak of the harvest. For that reason, Reap had claimed with confidence, the communists would assume that they would stay close to the villages—a perfect night for a roving patrol, a mobile ambush. He had gathered up a half-dozen men, three of them from Sem Ly's reconnaissance platoon, and set out in the dark. They were the best of his men, all as eager as he was to gun down some *yuons* and spread a little fear on the mountain. He gave Sem Ly a rough idea of the route he planned to take and left him in charge. No need to tell the Americans, he'd said, they would just worry. He would be back in the morning with a few trophies.

They checked on two of his company's outposts at the foot of Coto Mountain, picking up a couple of volunteers from each of them. On their way to the third at Wat Triek, traveling too quickly along the edge of the blasted forest, they ran head-on into a well-armed communist carrying party. Reap's bodyguard said that everybody fired at once and threw grenades. Reap yelled to charge them, and when he did, a piece of shrapnel from a B40 rocket tore through his lower jaw, severing bone and muscle, scattering bloody teeth.

A runner from the command bunker shook Strait awake. He was in tears.

"Captain Reap had his face shot off," he cried. "Oh, please!"

They brought him back in a hammock slung beneath a bamboo pole and laid him on a stretcher in Sirois's little dispensary. A soft, gurgling, moaning noise was all the sound he made. Sirois shot him up with morphine and slowly untied the bloody sarongs that held his face together. He cleared the mess of severed tendons and nerves, clamped off the bleeders, started an IV, put a pharyngeal tube down his throat to clear an air passage, and redressed the wound. He swore softly and turned to Strait, who stood behind him.

"He won't live if we don't get him to an American hospital. The Vietnamese can't handle something like this; he's got to go to Saigon."

Strait had already called for a medevac, making the request a Priority One, for a critically wounded American.

"I told them it was you."

"They won't take him."

"Fuck that," Strait said. "I'm going with him if I have to. You watch me here."

"He was so goddamn good-looking," Sirois said. "He might make it; but I tell you if he does, you won't ever see that smile again."

For three months American army doctors worked to rebuild Reap's jaw with bone grafts from his pelvis. On his first visit, Strait tried to talk to him through the bandages. Reap's eyes were open and followed Strait's hand, but they were fixed inward. Strait told him that Kim and the children were fine, and that he would be, too, but he got no response. In the third month, when he first saw Reap's horribly raw and rearranged face, Strait held his hand and wept silently. Reap recognized his voice but chose not to look at him. Strait feared then that Reap would never return, would never be able to surface into the frightful light of the hospital ward, where the only familiar sounds were the groans of the wounded; the only access to the waking world, the soft voice of a woman who said her name was Xhen Ni and her hand beneath his head as she fed him from a spoon.

Lt. Jenny Stevens, "Xhen Ni," told Strait that she believed she could restore Reap only to a point. She could get him on his feet and functioning, but it would take his wife and children, all his family, to rekindle his mind and spirit.

For Reap those months in the hospital were a single, recurring, hundred-day dream from which he did not even try to escape. In various distorted versions, he relived memories of his childhood.

When he was five years old his father had come home from the fields early one morning and lay down on the floor as if he were dead. Sok was forty-four years old, his wife Phim, forty; Reap was their youngest son, the child of their old age. For twenty years as village chief, Sok had struggled to save his people, his family, and his own life from the butchers on both sides of the Vietnamese war. On that day in 1947 a runner had come from Tanop Tasor to tell Sok that his only surviving brother had been killed by the Viet Minh the night before. His brother had sounded the drum to warn the others. They tied him over the drum and impaled him, hammering a pole as thick as the messenger's wrist into his anus with mallets until he died.

Sok sold his valuables and ordered a *stupa*, an ornate memorial, built on the temple grounds for his ashes. He took Reap with him on the long journey to Phnom Penh to purchase religious supplies for the dedication and blessing of the monument. On the third day, on a bumpy road south of Phnom Penh, four armed men stopped their little open bus and ordered Sok and Reap and the others out. The men were dark Khmer and wore the black pajamas of peasants; they were barefoot and tattooed in Sanskrit. The one in charge waved a huge French revolver that was attached to his belt by a lanyard. Of the seven passengers, Sok was the only adult male; the others were women going to the market in the city, one carrying an infant and dragging a frightened little girl by the hand.

The men said they were not bandits; they were Khmer Serei, freedom fighters who served Son Ngoc Thanh and would liberate Cambodia from the French. Two of them were armed with long rice knives; one of them held a huge British Enfield, a rifle almost as large as he was. The ones with the rice knives were in their early teens, not much bigger than Reap; they were skittish, brandishing their knives at the cowering passengers, clearly exhilarated to be inflicting fear.

The leader tucked his revolver into his armpit as he inspected the women's papers and pawed through their bundles. One by one he let them get back onto the bus, accepting with a bow a donation from each.

Then he turned to Sok, who was holding Reap's hand.

"We don't want to see your papers. They're forged. You're a spy for the French. You come from the south; you're a traitor."

"Let's take him for a little boat ride," said the boy with the rifle.

The blood drained from Sok's face; his knees buckled and he swayed slightly. Reap felt his father's hand turn cold and damp as it shook uncontrollably in his. He fell down, embraced his father's feet, and begged the men to spare his life. He "cried and cried."

The man waved his revolver, motioning to Sok to collect his son and get on the bus. When one of the men protested, he hissed, raised his gun, and ordered them back into the forest.

They rode in silence. The women sitting across from them averted their eyes from the pale old man who held his son's head against his chest and struggled to hold back tears himself. After a polite interval, one of the women passed a clean cloth to Sok, who wetted it in his mouth and wiped the dust and tears from his son's face.

When they got home, Sok lived for two days before he joined his ancestors while sleeping.

In the hundred-day dream Reap was sometimes his father, weak-kneed, being pulled down to the earth by a shapeless weight, but the child crying at his feet was his daughter Chandha. Or it was he who lay down on the floor of his house, and it was his wife Kim who was pale and had large gentle hands, kneeling beside him, mopping his brow, and holding his head to feed him. Sometimes the man with the revolver was Uchs, his face painted like a temple dancer's, waving his Chinese pistol; sometimes he was the man waving the revolver, and he was ashamed of the pleasure he felt from wielding such power over his fellow Khmer Krom. At night he sometimes dreamed he slept on a ledge inside the *stupa* with Sirois at his side; on a wall there was a chain-of-command chart with photographs of the district unit officers, but his own photograph, above 188 Company, had been replaced by his brother Dom's. In all the versions, at some time or other, he lay on his back, arms at his sides, in a little sampan, floating quietly in the dark while something huge and horrible swam patiently back and forth beneath him. More than anything, in all the versions, whether he was his father or his young self, the greatest dread came over him when he returned home. His mother wept at the sight of him and wrung her hands. A child ran away from him terrified; his father tried to touch his face, but could not. Sometimes there were European soldiers in his house, tall white men with mustaches, neither French nor American, but foul-smelling and noisy; they had been having sex with his wife, who cried quietly but did not fight them; it wasn't anger that he felt, but a suffocating realization that this was what he deserved.

·

When he was awakened that morning on the Chau Doc promenade, it was by Sem Ly, who shook him hard. They were sitting on a stone bench; the hand that had been shielding his crooked face had fallen into his lap.

"Something is happening," Sem Ly said. "Look at all the people. It must be more bodies like those we heard about. Do you remember I told you about it in Saigon? Do you?"

Reap said yes, with a slight nod. The clucking sound made by his clumsy tongue embarrassed him and he hid his face again.

"Let's look."

The crowd at the railing had increased, but the noisy chatter had been subdued to whispering by the scene on the river. The bodies themselves were hard to see at first in the muddy water: they were naked and bloated, belly up, as wet and brown as the river that carried them. Two men in a sampan, one steering with the long-stemmed propeller, the other pushing with a pole, were nudging a round carcass that had once been a woman back into the current in the middle of the river. The hair of a gray, swollen, little girl had snagged on a sunken weir; when a boy in a small boat tried to free her, she rolled once, then again, revealing that she, like the others, had been bound with her hands behind her back before she had been shot. There were more than a hundred, the spectators guessed, in the swollen flotilla that drifted slowly past Chau Doc. Boats of all shapes accompanied the bodies on both sides, herding them into the middle of the river, men prodding, examining, fanning the stench from their faces. The dead ones had floated across the border into Vietnam that morning, and would, from all reports from upstream, take all day to pass the city on their slow trip to the South China Sea. A week before, the people of Tan Chau had seen the same thing on the Mekong a few miles away. Now there were these, and everyone watching believed that there would be more.

They were Vietnamese civilians or, more accurately, Vietnamese citizens of Cambodia, and they were the first victims of Gen. Lon Nol's purge of "Vietnamese Communist agents" in Cambodia. Some were Chinese; all were merchants, farmers, bureaucrats, and their families who were accused of being communist sympathizers, but whose real crime was that they were not Khmer. While Prince Sihanouk was visiting France "for health reasons," the general and his followers unleashed a campaign against the hated Vietnamese inside Cambodia. It was a long-smoldering fire of racial hatred that was easily rekindled. He ordered his army to attack the North Vietnamese staging areas in the border regions, and to arrest and detain all enemy agents everywhere.

In his home province of Prey Veng, long occupied by the North Vietnamese who were operating across the border against South Vietnam, a popular uprising was staged against the Vietnamese occupation and Prince Sihanouk, whose neutral policies had for so many years permitted such an outrage. In cities like Neak Luong upriver from Chau Doc, thousands of Vietnamese were rounded up by Cambodian soldiers and police; untold numbers of them were marched to the river, herded aboard old LSTs, shot, and dumped into the current. The battalions of Khmer Krom mercenaries sent to Phnom Penh from American Special Forces camps by Son Ngoc Thanh were rumored to be employed in a purge of communist agents from the ranks of Lon Nol's army and from the government in the capital. A mob of unemployed students, bearing framed portraits of Sihanouk, demonstrated outside the embassies of the North Vietnamese and Viet Cong, then sacked and burned both buildings while uniformed police watched from the sidelines. "Dirty, silly Viet Cong," their banners said, "give up your ridiculous ideas."

The attacks on the North Vietnamese troops in the sanctuaries were futile; poorly trained and ill-equipped units of the Cambodian army were no match for the hardened North Vietnamese. In the capital and the army, however, the roundup and arrest of Cambodia's "enemies," many of them Sihanouk sympathizers, was cruel and effective. From exile, Sihanouk fiercely condemned the arrests and massacres as atrocities; he called the Khmer Krom battalions who were securing the city "Lon Nol's *ton ton macoutes*." Surprised by the sudden ferocity of the populace and the speed of events, the small American contingent of military and CIA personnel in Phnom Penh watched warily, while "unofficially" encouraging Lon Nol and Sirik Matak in their campaign against the communists. In Saigon the South

Vietnamese government was equally wary, pleased to see new pressure against their communist enemies but seething with bitterness over the reports of the Vietnamese bodies floating downstream. The people watching on the promenade in Chau Doc, Vietnamese and Khmer Krom alike, knew what no officials of any stripe were saying: that the bodies were a sincere carnal message from the awakened Khmers to their *yuon* neighbors.

A soldier in nondescript fatigues tapped Sem Ly gently on the shoulder.

"I think the captain is sick," he said.

Reap had leaned forward onto the railing, supporting his weight with his forearms. Sem Ly helped him stand.

"Let's go to a restaurant. You need to eat something."

Reap covered his face and shook his head no.

"Please. I insist, Reap. You need food to strengthen you. Some soup."

"Go to the Cuu Long," the soldier said. "They have shark's fin soup, for virility. It's expensive, but maybe you should spend the money now. When those bodies reach the ocean, the sharks will eat them and get polluted."

15

THE GOOD NEWS, so long prophesied, so long awaited, spread through the Khmer Krom villages, hamlets, fighting camps, and marketplaces as fast as bare feet and the human voice could carry it. The long wait was over; the time had come. Little groups of itinerant monks in pale worn saffron robes brought tidings of a new government in Cambodia, one blessed by their superiors, that would rid the kingdom of the godless communists and restore the national religion, peace, and a brotherhood of believers. Cattle drivers crossed the border with news that, yes, indeed, the government was collecting all of the old 500-*riel* bank notes and replacing them with new ones to make it impossible for the communists to use cash to buy Cambodian rice for their armies.

Traveling at night along footpaths and worn paddy dikes, revered *krus*, long in hiding, brought word of the return of the White Crocodile. Sighted by dozens of holy men at different places along the Mekong, the pale beast was he who was present at the birth of the kingdom, and was believed to be the Dragon King himself, father of kings. The White Crocodile controlled the tidal flow of the Mekong; he appeared only at a time when Cambodia was on the verge of great change. The ancient palm leaf inscriptions foretold that the old king would fall and be replaced by a new one when the Golden Palaces at the junction of the river were destroyed, and now Sihanouk's golden gambling casinos at the same location had failed and were closed. In Sihanouk's absence, the Queen Mother had drawn the sacred royal sword from its scabbard and found its beautiful blade corroded by a black bloody substance: no sign could be worse for the royal family.

Khmer Krom soldiers in civilian clothes carried messages from the battalions in hiding to the Special Forces fighting camps and the villages beneath Coto declaring that Chau Dara, the secretive leader of the FLKK, was none other than Lon Nol himself, and his alliance with Son Ngoc Thanh was a signal for all Khmer Krom to unite and prepare the way for the new government. There were those among the holy men who whispered to their adherents that Chau Dara, Lon Nol, was without doubt the *Aysey*, the immortal White One from the mountain, the Messiah himself made flesh.

•

Early in the second week of March 1970, Col. Michael Healy, "Iron Mike," the commanding officer of the 5th Special Forces Group, Vietnam, received a secure message from Major Zachary at Moc Hoa, a CIDG fighting camp on the border west of Saigon. "Something was going on" among his Khmer Krom troops, Zachary said. "Something big." Son Ngoc Thanh had just visited the camp, unannounced, and there was talk among the men about going to help Lon Nol. From Maj. Lee Mize, commander of Detachment B-36 at Long Hai, the headquarters of the 3rd Mobile Strike Force, Colonel Healy received the same message: his Khmer Krom "strikers," the majority of his three battalions, were antsy, excited, holding open meetings about setting out for the border .

In the early sixties Colonel Healy had been operations officer for the 5th Special Forces Group. He had been one of the architects of the CIDG program, with its emphasis on manning border camps with indigenous troops to deny the communists infiltration routes and more importantly to deny them the local populace. "Iron Mike" had an intellect as bright and fierce as his blue eyes. He had an Irish temper, a finely tuned bullshit detector, and a nearly legendary reputation as a fighting infantry officer, earned as a battalion commander with the 173rd Airborne Brigade in the highlands. He created the Mobile Strike Forces, dubbed "Mike Forces" after him, and filled them with Khmer Krom soldiers he knew to be loyal to their American officers and fierce in combat. "The Khmer Krom are gentle people, it's true," he said. "But they will fight. Oh, how they will fight."

In IV Corps, the Mekong Delta region, Colonel Healy was able to fill his camps and Mike Forces with Khmer Krom soldiers because Son Ngoc Thanh provided him with a continuous flow of recruits. Healy and Thanh formed what they fondly called the "Old Friendship School" for the training of Cambodian Special Forces. Their alliance provided Healy with crack troops, and it provided Thanh with an experienced, well-trained and -equipped army of ethnic Khmers for his "National Revolutionary Movement." Over the years, Thanh had "spotted" his Khmer Krom leaders in all the fighting camps and Mike Force units in the delta, so that when the time came for Thanh to return to Cambodia, his forces would have their own secret chain of command within the structure of the CIDG program.

"Dr. Thanh knew more about the CIDG in IV Corps than I did," Healy said.

Hours after he had heard from Majors Zachary and Mize, Colonel Healy and his bodyguard drove to Thanh's little apartment in the Khmer pagoda in

Saigon, not far from Chasseloup-Laubat high school that he and Sihanouk and Lon Nol had attended. A small round-faced man with horn-rimmed glasses, a high forehead, and serene expression, Thanh was every bit the elder statesman in exile. He greeted Colonel Healy warmly, knowingly, and the two sat down to discuss the situation over tea. "And, as always," Healy said, "he was the instructor and I was his student." Since 1945, when Sihanouk deposed him as the Cambodian prime minister, Thanh had been in exile in Japan, Thailand, and South Vietnam, supported by Sihanouk's enemies and reviled by the prince as a traitor and westernizer.

Thanh told Healy that he wanted to accept Gen. Lon Nol and Sirik Matak's offer to join their new government when they carried out their coup against Sihanouk in the next few days. The new government would appeal to the people of Cambodia because it vowed to rid the fatherland of the hated communists and Vietnamese, but it must move quickly to find a middle path of reasonable government and economic recovery and to create a working republic to which Sihanouk could return as titular head. If the vengeful, xenophobic crusade was not stopped soon, Lon Nol would rise to power on the shoulders of his army. Lon Nol was "a weak man," too fond of simplistic solutions and too much under the influence of spiritualists. Colonel Healy agreed. What did Thanh have in mind?

He had two plans; both required an initial force of three thousand Khmer Krom CIDG soldiers and an additional six thousand in the next three months. Lon Nol's ethnic fever had blinded him to the danger of the nascent Khmer Rouge, or Cambodian communist movement, in the northern provinces. Like Sihanouk, Lon Nol dismissed them as Khmer "Reds," lackeys of the *yuon* communists whom the pure Khmers would never follow. Thanh knew that the Khmer Rouge, trained in recruitment and propagandizing in North Vietnam, would grow quickly among the disaffected Khmer peasantry. There were only 3,800 of them so far, Thanh said, and he knew exactly where they were. With American planes or helicopters—from Thailand or South Vietnam, it did not matter—he could annihilate the Khmer Rouge with his little army of Khmer Krom. Once they had crushed the Khmer Rouge, his troops would go to Phnom Penh to join the campaign against the Vietnamese.

"We will eat this elephant one bite at a time," he told Healy.

Or they could airlift him and his three thousand men directly to Phnom Penh, where they would await the arrival of the other six thousand and together be the spearhead of a full-scale assault on the North Vietnamese staging areas on the border from the west, while the Americans and South

Vietnamese attacked them from the east. They would cut the communists' supply routes, isolate them, and with American air support end their ability to wage war in the south.

"The Americans want to leave Vietnam," he said. "If they leave before they help us do this, they will lose their honor and we will lose our freedom and our lives."

Colonel Healy was not surprised. He shared Thanh's opinion of Lon Nol, whom he did not believe had the ability to govern or to wage full-scale war. He believed that Thanh and his troops could punish the communists severely, and that he and Sirik Matak, both of whom were much admired by the Americans who knew them, could govern Cambodia as an ally against the North Vietnamese. He also believed Thanh when he said, "If Lon Nol goes to the left or right, I will kill him. If he goes straight ahead, I will support him."

Gen. Creighton Abrams, commander of the American forces in Vietnam, told his old friend Colonel Healy that his plate was too full to commit U.S. logistics and the Khmer Krom army against the Khmer Rouge. It sure as hell would not be approved by Washington. But Abrams agreed to release nine battalions of Khmer Krom, three battalions at a time, from the CIDG program, "to go where they want."

Officially, the CIDG program was under operational control of the South Vietnamese Special Forces, so Colonel Healy's next stop was their headquarters at Nha Trang, where he and Gen. Phan van Phu, the commanding general, took a long walk on the beach. General Phu said it was impossible. If the Khmer Krom troops went to Cambodia, his fighting camps and the Mike Force in the delta would be "denuded." Camps like Ba Xoai would be left with less than 40 percent of their fighting men; not only would they be undermanned, but they would be emasculated and eventually wiped out by the corruption of his officers and the communist infiltrators in the rank and file. Healy promised General Phu that he and Son Ngoc Thanh would replace the Khmer Krom CIDG troops with new Khmer Krom recruits from the regional and popular forces. General Phu knew that General Abrams had already agreed to the plan, and he knew Healy to be a man of his word. He gave his reluctant approval.

In the next five days Healy and Thanh visited many CIDG camps by helicopter, from Long Hai on the coast to Ba Xoai on the border. While Thanh conferred with his Khmer Krom officers in private and Healy met with the Americans, the Vietnamese Special Forces officers looked on with helpless anger. The three Mike Force battalions at Long Hai would be brought up to full strength by fillers from various camps and would be the first to go. Smaller units from the camps would be moved to Long Hai and Ba Xoai to be consolidated, trained, and outfitted with the best American equipment available, then would follow the first three battalions as a second brigade, a third to follow as soon as possible.

Phase Two began simultaneously, as Healy had promised General Phu it would. American CH-47 helicopters began to land at designated regional force outposts to pick up Khmer Krom replacements for the camps. When Healy landed with his helicopters, the replacements were already formed up in ranks wearing only sarongs, each man behind a neat pile of the inferior South Vietnamese weapons and gear that would be replaced by the American Special Forces at the staging area. John Paul Vann, the controversial senior advisor to IV Corps, called General Abrams, "screeching" and "demanding" to be told who was the son of a bitch in tiger fatigues and no rank and no fucking name tag, like a goddamned French Foreign Legionnaire or something, that was landing at his outposts in unmarked helicopters and stealing his goddamned troops. General Abrams, who loathed John Vann, said he did not have the foggiest idea who the man was.

At their last meeting before his departure to Phnom Penh, Dr. Thanh asked Colonel Healy if he would provide him with six copies of the United States Constitution, which he planned to use as a blueprint for the new government in Cambodia. He had one copy, he said, but it was an old one; he wanted to have "the latest revisions." There were no recent revisions, Healy told him. Would he want a copy of the Bill of Rights as well? Oh yes, said Thanh, they would definitely want a Bill of Rights; what could be more important?

.

At Detachment C-4 in Can Tho, where the 4th Mike Force was headquartered, Sgt. Robert Steppe, team leader and adviser to the detachment's reconnaissance platoon, met with the platoon commander, Sgt. Son Ha, the man whom Chau Got had briefed on Coto Mountain two years before. Son Ha's platoon was forty-eight men strong, well disciplined and spirited, young, and experienced in airborne assaults and cross-border operations. Sergeant Steppe, whom Son Ha "loved like my brother," had orders for the recon platoon. They were to board a C-130 the next evening. They would land at an airport and secure it, until relieved. Steppe didn't know what airport or where, and he was sorry to say that he would not be going with them.

When they boarded the C-130, Sergeant Ha and his men "had a very good idea" that they were headed for Cambodia, but when they touched down in the darkness and spread out to form a defensive perimeter, they were just as surprised as the Cambodian soldiers they found there. They had arrived at an isolated strip at Pochentong airfield, from which they could see the lights of the Royal Cambodian Air Force Base and Phnom Penh in the distance.

"At first we didn't know who the soldiers were. We could only see that they were carrying AK 47s like the communists and they were scared of us. But they shouted at us in Khmer and we answered them, and right away everything was fine."

In the morning, soon after dawn, Sergeant Ha greeted a team of American civilian engineers who had come to oversee preparation of the airstrip. Within hours, a convoy of Cambodian army transport trucks began to arrive and line up along the airstrip. With them came buses and cars filled with girls and schoolboys bearing food, flowers, and musical instruments—the welcoming committee for Sergeant Ha's platoon and the 1,800 men of the three Mike Force battalions who were inbound on South Vietnamese Air Force transport planes from Long Hai.

"The girls were so beautiful," Sergeant Ha said. "They were all Khmer, dressed in sarongs, blouses that showed their breasts. When the planes landed, there was singing and flowers, food and cold beer. All along the way when we were riding in the trucks to the city, people cheered us, greeted us with *sompeah*, like for kings or heroes coming to save them. That's what we felt like. They took us to the *Cercle Sportif,* the sports stadium, where we would stay and wait for the others. Everyone was celebrating."

•

Captain Uchs had had the letter for more than two weeks, and during that time every soldier, mother, and child over six in the villages had heard it read so many times, heard parts of it recited so often, that they thought they knew its contents by heart, as Captain Uchs seemed to. He and his bodyguards treated it like a sacred script of some kind, like it had been written by a saint and delivered by a god. For some that was partly true: Col. Nhoc Lon, its author, was indeed one of Lon Nol's closest advisors; he was the new commander of the Khmer Krom battalions in the mountains and—now it could be said aloud—Lon Nol's choice to be the leader of all the Khmer Krom.

Mounted on polished teak and covered with cellophane for preservation, the letter, dated 21 February 1970, said that Gen. Lon Nol would very soon stage a coup d'etat in Phnom Penh to seize control of the government and country. He, Lon Nol, invited Captain Uchs to prepare his officers and men to come to Phnom Penh when called. Captain Uchs would be "treated with prestige" and promoted; he would help secure the capital and capture and destroy the communist agents in the army like those being executed in Kompong Trach the very day that the letter had been written.

Uchs had new uniforms made, with wide collars to accommodate his new rank. He sent two of his cousins to Phnom Penh to find him suitable quarters and arrange for a vehicle for his use. He consoled his wives, feasted his friends, changed his Vietnamese scrip for gold and greenbacks, practiced speaking high Khmer, and in exchange for gifts of livestock, accepted the blessings of every monk and *kru* within sight of the mountain. His only regret, he liked to say, was that the casinos had been closed; perhaps they had closed because they had heard that he was coming and they were afraid to lose all their money.

Nhoc Lon's letter also said that he hoped Captain Uchs would use the considerable influence he said he had with the Americans to gain their assistance. But Uchs said nothing about the letter and their imminent departure to the American advisors or to the South Vietnamese authorities in Tri Ton. He counseled his people not to mention their plans to either, explaining that this was a "Khmer national matter" and none of their business. The meetings he held to recruit men and make operational plans with the officers were quiet and kept small. A month before, Captain Strait had been sent to Tri Ton to replace the new American district advisor, who had proven to be a drunkard, and then he, Strait, had come down on orders for the 82nd Airborne Division at Fort Bragg, and he was gone. Sergeant Sirois was gone too, leaving only two enlisted men and a fresh young lieutenant on the advisory team at Pratheat pagoda in Olam. These Americans kept to themselves, rarely venturing far from the safety of their bunkers; they did not seem interested at all in the affairs of the villagers and were useful to the companies only because of the supplies they provided.

Who would go with Captain Uchs to fight for the fatherland, to follow *Aysey* into battle, and who would stay to defend the villages from the North Vietnamese? The young men without families would go, as would many others who were ambitious or adventurous. The true believers would go; so would those who were in some kind of trouble at home or in the village.

It was decided that Reap would stay and assume command of the three companies. He had recovered from his wound and the deep depression that had followed it. From his wife, who had never once even blinked at the sight of his scarred and twisted face, he had regained his strength. His deformity was a badge of honor to his troops, proof of courage far greater than the American Bronze Star he wore to weddings. The departure of Captain Strait had been a bitter disappointment, but one that Reap had known was coming and had steeled himself for. Strait had left them well supplied, and as a consequence stronger and more independent than ever. Reap would stay and protect their land and villages with every drop of his blood if need be. Sem Ly would stay as his executive officer. Uchs urged Chau Got and the Scouts to slip away and join him; Chau Got said he would stay, but he gave Krech and two others permission to go.

When the coup in Cambodia was finally announced on Radio Phnom Penh and the villagers learned that it had been orderly and bloodless, many thought that it was merely a "political scheme" by Sihanouk and Lon Nol. While the prince was out of the country, they speculated, Lon Nol and his supporters would rid Cambodia of leftists and Vietnamese and make an alliance with the Saigon government and the Americans; then Sihanouk would come back and reward Lon Nol by sending him and his army to reclaim the land of the Khmer Krom for Cambodia. Lon Nol had always been loyal to Sihanouk; he would never betray him. "The two were like bats and bananas." Some were skeptical of the claims that Lon Nol was Chau Dara himself, the mythical Bright Star; it could only be Samdech, "Our Father," Sihanouk, who could liberate them.

In a little black Citroen with bodyguards on the running boards, Col. Nhoc Lon rolled into Kraing Chey hamlet, where he met with Reap and several of the men from Olam who had once served under him in the mountains. Captain Hien, who commanded the Khmer Krom troops staying behind at Ba Xoai, was also there. Reap and Hien were to cooperate with the South Vietnamese army as long as possible, stay loyal to their Americans, especially the Special Forces at Ba Xoai, and make every effort to send weapons to his Khmer Krom headquarters in Neak Luong in Cambodia. If the North Vietnamese gained the upper hand in Chau Doc, and it looked like they would, Reap and Hien were to disperse their people and bring their soldiers to Neak Luong. He gave them each a certificate of merit signed by Lon Nol himself and adorned with his seal: a human skull supported by two royal sacred swords. The skull represented the Khmer Krom whose heads were used to boil the Vietnamese masters' tea; the swords stood for the Khmer Krom struggle for liberation.

On the evening of 21 March, the 180 men who were to leave that night gathered with their families in the villages for quiet farewells and a last meal. While the men proposed toasts to the future kingdom, the young wives wept and their children cried to see their mothers' tears. Women packed and repacked knapsacks of food and extra clothing. The youngest of the crusaders strode in full battle gear under the lanterns in the village centers, exciting wonder among the children. After midnight, while the American advisors slept, the men went in twos and threes to the temple to be blessed, then slipped away into the dark paddies toward the rendezvous point across the border.

16

A **"SIMPLE MAN,"** a man more in the other world than in this one, more a soldier than a diplomat, more an animist and Hindu than a Buddhist, Lon Nol avoided involvement in the political wrangling in the Cambodian National Assembly and among the new leadership. He withdrew to the Chamcar Mon Palace, where he surrounded himself with trusted military officers and religious advisors, and surrounded the palace with Khmer Krom guards who would gladly die in the defense of Chau Dara, the *Aysey*. While listening to his advisors he was "as silent as a carp" and was known to sometimes slip into a trance where he listened to the voices from the spirit world, often tape-recording his own responses to the spirit voices for later reference. Twice a week, in private sessions that lasted as long as four hours, he convened with the quasi-Buddhist monk and *kru* Mam Prum Mani, who had harnessed his considerable influence with the spirit world to Lon Nol's chariot. In the same harness was the promise of massive American economic and military aid that guaranteed the general the loyalty of his officers and success on the battlefield.

His spiritual advisors, whom he had revered since he was a boy, had little trouble convincing him that he was the great king predicted by the ancient and unchallengeable *Kbuon*. Sometimes known as the palm leaf inscriptions, the *Kbuon* are god-given formulas or rules that were used to govern and guide the ancient Angkor society and create the perfect kingdom called Chen La. There are *Kbuon* that explain and dictate the use of astrology, others that can be used to predict the future, and one that governs strategy or tactics. The last, the manual for waging war, had long ago been carried off by the Thais in the statue of a cow when they sacked the city of Angkor. But it had been recovered recently and its return to Cambodia had been authenticated by the sighting of flying cows by soldiers in the western provinces.

The behavior of the chosen one in war must be governed by the four-part formula in the *Kbuon* named *Reacha Sey*, which says that the king should not allow himself to suffer shame, should not feel the need to be true to his sworn oath, should disregard justice, and should give no enemy any chance to resist his will. The specifics of the formulas must be kept secret, as any time a nonbeliever or person without the power to interpret them learns the rules, the power of *Kbuon* is diminished. If all his actions were in accordance with *Kbuon*, Lon Nol believed, the Khmer people would be victorious in their war against the Vietnamese and the ancient kingdom would be restored in all its glory. Although the educated elite in Cambodia gave little or no credence to the power of *Kbuon*, the common people, especially Lon Nol's fellow Khmer Krom, whose loyalty he courted, believed wholeheartedly in its power, and hence in his.

Soon after the arrival of Sergeant Ha's recon platoon and the first contingent of Son Ngoc Thanh's troops, Lon Nol ordered his helicopters to spread consecrated sand around Phnom Penh, making it invulnerable to attack. He then ordered that the army's garden of magical plants near the Pochentong airport be dug up and pieces distributed among the young men being recruited for his greater army. Wearing a piece of one of these plants, and drinking a concoction distilled from them, would protect these inexperienced troops from harm in combat. The spiritual power of the plants, combined with the ancient magic inherent in the amulets and sacred white scarves that they already wore, made Lon Nol's soldiers morally ascendant and invincible. His draft of the new constitution, which emphasized the importance of racial purity in the government and countryside, like his dissolution of the National Assembly and assumption of the title of president, were all in accordance with *Kbuon*. So was the General Mobilization Program for the new army, which included six practices that should be followed to ensure victory:

1. Cutting of the skin to allow Buddha to enter the body and bring strength, or sewing precious stones or ivory statues of Buddha into the incisions for greater power
2. Making of clothing or scarves with holy inscriptions
3. Securing the blessing of a *kru*
4. Magical creation of the illusion of many soldiers when only a few exist
5. The transformation of leaves of grass into soldiers
6. Strict adherence to the five basic principles of Buddhism, without which the above were ineffective: Do not lie. Do not steal. Do not commit adultery or have adulterous thoughts. Do not drink alcohol. Do not kill any living creature, with the exception of the enemy.

"We use the occult sciences practiced by our ancestors," Lon Nol wrote. "Out of stones and wood we can make beefsteak, cloth, and other useful objects, we can travel through space to the stars, use an electronic brain, communicate across oceans, and go round the world in less than 24 hours."

In his speech to the country on Radio Phnom Penh upon assuming power, Lon Nol delivered his manifesto for religious war. He explained that Buddhism was at the halfway point in its five-thousand-year cycle and was threatened by the Vietnamese communist infidels who would destroy it "with little concern for justice and morality." The Khmer people, true Buddhists, must stand up to the Vietnamese communists; they would win victory in this war of aggression, "as predicted in the oracles," the *Kbuon*.

The modern enemy were nothing but the children of the Vietnamese who had conquered Kampuchea Krom, the most cruel and barbaric enemy in history. "During five centuries our people have known miseries and calamities, but in the face of all these vicissitudes—occupied territory, people under domination—the Khmer, thanks to their determination, to their indomitable courage, have lifted their heads and are recovering liberty. . . . We can restore our historic glory that gave our country the titles 'the island of power' and 'Chen La the rich.'"

Swollen to the bursting point by more than a million peasants who had come to escape the American bombing in the eastern provinces and the fighting in the north, Phnom Penh was in as much danger from internal chaos as it was from the Vietnamese communists who controlled the outlying provinces and were moving, with their Khmer Rouge allies, closer to the city every day. The unemployed children of the middle class, starving peasants, and high school students who answered Lon Nol's call hurried by the thousands to have prayer cloths blessed, bedeck themselves with amulets, and join the army. Without uniforms or training, with ancient weapons for which there was little or no ammunition, they rode cheering out of the city, packed in civilian cars and crowded onto confiscated buses, to confront the Vietnamese. With no direction, no discipline, no inkling of how to fight an infantry war, they were easily slaughtered by the North Vietnamese regulars, who were being driven closer and closer to the city from the Vietnamese border by the bombing and incursions of the American and South Vietnamese armies, Cambodia's new allies. The South Vietnamese troops who crossed the border in April before the American invasion were quick to "recapture" the Vietnamese villages and property that had been confiscated in the purges of Vietnamese citizens by Lon Nol's government; they took vengeance for the bodies that floated down the river by taking everything of value they could carry or transport, and with their plunder, shooting their way past Cambodian troops who tried to stop them.

Lon Nol and his government had no control over, indeed no knowledge of, the communist targets inside their country chosen for destruction by the American B-52s and bombers of the South Vietnamese Air Force. But the invasion and the bombing in his border provinces gave Lon Nol time to consolidate his power in Phnom Penh and raise an army. The "faucet of American dollars," which had been turned off by Sihanouk in 1963, was back on, its valve wide open, and American military hardware was pouring into the city. There would be no American troops, but there would be unlimited air support and two billion dollars in aid of all kinds, which would mean victory for Lon Nol's army and would provide President Nixon with a "side-show" in Cambodia that would engage the North Vietnamese in a new war and give the Americans time to withdraw their troops from Vietnam with minimal casualties: "the Nixon Doctrine in its purest sense."

Crucial to Lon Nol's plan in its early stages was the incorporation of the Khmer Krom units into his army. This had to be done quickly to be sure that the Khmer Krom units would not act independently under their own leaders, and so that Son Ngoc Thanh could not use them as a private army to gain power or wield influence. In public ceremonies Lon Nol reviewed the crack Khmer Krom units and accepted their disciplined displays of loyalty to him and the republic. Close to six thousand Khmer Krom CIDG troops arrived in Phnom Penh in the spring of 1970, with more being trained and equipped in the camps they had come from. They were billeted in the *Cercle Sportif*, the stadium and sports complex, where those not sent out on special missions awaited their orders and their pay.

Like many of the other Khmer Krom officers of his rank and higher, Captain Uchs kept a comfortable apartment in the commercial district and visited his men in the stadium only occasionally, when he was not "busy with planning strategies" at the bordellos, gambling houses, and nightclubs. While he waited for the promotion he had been promised and watched in every direction for signs of things to come, Captain Uchs maintained his lifestyle with the pay of his "ghost soldiers." Allotted the equivalent of thirty dollars a month for each man in his command, Uchs submitted as a payroll a roster of the names, ranks, and serial numbers of two hundred men, including Captain Reap, Lieutenant Sem Ly, and many of the others who had stayed behind. In truth he could claim little more than a hundred men present for duty, having lost forty to desertion and death. His officer friends in the Cambodian army were doing the same thing. It was American money, they said, so the practice harmed no one—unless of course some naive general committed Cambodian units he thought were at full strength against North Vietnamese units of equal designation that were: a Cambodian battalion of under 200 against a communist battalion of 450.

When the euphoria that accompanied their arrival—the bouquets, the gifts of food, the soft-breasted girls—wore off, the men of the Khmer Krom battalions found themselves seemingly forgotten and abandoned. They were living crowded into the sports complex, which offered little shelter, almost no plumbing, and an increasing miasmic stench that clung to their clothing and skin. Outnumbered by the better-trained and -equipped Khmer Krom from the CIDG camps, those who, like Captain Uchs's men, had come from the mountains and the villages were forced to live in makeshift shelters in the open; only a few of them, such as Krech, had the option of living with distant relatives in the city. There were no food rations and no medical supplies; they had been equipped by the Special Forces for a limited civic action, the securing of the city. The vendors and cafe owners in the vicinity of the complex, their only source of food, charged outrageous prices, and their money was running out. The Khmer Krom medics and five female nurses from Long Hai set up a hospital of one hundred beds in a corridor, but the drugs and medicines they had brought with them dwindled quickly, consumed or sold for food. They sent word back to Long Hai through the monks, asking for resupply.

Many extorted money and food from the merchants, not too hard a task for men better armed and far more numerous than the local police. Some turned to pimping, others to outright robbery. Resentment by the Cambodian army and citizens, many of whom were starving, flared into ethnic slurs against the Khmer Krom who were "not Khmer but half *yuon*," who were arrogant and spoke with a foreign accent. Fights erupted between Khmers. Sergeant Ha, insulted and threatened by a Cambodian lieutenant in a restaurant, shot the man's feet to smithereens with his .45, then thrashed him soundly.

Though very little food, and almost no medicine, was provided the men in the sports complex, there was plenty of spiritual sustenance, much of it provided by visits from the Venerable Maj. Mam Prum Mani. Said to have come from all of the mountains of Cambodia, Mani, a chaplain who led but did not command a brigade of his own, had great affection for the Khmer Krom, his fellow believers. He arrived often, unheralded, riding with his attendant monks in a brightly buffed orange Opel 1700, an emissary from Lon Nol himself bearing predictions, pronouncements, and news of the "true" situation. While he received the adulation of the troops, his assistants handed out yellow cloths bearing his signature and title in Khmer and

French: "great intellectual of pure glory." The cloths, he said, were blessed by him and were all-powerful.

"I'm watching the military situation very closely. And if the war grows in intensity, a 10 percent escalation for instance, I'll increase the power of my scarves by 15 percent. If it goes to 15 percent, then I'll increase by 18 to 25."

He told them that they would soon go into action and warned them that the North Vietnamese, who were already desperate, were known to be placing naked Vietnamese women in their front lines to inspire adulterous thoughts in the Khmer soldiers and hence invalidate the magic of their scarves. They must follow all the moral precepts, break none.

"When a man violates the rules," he said, "we say that that man has killed himself."

He predicted that the war would end in seven months and twenty-six days, and reminded them of Lon Nol's promise to lead an army to liberate the Khmer Krom homeland and reunite it with Cambodia. The men listened reverently, and some were encouraged, but most shared Sergeant Ha's sentiments: "Yes, I was very happy to have his protection. But it's even better to dig a deep foxhole as well."

It took less than five days for the monks to carry the request for resupply to the Americans at Long Hai, almost 150 miles away. The message was directed to an American master sergeant who prefers not to be named. The sergeant knew that an official request for resupply through channels would be denied because the battalions were no longer under American or South Vietnamese control. He also knew how to use bolt cutters. He gathered a group of Khmer Krom from those who were about to graduate from the first training cycle and would soon join the three battalions; with them he conducted a training mission, a "graduation exercise in field expedience." In civilian clothes, armed with concealed pistols, the group paid nocturnal visits to nearby South Vietnamese army bases. Within two weeks they had "collected" forty-five vehicles, most of them 2 1/2-ton troop carriers and dump trucks, all American-made, all painted with South Vietnamese unit designations. They loaded them with "requisitioned" weapons, food, medical supplies, and ammunition, painted them with Vietnamese Special Forces markings, and convoyed them under heavy guard across Vietnam and Cambodia to the sports complex.

The medical supplies were appropriated by Kien Rinh, the NCO in charge of the hospital. He would not see his fellow Khmer Krom reduced to paying for clean bandages and drugs like the Cambodian soldiers had to do. The weapons, small arms still packed in cosmoline, were uncrated and sold on the black market; pallets of C-rations were broken down and sold meal by meal. A pair of new jungle boots of any size brought nearly a week's pay; a steel helmet, a night on the town. The trucks were kept at the stadium; their counterfeit markings were painted over and replaced with "43rd Brigade," the new designation for the battalions as part of the Cambodian army.

In late August, the 43rd Brigade loaded into its trucks and started up Route 6, the spearhead of the army's column sent to relieve the communist siege of Kompong Thmar, eighty-five miles to the north. It was the first major campaign of the army of Lon Nol's Khmer Republic, and it was called "Chen La."

17

THE CROWD THAT milled quietly around at the entrance to the little graveyard beside the road in Nam Qui was mostly children, among them here and there an ancient man leaning on a stick. The women were lined up on both sides of the road with the family members to await the procession. Captain Reap and his brutish bodyguard Hom, both in freshly starched fatigues, stood aside in the shade of palms with eight other members of the Olam companies at parade rest in two ranks behind them. They were all friends of Ut Le's, had been since the old days when they were Viet Cong with him in the mountains, and they had come to represent the companies.

It had been Hom who had found Ut Le at dawn on the day before, while on his way back to Olam from a visit with his family. The way Hom told it, two terrified naked boys, each pulling him by a thumb, led him past a thicket to a bamboo fence along a footpath where Ut Le was propped up, shot full of holes. He had been shot five times at close range, three in the chest, twice in the stomach through his web belt, all by a heavy weapon, probably his own .45, as he was wearing the empty holster. He was still very handsome, Hom said; he looked like he had been laughing when he was shot, but he probably was not. No one knew who had killed him. It could have been communists. It could have been an old debt settled. Most believed that it had been a jealous husband who had caught him with his wife. Ut Le had probably known his killer. The man must have been armed; how else could he have gotten Ut Le's pistol? To Reap it did not make any difference who had killed him, but to Chau Got it made all the difference in the world, and there would be vengeance sevenfold when he found out.

The procession was led by a withered monk. Behind him came the musicians with a gong and muffled drums. Walking before the jeep that pulled the casket, Ut Le's mother sowed the ground with rice. The casket, painted in red and green floral patterns and covered with a South Vietnamese flag, was riding atop a trailer pulled by the jeep. Chau Got and his men walked alongside, steadying the casket, until the jeep stopped in front of the crowd. Chau Got looked like he was about to pounce on someone and beat him to death. Among Chau Got's men—there were about ten—Reap only recognized three; the others were strangers, recruited from Tinh Bien to replace those who had been killed or gone off to Cambodia, like Krech and gentle Con had. Five Americans from the compound in Tri Ton got out of the jeep and stood around with mournful expressions on their faces; the flag must have been their idea, well-meant but misguided.

Since Strait had left, Reap had not spoken one word of English, except maybe once or twice with Major McGuffin, the new district advisor. The Americans came and went so fast. The mobile advisory team in Olam was sometimes gone for weeks at a time, and when it returned, it was often made up of different men. Around them, Reap pretended that he did not understand; he talked Vietnamese with their interpreter when he needed to. The Americans who stayed in Tri Ton had all changed over at least twice, and some were not being replaced. Even their counterparts, the men Reap had learned to trust, had changed: Major Quyen was gone to the 7th Division, Aziz sent to Can Tho. Cop, their cowboy interpreter, had gone to Cambodia; the new interpreter, a Vietnamese sergeant, spoke to Reap and his officers like they were shit-spreading vermin.

Reap missed Strait, not just for his friendship, but for his interest in the companies and the villages, his shared commitment to them. People said that these new Americans, Major McGuffin particularly, were good men, and Reap believed it. Two weeks before the funeral, Chau Got had gotten into a drunken row with a Vietnamese village chief; they traded racial insults, then the village chief said something about Chau Got's mother, so Chau Got shot him dead. Chau Got claimed that he had only fired a warning shot that glanced off a headstone and hit the man; witnesses said otherwise. The Tri Ton police arrested Chau Got and were going to try him for murder, but Major McGuffin got him released. He, the major, wore dark-rimmed glasses with green-shaded lenses clipped onto them.

Ut Le's family, in funeral white, laid the casket next to the open grave, removed the flag, and gave it to an American. While his mother lay across the casket wailing the familiar refrain of loss and fear, the Americans stood nearby, heads bowed or hands on hips watching the native mourners for signs of how to behave properly. The family covered the grave with a blanket of thorns to keep Ut Le's restless spirit from wandering and started down the footpath to the hamlet, where the music for the funeral feast could be heard.

There were no feasts when they buried their common dead in Olam, Coto, and An Tuc villages; the people could not afford them. Even if they could, there were so many funerals now—soldiers killed in ambushes,

children killed by mortar shrapnel, families decimated in rocket attacks—
that people had begun to offer a few gifts of food to the monks in the de-
ceased's honor rather than give a feast.

The North Vietnamese on Coto Mountain had become so numerous and
strong that they had driven Reap's outposts from the foot of the mountain,
shrinking his perimeter. They mortared the village fortifications and outlying hamlets at will, sometimes sending a rocket smashing into a cluster of
houses. The jeep-mounted recoilless rifle that Strait had stolen for the
Khmer Krom companies had been confiscated by the South Vietnamese,
leaving Reap's people with only mortars, and damn few rounds for them. In
November the communists launched a full-scale ground attack on the village defenses: first the barrage and the sappers in the wire, then the bugle
and the infantry assault. They breached the wire once, but were driven back
with heavy losses. At dawn they withdrew, dragging their dead and wounded
back to the mountain. The Khmer Krom lost nine killed, the North Vietnamese ten times that number. They attacked again eleven days later with
the same results. But they would come again. Reap and Sem Ly worked tire-
lessly to keep the companies resupplied and to hold the men together. One
at a time, families left the villages for Tri Ton or to live with relatives in
Cambodia. They had "too many wounded to count." Reap wanted to lie
down and quit, like he had with his father in the hundred-day dream, but he
could not.

There was hope from Radio Phnom Penh. Lon Nol announced that the
Chen La operation to liberate Kompong Thmar had been a great success. His
army was on the path to victory and the Khmer Krom brigades had fought
heroically; the communists were retreating to the north. But during the
making of palm sugar in Olam, two men who had deserted from Captain
Uchs's unit to come home told a different story about the Chen La operation. They said that Lon Nol had sent the whole army north on one road,
creating a convoy several miles long that rarely moved faster than a man
walking. There were hundreds of vehicles and artillery pieces and trucks
full of soldiers and their dependents; they could not maneuver off the road
because the paddies were flooded, so whenever something held up the column ahead, they just sat there. No flankers, no defenses. Units were spread
out all along the road, mixed up; most of them were leaderless. At first the
North Vietnamese had been surprised and withdrew, but they regrouped.
One time enemy resistance stopped the column and they camped on the
road for a week. American B-52s bombed the communists all day and all
night. It took the lead elements three months to reach Kompong Thmar;

most of the column never saw the town. Then they turned around and started back to Phnom Penh. There was no battle, no victory, no big communist retreat—only confusion and arguing and broken-down trucks.

The men confided to Reap and Sem Ly that Captain Uchs had not gone to the field with his company. He had stayed in Phnom Penh, but he was not there when they got back. Two Cambodian colonels who knew that Uchs was padding his payrolls had been blackmailing him. When they came to collect the third time, Uchs and his bodyguards ambushed them, killed them both and took their jeep and money and disappeared. Some of his men joined other Khmer Krom units or were drafted, some just disappeared like Uchs did; there would be more coming home soon, they predicted, perhaps among them Krech, who had been shot in the knee and was last seen in the hospital at the stadium.

The few others who did come home said that the government's radio report of the attack on Pochentong airfield was grossly understated. It had been a sapper attack, all right, but the slight damage reported by the government was in truth the complete destruction of the Khmer air force. Every single combat plane had been blown up in place. Further attacks by the same communist unit on villages west of the city emphasized the vulnerability of the capital itself and spread fear and near-panic among the people and troops in Phnom Penh. Then on the night following the attack, Lon Nol suffered a stroke that paralyzed half his body. A few days later he was evacuated by American aircraft to a hospital in Hawaii.

All this news spread among the hamlets and the three villages like the foul swamp vapors in the rainy season. How could Lon Nol call a fumbled campaign a victory? Were not his plans in accordance with *Kbuon* and blessed by holy men? What about the circle of sacred sand around the city? How could Chau Dara lose control of his soldiers? How could the *Aysey* suffer a stroke? Some argued that mistakes must have been made in the astrological calculations. Others said that here was proof that Sihanouk, and not Lon Nol, was the *Aysey*. Sem Ly said that the people should stop talking about spirits and messiahs and get back to work filling sandbags and repairing the barbed wire.

The Special Forces camp at Ba Xoai where Captain Hien had taken his Khmer Krom company was hit hard by the North Vietnamese. Sappers got through the wire with grenades and satchel charges, and along with pinpoint preplanned mortar fire, destroyed the generator bunker, the communications bunker, the mortar pit, and the team house. The Vietnamese officers and NCOs in charge of the camp took cover, but the Khmer Krom, led by Captain Hien and an American captain named MacDonald, stayed on the wall and in the machine gun emplacements and fought until gunships came to drive off the attackers. Two Americans and ten Khmer Krom were killed; eleven dead communists' lay tangled in the wire and many bloody trails were found. There were no casualties among the Vietnamese in the camp. Captain Hien knew that at least some of the bunkers had been sabotaged by communist infiltrators among the Vietnamese Special Forces, that someone, somehow, was directing enemy fire from inside the camp, and that the reserve generators to power the searchlights had been sold on the black market. He sent word to Reap and fled into Cambodia with his company.

At Chi Lang, five miles away, where the Americans were training the newly formed Khmer Krom battalions to go to Cambodia, relations between the Americans and Khmer Krom on one side, and the Vietnamese Special Forces on the other, had gotten so bad that the Vietnamese major in command of the camp had told his men that no one would be punished for stealing from the Americans. The Khmer Krom recon platoon, with two Americans, stumbled into a company-size communist unit on the western slope of Ta Bac mountain and was quickly surrounded. When the American in command radioed Chi Lang for assistance, the major told him that all his elements were "too busy" to respond. Only a few of the Khmer Krom recruits escaped; neither of the American officers was seen again.

When his first son Vith Chon was born, Reap prayed that the child would live to become a monk, would live long enough to see peace and to take care of his sisters and his parents in their old age. But he knew that the period that he would later call "the happy time" had come to an end. Even the village *krus* admitted that they were worried that instead of a kingdom to come, they would soon see a time when garbage floats, and gourds, things useful, sink.

18

I WAS SPRINKLING rock salt on the front walk when General Taylor's car made the wide turn in the cul-de-sac and pulled up to the front steps. I had not expected him until five-thirty or so, but here he was, at four, and the walk was still icy and he would get those white salt stains on his good shoes. It had been dark, cold, and drizzly all morning, an average sort of day for January in D.C., but that afternoon while I was in the library, it had turned unusually cold in a couple of hours, making the campus sidewalks skittery. The trees in the park on the way home were bent under the weight of the ice and hissed and crackled when the wind stirred them. While I watched the general switch off his little reading light and gather his things from the back seat, I wondered if I should offer him a hand on the steps, and decided I should not. He and his driver laughed about something, then he greeted me as he emerged from the car and I stood aside on the frozen lawn. In gray suit, white shirt, and tie of bright Air Force blue, he looked more like a scion of a fine Virginia family, bred to squash courts and fox hunting, than a retired three-star general finishing his career with the CIA. Tucked under the handle of his briefcase was a cardboard tube.

"Are you busy?" he asked. "I've got something for you. Come on inside."

•

I had been out of the army for a little over a year. When I got back from Vietnam I spent my last six months in uniform commanding a basic training company at Fort Lewis. My wife, who had become deeply committed to the antiwar and women's movements, stayed with me at Fort Lewis for a few months before she went back to her friends on the east coast. I had changed in ways I could not understand and would not admit. She and the culture I had left behind had found a new and higher consciousness than mine, had reached a higher moral plane to which I could not, in their way of thinking, even dare aspire. Like the North Vietnamese, they believed that the war in Southeast Asia was a struggle for Vietnamese independence against American colonialist oppressors—a noble peasant struggle, a peoples' war for liberation and equal rights, not unlike the cultural war they were waging in this country against the same enemy. Like every other returning veteran, I had been warned that we would be vilified by some, cursed and loathed for having served, sneered at for believing the lies about the war being one for democracy and self-determination for the South Vietnamese. I believed that once I had a chance to explain our side of the story, Reap's side, Aziz's side, that they would understand that there was human truth to both sides: that we could not befriend, arm, and organize people with promises to stand by them in their fight for self-determination and then walk away; that when we fought we did so not for an ideology, but for one another; that honor and loyalty are worth fighting and even dying for, no matter how corrupt the governments that wage the wars.

I was wrong, in the main. They listened but found what I said unacceptable, simply wrong-minded. Oh, it wasn't the veterans' fault, they said: we had been victims of right-wing propaganda, had become pawns and cannon fodder and worse, morally unredeemable for having killed patriotic Vietnamese soldiers and innocent peasants. At times I believed them and felt lost as a man, then I hated myself for having done so. I wanted security, a chance to gather myself. I wanted to find refuge in a private and conventional life. My wife wanted change, motion—anything, absolutely anything but a conventional life. It was the Age of Aquarius, a time of personal becoming and political liberation, and I was talking about lying in a hammock in some village or mowing the fucking lawn. We agreed to separate temporarily, to find ourselves on opposite coasts, then try a reconciliation in the near future.

General Taylor and his wife lived alone in an imposing brick Georgian house at the end of W Street on the edge of Cleveland Park. Their neighbors were high-ranking diplomats, Rockefellers, Posts, and Buchwalds. Though the Taylors only planned to be in Washington for a couple of years, they needed a large and stately house for entertaining. They also needed a caretaker. This was the second marriage for both of them, and their children, both in their early twenties, were pursuing alternative lifestyles out west; one of them was breeding buffalo. The Taylors advertised at the universities for a graduate student to live in their basement apartment, and I answered the ad. I paid rent by doing yardwork and some housework and staying in the house while they were away.

My apartment was in the basement of the house: two bedrooms, living room with a fireplace, a bar, and sliding glass doors leading to a private patio that looked over the wooded slope to the creek in the park below. I kept irregular hours at school; when not in class I was in the library or doing chores for the Taylors or reading and writing, or watching the evening news.

When Walter Cronkite did his daily segment about Vietnam, his backdrop was a recruiting poster for Officer Candidate School that I had posed for at Fort Bragg years before. In the photograph I am on one knee, mouth wide open in some imagined heroic cry, waving my troops into action. The photographers had splashed water in my armpits and torn my helmet cover; smoke rolled around the machine gun crew by my side. In magazines and in front of post offices, the poster had said "Learn to Lead," a promise that CBS had removed for the news hour. When it first appeared behind Cronkite's deeply concerned shoulder I had been amazed, then bitterly amused that a faked photograph was being used to enhance the drama of a war that was as real to the television audience as the poster was. To me it was fitting in an odd and appropriate way: it was as true as the exaggerated numbers of enemy killed being reported by the generals, or the payrolls of men like Captain Uchs. To some it was appropriate because it advertised and hence increased my guilt for having posed for a recruiting poster and then served in Vietnam. My veteran friends who saw it smiled knowingly and called me an asshole. In early 1972, when I watched Cronkite in the Taylors' basement, the colors of the poster had become psychedelic, as though some grooved-out stage manager had caught on to the sorry joke.

I saw Mrs. Taylor often and she oversaw me as I pruned the boxwood and guided the clematis, but I rarely saw the general. In the fall I had asked him if he would help me find out what was happening to the Khmer Krom who had reportedly gone to Cambodia, and maybe even find out what was going on in Tri Ton. He had said that his job was to chair a committee on internal security. He was not privy to tactical intelligence, but he might be able to help me; he had a friend. In the following months I saw him only when he came downstairs to fetch a bottle from the wine cellar. He did not mention the Khmer Krom or my request and I was too shy to pester him. Since *The New York Times* had reported the first Mike Force battalions arriving in Phnom Penh over a year before, I had not been able to find information anywhere about them or the situation in Tri Ton.

•

We wiped the salt from our shoes at the front door, and I followed General Taylor into the dining room where he unrolled a map on the table and pinned its corners with coasters and candelabra.

"This wasn't easy to get," he said. He took a sheaf of handwritten notes and his reading glasses from his briefcase.

It was an Army Map Service topographic map of the area north of Phnom Penh, titled by hand at the top: "'Chen La II': Ground Operations." On it were drawn conventional military unit symbols and arrows that advanced, clashed, and veered off, red ones for the communists, black ones for the Cambodian Army. Someone, the general I assumed, had circled several of the brigade and battalion symbols in blue ball point.

He said he was sorry it had taken so long. Intelligence from inside Cambodia, especially from the fighting north of the capital, was hard to come by and rarely considered reliable. I would want to listen carefully—he would take it slow—because he could not let me keep the map or notes. The information he had brought had not even been classified yet, so he would appreciate it if I would keep it to myself.

Against the advice of his General Staff, and for reasons that nobody really seemed to understand, Lon Nol had launched another offensive up Route 6 to retake Kompong Thmar, which his army had abandoned after the first Chen La operation. The tactics of Chen La II were identical to those of its predecessor, the results far worse. This time the communists let the column spread itself out along the road again. "My friend calls it a front twenty feet wide and forty miles long," the general said. This time the North Vietnamese numbered more than twice as many as the last time; their strength was estimated at fifty thousand. And this time Cambodian communists, several thousand Khmer Rouge, fought with them. Behind artillery barrages, full-scale infantry assaults on the column isolated and annihilated entire units on the road. The bridge at Skoun had been destroyed, blocking resupply and denying retreat. Many units simply disintegrated: the officers and men fled in every direction, shedding their uniforms. The equipment they abandoned, including artillery pieces, had to be bombed by American fighters to keep it from falling into communist hands.

The official Cambodian after-action report claimed ten battalions of personnel and equipment lost, as well as the equipment of ten additional battalions. On paper, four of the brigades were Khmer Krom, about 6,000 men. Cambodian army losses were 3,000 killed and 15,000 missing; no one knew how many of either statistic were Khmer Krom. He said that his friend, who knew the Mike Forces and the Khmer Krom, guessed that they had fought rather than run and consequently had taken many casualties. We did not know the fate of any of the Khmer Krom units, but word in Special Forces channels was that one unit of 3,000 was trapped by a river and annihilated.

The only good news, the general said, was that the massive American bombing in support of the operation had done serious damage to the North Vietnamese 9th Division, one of two divisions in Cambodia preparing for an invasion of South Vietnam from the west. Lon Nol's debacle, launched in accordance with *Kbuon*, had bought time for his new friends, the South Vietnamese.

According to official reports the general had read there was no such thing as a team of Kit Carson Scouts in Tri Ton. On paper the American advisors were not authorized a team and were not paying one. I said that that did not mean they were not still there, and he nodded in agreement. Officially, Reap's three companies at Olam were still at full strength, but according to the general's sources, they were far less than that, a thin outpost completely surrounded by North Vietnamese regulars. The American advisory team in Tri Ton had been reduced to four, and they were due to withdraw to Chi Lang by September, leaving the district and soon the entire province in Vietnamese control. It was likely that many Khmer Krom from the Seven Mountains regional forces had gone to Cambodia or were on their way; the training centers were still taking Khmer Krom recruits from the area and filling units to be trained and sent across the border.

"You knew these guys. You can probably guess better than any of my sources which ones went and which didn't."

I said I could not.

When he lifted the coasters, the map rolled itself up to the candelabra with a snap.

"You'll have to forget them, or, no, put them out of your mind," he said. "Assume the worst; lay it to rest, then push on. That's what they're doing, isn't it? There's nothing else for it. I recommend you start right now, tonight. Betty's out for the evening and I'm looking forward to a quiet little dinner by myself—a perfect lamb chop, a nice bottle of wine—and with any luck I'll fall asleep in a good novel. You ought to do the same. That new Vouvray is especially good. Leave a bottle at the top of the kitchen stairs for me and take one for yourself."

I thanked him. He shook my hand, held my eyes for a second, then let me go.

"Let it breathe for at least half an hour."

"Yes, sir."

19

WHEN LON NOL'S spiritual advisor Mam Prum Mani's prediction that
the war in Indochina would end in June 1971 proved to be wrong, he revised
it. It had not been his prediction that had been wrong, he said, but the way
that people had interpreted it. He had not meant that the war would end by
then, but that it would begin to "fade." The stars and spirits told him that in
January 1972 signs would appear that would herald the coming of peace in
the year 1975. Mani, whom the Americans in Phnom Penh called Friar Tuck,
was serene about his influence over Lon Nol and consequently over events
like the abysmal Chen La I and II operations. Those who looked for flaws in
his predictions were simply jealous; what could he do about that? After the
coup, he had said that Sihanouk's political career in Cambodia was at an
end. When Sihanouk emerged from Beijing as the titular head of the Khmer
Rouge and he and his divine image were used by the communist leadership
to swell their ranks with disillusioned peasants, those who doubted Mani
asked him about it. He smiled seraphically and reminded them that he had
also said that Sihanouk would *try* to come back, but that he would fail in the
end. An American journalist asked him cautiously about the charms—the
scarves and amulets—that he had seen on so many dead Cambodian soldiers. Mani closed his eyes and shook his head sadly. Those men had not
followed the moral precepts that were necessary to empower the charms,
or they had put their faith in charms that were false or improperly blessed.
Those men had killed themselves. The journalist simply did not understand.

"General Lon Nol acts on the matters that I advise because he is aware of
my powers. I'm not frightened by such a responsibility—if anything goes
wrong because of what I recommend, it's the other person's fault; my advice has simply not been carried out properly."

·

Those who looked for the ominous gestures from the spirit world that Mani
predicted for early 1972 were disappointed. Those who followed the events
of this world were disappointed, too, but for different reasons. Col. Thach
Quyen was raised a Buddhist and considered himself a religious man. Like
many other educated Khmer Krom, he knew about the animism and heavy

Hindu influence on Buddhism in the Seven Mountains region; he thought it interesting and sometimes found it attractive. But when he was district chief in Tri Ton, he had been surprised by the importance attached to spiritualism and magic he had found there. He had never heard of Mani, but he knew that Lon Nol was a mystic, and this was something that worried him and other Khmer Krom he talked to.

When he had left Tri Ton a week before Ut Le was murdered, Quyen was promoted to lieutenant colonel and appointed garrison commander of Dong Tam, the home of the South Vietnamese 7th Infantry Division. His immediate superior, General Hai, was known as an exceptional officer, a clear-eyed tactician who had risen through the ranks because of his ability rather than loyalty or favoritism. He was uncorrupted politically and beyond graft. He found the same qualities, brightened by military pride and an abiding sense of honor, in Colonel Quyen. General Hai tried to promote Quyen to a staff position, but was told that as a colonel, Quyen was already higher in rank than any Khmer Krom should be; so Hai sought Quyen's advice unofficially, and often in front of his Vietnamese colonels. Some were jealous, others discomfited; General Hai ignored them. Quyen obeyed his commander.

In January 1972, the 7th Division was preparing contingency plans for what intelligence told them would be a major North Vietnamese invasion from Laos and Cambodia in the coming months. Because of the current positions of the North Vietnamese divisions, it was assumed that the attacks would be against the northern provinces and the bases in the highlands. Dong Tam, way down in the watery mouth of the Mekong, was not in jeopardy, but the division had to be ready to move to reinforce other units, and at the same time be prepared to respond to attacks by communist units in the delta who might exploit the weakened conditions of bases and provinces like Chuong Thien and Chau Doc. In official and casual conversation General Hai and Colonel Quyen agreed that the fighting would be on a large scale and very difficult, but even with only a few thousand American combat troops left, the South Vietnamese army could grind down and push back the invasion with its sheer numbers and firepower.

"But then we learned that night, I don't remember which one it was, that President Nixon was going to China, and we knew that this meant the end for us. The Americans were going to talk their way out and leave us alone to face the North Vietnamese with China behind them. The Americans had lost their will to fight, and now even to support us. They had bilked us. Nixon would be reelected. Indochina would be communist. We could see it as clear as a future map."

The intelligence reports proved all too true. The North Vietnamese invasion that spring was massive and bloody and sustained far longer than the South Vietnamese ever imagined it would be. The damage to cities and main force units and South Vietnamese morale was staggering. The North Vietnamese were driven back, with great losses to both sides, but as Hai and Quyen had feared, much of the delta had been lost to communist units, and the rehearsal for the final invasion and fall of South Vietnam had been a success for the Northerners.

While the main force units fought a conventional war in the northern provinces, the local communist guerrilla forces in the delta, brought to full strength by North Vietnamese regulars, attacked outlying posts and fortified villages, driving the regional forces or militia into the towns and cities. The training camp at Chi Lang was overrun, then retaken by South Vietnamese regulars. Refugees from unprotected hamlets and villages flooded into the provincial capitals, leaving no doubt of communist control of the rural areas and populations. In Tri Ton, Maj. Kien Keo, the new district chief, pulled his regional forces into a perimeter around the town, leaving Reap and his companies almost completely cut off in the villages. Resupply, when it came, was by helicopter that arrived and departed under heavy mortar fire from the mountain.

After one particularly ferocious ground attack, which left the barbed wire and bunkers around the Pratheat pagoda in Olam littered with North Vietnamese dead, Sem Ly decided to send his family back to live with relatives in Soc Trang. Reap sent word to his wife in Tri Ton telling her not to try to visit him, to stay put there with the children. His mother and his brother Dom and his family stayed in Olam, as did many dependents who had no other place to go, or who were determined to die in their native hamlets rather than flee to the mountains yet again.

Uchs returned to Tri Ton, appearing quietly in a freshly painted jeep. He brought with him, it was said, "seven sacks of Cambodian gold coins" and set himself up in the town with several Vietnamese officer friends, "gamblers and pimps," in a large house. He made no attempt to contact his Khmer Krom companies but wore the uniform and rank of a major in the Cambodian army, and in the house held a lavish court, fit for a little king, dispensing favors, receiving and sending messengers across the border. He still claimed command and control of the FLKK forces in Olam, the camps, and the border region, and he was treated by South Vietnamese and Cambodian officials as though those forces were considerable. His bodyguard, the big man with the hand axe, had grown so fat that he smothered a whore when he passed out on top of her, a story Major Uchs found hilarious.

The district advisory team in Tri Ton was ordered to prepare to withdraw completely by the end of the year. Major McGuffin received orders to disband the Scout team within ninety days and integrate them into the South Vietnamese forces. Though McGuffin did not tell Chau Got at first, the Scouts found out, and weapons and equipment began to disappear. McGuffin thought the thieves were the two new Scouts from Tinh Bien, but before he could press the matter they had deserted to Cambodia.

Chau Got was embarrassed and outraged. McGuffin assured him that the thefts were no reflection on him as a leader because the guilty ones had been Scouts that he, McGuffin, had recruited. Chau Got did not want his remaining Scouts to get drafted into the South Vietnamese army and sent away, nor did he want to go to Cambodia, but rather wanted to stay in the Tri Ton area with his families. Maj. Kien Keo, a Khmer Krom himself, was wary of Chau Got, but he believed him and his men to be loyal, so he agreed to use the Scouts as a local intelligence platoon. With Chau Got still in command, they were assigned to nearby Salon hamlet, there to establish an outpost, conduct ambushes, and protect the villagers. They could keep their weapons and would be supplied by the Americans. Within a month they had triggered two successful ambushes, endeared themselves to the villagers, and earned the respect of the district chief. But when the Americans withdrew at the end of the year, the Scouts' weapons had to be turned in and replaced with inferior regional force weapons, and their resupply came through Vietnamese channels. They were no longer strong enough to conduct ambushes, but Chau Got was determined to stay to protect their families or die with them.

News from Cambodia, carried by the monks who still managed to travel by foot during the day, was sparse and increasingly grim. First came word that the units being trained by Americans in the camps like Chi Lang were no longer Khmer Krom, but regular Cambodian recruits flown across the border to be trained and returned in six weeks. The Khmer Krom who had been in the CIDG camps, and those recruited from the regional forces, had been expended, and there were no more to replace them.

In July two young monks, barely in their teens, came to Olam with a message for Major Uchs from Lon Nol's advisors, ordering him to return to Phnom Penh. They told Reap that the 48th Khmer Krom Brigade, the last major Khmer Krom unit intact, had been surrounded by North Vietnamese and Khmer Rouge on Route 1 south of Phnom Penh, outnumbered ten to one. They fought well, but then started to run out of ammunition. They called for air strikes, but none came. Finally, as they were being overrun, they called for artillery fire on their own position. Of six hundred men, thirteen escaped alive.

Lon Nol, whom the messengers no longer believed was Chau Dara, much less the *Aysey*, had used up all the Khmer Krom, not just the FLKK who had gone, but all the CIDG and Mike Force units sent by Son Ngoc Thanh and General Healy. Maybe Lon Nol had sent the Khmer Krom units into the worst fighting intentionally, to destroy any claims to political power that Son Ngoc Thanh once had. After all, Thanh had returned to Saigon, where he was staying with his wife.

Captain Hien, who had taken his company from Ba Xoai, was still at large in the border area, and a few Khmer Krom from the decimated units were joining him. Those who joined Cambodian units or tried to blend into the countryside were treated as less than pure Khmer, despised for their lighter skin, strange accent, and vocabulary. The entire Cambodian 7th Division, the bulk of Lon Nol's army, had gone without pay for three months and was walking back to Phnom Penh to demand food and money. Lon Nol feared a soldier uprising, and this was why he wanted Major Uchs to return, with as many men as he could.

Reap instructed the messengers to tell Uchs that he, Reap, could spare no more men; Uchs would have to get them elsewhere. Reap would see no more of his few remaining FLKK soldiers wasted by corrupt and incompetent officers. He and his companies would stay to defend their villages and temples, their fatherland. No more deals with Uchs, never again. He made arrangements to have his father's monument repainted; he fought off the old dark temptation to lie down with his father by staying busy, keeping discipline and order among his men.

The North Vietnamese Army began its final invasion of the south in January 1975, and the Khmer Rouge, who were then in control of most of Cambodia, pressed their siege of Phnom Penh to its conclusion in the same month. The South Vietnamese divisions north of Saigon were crushed and scattered by the communist armies. In the final days, the American ambassador to Cambodia offered to evacuate Lon Nol and the other leaders of his government in hopes of placating the Khmer Rouge. Lon Nol accepted and escaped, but the others chose to remain. Speaking from Peking, Sihanouk said that there would be no deals, no negotiations. On 17 April, when the city was taken and ordered emptied by the Khmer Rouge, Sirik Matak and several other "super-traitors" who had been involved in the overthrow of

Sihanouk, were taken from the French embassy to the *Cercle Sportif,* where the Khmer Krom had once gathered, and were executed, the first victims of what would prove to be the most brutal program of auto-genocide in human history. Sirik Matak sent a letter to the American ambassador explaining why he refused to leave his country: "I never believed for a moment that you would have this sentiment of abandoning a people which have chosen liberty. You have refused us your protection and we can do nothing about it. . . . I have only committed this mistake of believing in the United States."

Thirteen days later Saigon surrendered to the North Vietnamese.

•

Colonel Quyen, General Hai, and a half dozen other field-grade officers crowded into the communications room at division headquarters to listen to radio reports from the fighting in Saigon. When the broadcasts from Saigon headquarters ceased, two of the staff officers left the room, as though they could not bear to listen any more. A silence followed, "more than an hour" in which the remaining officers smoked cigarettes and drank cognac. The silence was broken by commercial Saigon radio. The announcer, who did not have a northern accent, said that General Minh's surrender had been accepted. Saigon was liberated. He said that the people had nothing to fear. "Between Vietnamese there are no victors and no vanquished. Only the Americans have been beaten. If you are patriots, consider this a moment of joy. The war for our country is over."

The officers who had left the room returned wearing communist rank and asked General Hai and Quyen and the others to surrender their pistols. They were to stay in their quarters, under house arrest, while the camp was turned over to communist control. A naval officer friend of Quyen's, whose name also appeared on the list of officers to be "transferred," told Quyen that he had arranged an escape aboard a patrol boat. If they moved quickly, that night, they could go upriver to Can Tho to collect their families, then escape into the South China Sea. There was room for twenty or more. Quyen thanked him, but chose to stay with General Hai. Two nights later General Hai committed suicide in his quarters. Quyen slipped out of the camp and made his way home to his wife and children in Can Tho. Within a week a young communist officer leading a squad of six men came to arrest him. Bound and loaded into a truck with three other men, one a medical officer named Doctor Tinh, Quyen could not bear to look back at his wife and son and daughter in the doorway.

•

No one was surprised when the news that the war was lost reached Olam. "Everyone was only quiet," except Sem Ly, who asked angrily what difference this made. The bastards had them surrounded, yes, but they had been holding them off for years. Nothing had changed. They had plenty of ammunition. Reap said no, they had to surrender. He had to. If they fought, the people and the villages would be destroyed. Sem Ly had never lived through a bombing attack, had he? If there were any survivors, they would starve or be hunted down and killed. Maybe some more could get away to the mountains over the border; that was their choice. Reap would go home and wait to see what happened. He wanted to go to Tri Ton to see his wife and children, but he feared that his presence would cause them to be treated more harshly. He went to his mother's house where he had been born. Unlike Tri Ton and almost every other village in South Vietnam, the three Khmer Krom villages did not have a clandestine communist infrastructure in place, so communist cadre had to be dispatched from Tri Ton, affording a few men like Reap's brother Dom a chance to disappear.

A lieutenant and two sergeants in the headquarters compound in Tri Ton changed their insignia and demanded Major Keo's surrender. The lieutenant, a Vietnamese artilleryman, had long been plagued by Keo and his Khmer Krom predecessors who had interfered with his market in brass shell casings and treated him with no respect. He laughed as he ripped the brass from Major Keo's collar and ground it under his foot. The district interrogation center and police jails were emptied and quickly refilled with the lieutenant's enemies, the enemies of the people. In Salon hamlet, Chau Got and the four remaining Scouts were surrounded by two squads of North Vietnamese while the communist village chief, a fisherman from the next hamlet, looked on. They were disarmed, bound, and led to Tri Ton for trial.

The men who came for Reap were local force guerrillas from Coto Mountain, five of them, one he had known from his years with the Viet Cong. They were polite to his mother and calm and respectful to him at first. But as they went through the house looking for evidence and found first the American Bronze Star in its felt case, then a framed photograph of Reap and Strait, arms around one another, they became filled with righteous indignation. As he lay bound on the floor, they struck his ears with cupped hands, pounded his hips with rifle butts, and spat on him, all while his mother wept. Reap and a half dozen of his NCOs, bound together at the neck, were led out of the village, away from the smell of burning rice and thatch and the sound of their wives and daughters screaming for mercy.

•

In the week following the arrest of officers and officials of the old government, the towns and villages of the Seven Mountains region were crowded with jubilant communist soldiers who had come down from their mountain strongholds to disarm the regional soldiers and secure key installations such as Chi Lang, Tri Ton, and Chau Doc for the arrival of the new administrators. Those who had collaborated with the Americans—interpreters, agents, secret police operatives—escaped to distant towns, where they changed their names and pretended to be hapless draftees from the old regime. Those who had served as common soldiers or bureaucrats, and families of those already arrested, such as Reap's and Chau Got's, waited quietly in their homes, motionless and dumb with fear.

The Khmer Krom soldiers and citizens knew to expect the worst. They had sided with the French, then the Americans, against the people of their "adopted" country, and then in the last few years with the traitors in Cambodia. With American weapons they had killed thousands and thousands of innocent Vietnamese on both sides of the border. Now the Vietnamese were masters again, and the Khmer Krom prayed that they would be merciful.

Not all would pray. Not all would lie down and submit. The night before Reap was taken from Olam, Sem Ly met with twenty-four men from his recon platoon to decide what to do. If they went to the mountains in Cambodia like Dom and the others, it would be too much like running. If they stayed at home, they would be disarmed and enslaved. If they were taken prisoner, they would be tortured to death. They were Khmer Krom and they would defy the *yuons*. That night they packed as much ammunition and food as each could carry and made their way to the top of Coto Mountain, skirting the remaining sentries, avoiding the caves they knew so well. At the summit they formed a perimeter and at dawn unfurled the flag of the Front for the Liberation of Khmer Krom in the very place where the revered old tree had grown so long ago. There they would die free men, serving no master.

Under the red flag of united Vietnam in the football field near the Tri Ton market, a gang of prisoners dug three deep post holes, and in them fixed large wooden stakes. Communist soldiers rode through the town in captured green-and-white police jeeps ordering the people to gather at the football field. When the crowd had assembled, Chau Got and Major Keo were led out of the interrogation center on a leash by the Vietnamese artillery officer. Their hands were bound behind their backs and their elbows pinned painfully together by wire, flags of the South Vietnamese government were stuffed into their mouths. At several places along the way, embittered citizens, relatives of men Chau Got had killed, rushed out and attacked him with fists and sticks before they were pushed back by communist guards. Chau Got and Major Keo were bound to two of the stakes, blindfolded by the flags taken from their mouths, and shot by a squad of "volunteers."

20

I WAS PACING back and forth in front of the blackboard, hands behind my back, trying to stir up a discussion about the effect of Turgenev's use of verisimilitude in one of his sketches. It was the first of May, early afternoon, and out the window on the broad campus lawn some boys were winging a Frisbee. Two girls, both barefoot and carrying their shoes, strolled by under the pin oak. One wore a garland of purple vetch in her hair; the other stooped to pick a dandelion and tucked it behind her ear.

"Mister Watkins," I said. Better to pick on one by name than ask the class; at least he would have to look at me and make a show of thinking. "Why does Turgenev bother to say, 'In the village of X . . . ,' instead of using real names, or creating fictional ones?"

Watkins looked at me like I was his cleaning lady and had just disturbed him in his bath.

"I'm sorry. Would you repeat the question?"

Those who were listening would have tittered at his response if they had not been afraid that I would call on them. They were prep school seniors. They had all been accepted by prestigious northeastern universities, had far transcended this middle-aged high school teacher in the midwest. But a couple of them *might* have done the reading. I moved to stand in the window between them and the vernal romp on the lawn.

It might have worked. I might have gotten a discussion going among a few, if I had not stolen a look out the window. The little old lady in my daughter's Babar books was coming up the admissions office walk with Krech on her arm. I had an overwhelming urge to crouch down.

Watkins asked if I was all right.

"I'm fine," I said. "Look, it's stupid to try and hold class on a day like this. Let's quit early. Use the side door and go quietly, please."

It wasn't Krech, of course. It was Socheat Som, who could have passed as Krech's twin: a dark-skinned, round-faced Khmer boy of about fifteen with the same lift to his walk, the same nodding chin. The little old lady was from the Jewish Community Service. A counselor at Socheat's inner city school had recommended him to the lady as a hard-working student who was not being challenged in the public system. He had not done well on the verbal portion of our entrance exam, but his math was above average. He would need a full scholarship and remedial work in English, but the lady's gentle pressure and humane arguments prevailed and a generous admissions committee admitted Socheat for the next year.

I introduced myself to him in the crowded hall during the first week of school. I told him I had once spent time living among Cambodians and that he reminded me of an old friend. He smiled politely, then moved meekly aside so that another student could get into her locker. If he had any problems, anything at all, he should come see me, I said. I would be happy to help. He looked at his schedule card, thanked me, and was gone.

"He has no idea what's going on, the poor bastard." His English teacher, Snavely, rubbed his eyes. "How can we expect someone who survived the killing fields in Cambodia, who was a malnourished slave for four years, to understand *The Catcher in the Rye?* What's he going to do when we get to *Midsummer Night's Dream*, for chrissake? It'll be like reading Steven Hawkins in Turkic. And his writing. . . ."

"He had A's in English at his old school," I said.

"I asked him about that. He got A's there because he showed up every day and he did the homework."

I stopped Socheat several times, urging him to come see me for help, but he did not. I thought he was afraid of me, or maybe did not want help. I wanted to tell him about Krech, how he danced his defiance in front of the caves on Coto that morning. After a few more tries I decided to leave Socheat alone; he was getting extra help from other teachers and a reading specialist. He was just too busy and probably too worried about school to sit down and listen to an old man remember.

As the end of the first grading period approached, it became obvious that Socheat could not possibly pass most of his courses. We waived his foreign language requirement and devised an easier English curriculum for him, but still he floundered. He went from class to class alone and ate lunch alone. He seemed to be shrinking.

One afternoon I found him sitting forlorn on the floor in a corner of the student center. I hit him with an obscenity in Khmer, suggesting he do something that even Krech would have thought vile, then walked away. The next morning he came to my office and asked if we could talk. He knew that he was in over his head and that he would have to go back to his public school. It was not so bad for him, he said, but it would be a terrible loss of face for his father, who had boasted of his son's success to his Cambodian friends in the refugee community on the west side of the city. Socheat could not bear the thought of disappointing his father. Maybe I could understand that nothing could be worse than that. I promised him I would do everything I could to find a way to keep him at our school. He would have to work hard, and put in far more time than the other students. He did not mind working, he said. He wanted to work; he just did not know how. I told him that that was our job and he could trust us to do our best. As he was leaving, I apologized for the obscenity.

"Don't worry," he said. "I've heard that one before."

.

The invitation was written inside a glossy red Father's Day card. The Som family invited my family to come to their house for dinner on Sunday afternoon. After my divorce, I had been single for a few years, then met and married Holly. Our daughter Sarah was three years old, and Holly was seven months pregnant.

"They want to thank you for helping Socheat," Holly said.

Would it be a Christmas party? Sarah wanted to know. We explained that the people we were going to visit did not celebrate Christmas. They were from another country far away, and they had moved to America to get away from evil men. There would be other kids there for her to play with, and lots of food.

"For a long time they lived with almost no food, some of them even died because there was nothing to eat, so now they celebrate by eating and enjoying being safe together. Even when they say hello to you, in their language it means, 'Have you eaten yet?'"

"Oh," was all Sarah said.

The Soms are from Battambang in northern Cambodia. Socheat's father Sambuoth had been an officer in the paramilitary police when the Khmer Rouge took over the country, which meant that he would have been arrested and executed as an enemy of the new regime if he had been caught. Sambuoth and a few others fled to the forest with their weapons, leaving his wife Ny, Socheat, and his three daughters in the town, where he could only hope they would be safe. In the forest he learned from others in hiding that the Khmer Rouge were not only killing anyone who had had any affiliation with the Lon Nol government, but were exterminating everyone who could speak a foreign language, who could read or write, had been educated, or wore eyeglasses. All doctors and teachers and monks were killed. They were out to take Cambodia back to the "year zero," to eradicate all traces of foreign culture. Gun-waving young guerrillas were driving the populations of cities and towns into the countryside, where they were herded into work camps. A man told Sambuoth that he had seen Ny and the children in a small hamlet south of the town and that they were about to be taken away, but when Sambuoth went to get his family at the place the man had described, it was a trap and he was ambushed by the Khmer Rouge.

He escaped with a bullet hole in his calf and returned to the forest to mourn his loss.

Ny was separated from her children at the work camp. There were to be no more families, only love and loyalty for the new order. Men and women were segregated in one part of the camp, boys and girls in another far away. At dawn everyone over the age of five was led out to work in gangs digging a new canal; at dark those who had not died of exhaustion and starvation were led back to the camp. Children caught trying to visit their mothers were butchered, the mothers often made to watch. When the second of her youngest daughters died of starvation, Ny slipped away in the dark of the moon, found Socheat and his sister, and ran away with them to the jungle. Several months later, almost dead of starvation themselves, they reached the refugee camp at the Thai border. A year later, they were reunited with Sambuoth; Socheat did not even recognize his father.

The Soms live in the lower portion of a duplex in a row of similar houses across the street from a plastics factory. There were at least twenty adults and half as many children in the little duplex. Sambuoth and Ny greeted us formally at the door with Socheat and his beautiful sister Sompeh at their sides. Sambuoth is a short, pleasant-faced man decorated with intricate Sanskrit tattoos. They introduced us to their relatives all around and invited us to come to the table that nearly filled the back room. The old familiar smells of *satay* chicken and tamarind and the musical rise and fall of spoken Khmer released in me a confusion of shapeless memories, a mixture of sorrow and gratitude. Holly knew that it is Khmer custom on formal occasions for the female guest to sit at the table with the men, but she insisted that Ny sit with her, much to Ny's delight. They sat back a little from the table, Sarah on her mom's knee in open amazement at the scene around her.

The women served us from the adjoining kitchen, and while we ate, course after course, they crowded in the doorway behind Holly and Ny to watch and discuss the meal in progress. Both Holly and Sarah have hair so blonde that it is almost white; their cheeks were flushed pink in the warm room.

"They look like ghosts," I understood one girl to say. "Like spirits."

A hand stretched from the doorway toward Holly's hair, but was pushed away by Ny who said something that made the woman move back.

I strained to follow the polite conversation among the men at the table. The few who did speak English did so haltingly and tried their best to translate what others said to me in Khmer. Some words came back to me, but only a few; when I tried to use the patois of English, Vietnamese, and Khmer that had worked with Reap and Chau Got, I only confused my hosts.

A tattered photo was produced and passed around. In it, Ny, hollow-eyed and ragged, stands with Socheat and his sister before a nearly naked crowd of Khmer children. His sister Sompeh looks about ten years old and barely strong enough to stand. Socheat, wearing only a tattered pair of shorts, has legs and arms like sticks, a distended stomach, and swollen joints.

"That was in the refugee camp, when they got there," the man next to me explained. "Look at them now!"

When Sambuoth rose to speak, first the table, then quickly the doorway and the kitchen, fell silent. He stood with his hands at his sides and spoke in measured Khmer as if he had memorized what he was saying or was reciting something long known. I understood a few words—school, *kru*, temple, father—the rest rolled by me. There were murmurs of approval and nodding smiles to me. Sambuoth finished with a question for me and waited for my answer, as did everyone else. I squirmed. I could not even remember how to say I do not understand. They were as embarrassed as I was, perhaps more so. Finally the man next to me put his hand over mine.

"He asks you to save only the boy's eyes and bones," he said. "He thinks you understand that."

I apologized to Sambuoth in English, and the man said something to the table in Khmer. A few whispered sympathetically.

"When a father in Cambodia gives his son to the monks to have them teach him, he gives them permission that they can do anything to him to make him learn. Anything. Even beat him. But only don't hurt his eyes or break his bones. This way he's asking you to take charge of Socheat for his education. Will you accept him?"

I looked at Holly, who nodded slightly, and said yes of course I would. Sambuoth bowed and thanked me. I said I was honored. The table was cleared noisily and tea and sweets brought out. Sambuoth opened a bottle of Hennessey's, and we stood for toasts.

Later we sat in the living room with the Soms and the few remaining guests, watching the children play on the floor. The man who had been next to me at the table sat on the couch between Sambuoth and me; he and Socheat translated for us. Sambuoth asked where I had been in Cambodia and when. What did I do?

I started to explain, and suddenly the man next to me cried, "Ah! I thought so! You had a mustache then! Ha, ha!"

I do not know what my expression looked like, but it made Sambuoth think I had been insulted and he said something sharp to the man. But the man laughed and explained in Khmer, then put his hand on my knee. In his explanation were the words "Mike Force" and "Coto." I must have brightened at that, as Sambuoth relaxed and smiled.

The man was Sergeant Son Ha, the recon platoon leader on the top of the mountain who had drunk gasoline and been briefed by Chau Got and Aziz. Did I remember him? I said I was amazed and so happy to see him. And to see him safe in the U.S.

Yes, he said, he was one of the lucky ones. He and his platoon had been broken up in the fighting north of Phnom Penh in 1970. He did not know what happened to the others, but he could guess. He had gone west to Pailin to rescue his adopted sister, who had been sold into prostitution. When the Khmer Rouge took over, he and his sister escaped across the Thai border on a motorbike. He straddled the arm of the couch to show us how he hid his M16 under a poncho and when the Khmer Rouge border guards threatened him, he shot them both, like that! The Khmer children laughed and applauded; Sarah left the others and went to sit with her mother.

I asked Son Ha if he could help me find out about my friends. He said he thought so and he would try. Those Khmer Krom who went to Cambodia to join their fellow Khmer as he did were probably all dead; those who stayed in their homeland and surrendered to the Vietnamese were put in jail, but most of them had been released by now, ten years later, and were beginning to escape by boat or across Cambodia to the refugee camps. He knew how to find them if they were alive.

Would I find an American soldier for him? he asked. His name was Robert Steppe. He wrote out his name and from memory his service number. I said I would try.

When we said good night on the cold porch, Ny knelt before Sarah and put her arms around her, pulling her close. After a long moment, Sambuoth touched her shoulder and gently helped her back to her feet.

21

A TALL, BULL-NECKED Irishman in blue uniform shirt and hip-high rubber boots was hosing down a black pickup in front of the firehouse. I pulled up onto the concrete apron in my pale little Japanese rental car. I was looking for North 127th Street; I had found 127th Street all right, but couldn't find *North* 127th. Would he tell me how to get there?

"Are you selling something? I wouldn't bother to get there if you are."

"I'm looking for a friend."

He shut off the hose and came closer to the car to bend down and have a look at me from head to knees, God knows why.

"You sure you got the right address?"

"Yes." I was ready to give it up and try elsewhere, but he explained how to get there, repeating himself to be sure.

"I tell you, I wouldn't go in there if I was you."

Tacoma's North 127th Street is only a detached segment of the longer street. It runs for a couple of blocks along the edge of a hill above a mangled landscape of junked trucks and fenced-in rusting rows of fifty-gallon drums. Built on the top of the incline, running parallel with the street, are two long two-story apartment buildings, the upper story entered from the street, the lower story from the parking lot behind. While the rest of the hilltop neighborhood is small square houses built on tiny lots and inhabited by Blacks, some Asians, and many Latinos, the two straw-colored apartment buildings on the hillside seem to have been added as an afterthought and they are inhabited entirely by the various surviving remnants of about forty Khmer Krom families from the three villages beneath Coto Mountain.

The frail solitary figure that I could see standing in front of the apartment building I knew must be Reap. The sun had gone down beneath the hill, but even in shadow and from a distance I could see that his face was twisted off center. Several of his family waited at a respectful distance behind him in the doorway to their apartment. Not far beneath the surface, I felt a tidal pull of sorrow and warned myself, almost aloud, to put pity in a private place and keep it covered there lest I insult my friend with it. When

I pulled over to the curb, he strained to see me, then started slowly toward the car, a slight hitch to his step.

In the photograph he had sent me I had seen his three surviving daughters, now young women, and his son Vith Chon in the orange robes and shaved head of a novice Buddhist monk. I had seen Reap's wounded face as well, and the rheumy, stricken eyes through which he could barely see. I thought I was prepared for the visit until I felt his diminished frame against mine when we hugged. To gain control, I fixed my eyes on his children arranged in the doorway, and we held onto one another in silence.

"How are you?" he asked in English. "How are your family?" He had rehearsed these lines and I thought that if it were not for his wounded mouth they would have been pronounced perfectly.

"Come eat." He took my arm. In the distance, lighted by the westering sun, I could see the snow-covered top of Mount Rainier over the apartment building.

I do not think there was ever a time during that visit with him and his family, except maybe when we went late to bed, that there were not at least a dozen pairs of shoes shed by family and guests in the doorway. Each family that came to say hello was invited to stay and eat something, and did. Perhaps four or five of the family groups were complete. Most were missing at least one member; some were made up of several individual survivors from other families come together to form another family. The few adult males were all former soldiers, either from the Khmer Krom companies in the villages or from the Mike Force; all the male survivors but Reap had gone to Cambodia to fight for Lon Nol and managed to escape the Khmer Rouge holocaust to the refugee camps in Thailand. They thanked me for coming, for Reap's sake. Each of the men asked me to contact or try to find his American, a Special Forces officer or NCO in most cases.

"Tell Major Topp that Chau Cowboy asks for him. Not for help or money, but only to hear his voice, maybe see him, to learn about his family."

For the evening meals, each one as varied and splendid as any restaurant's, a bamboo mat was rolled out on the living room floor and the men were served there while the women prepared food on the kitchen floor and served, or sat in chairs about the two rooms, talking, laughing, and scolding children. At the far end of the narrow living room the drapes were drawn over the sliding terrace doors, blocking the view of the littered landscape and the distant mountain; a large-screen TV showed one nature film after another with the sound turned off.

Reap and I were the center of attention at every meal, during every visit, in daylight and dark. People I had never seen or did not remember swore they remembered me vividly. One young man recalled the wedding at which I had fallen down while dancing the *Romvong*. He had been only a little boy who had been watching from outside, but he would never forget it, he said. He began a loud, animated rendition of that night, but a glare from Reap to the man next to him got him pulled back onto the couch and hushed up abruptly. We posed for what seemed hundreds of photographs: Reap and I together, his family and I, and each and every one of the families who visited us. In the corner of the hallway a video camera was set up on a tripod focused on the center of the couch where Reap and I usually sat. Every conversation and every mouthful was filmed. When guests arrived, his daughter Chandha filmed their entrance and our meeting; when the blinking red light told her that the tape had ended, she scurried from the kitchen wiping her hands on a towel to begin a new one.

One morning I sat in a folding chair while Kem photographed each of Reap's children standing next to me. His daughters, Chandha the eldest first, changed into formal dresses and posed by my seat with one hand on my shoulder like attendant ladies. They addressed me as *bu*, uncle, an affectionate and respectful term, and the ease with which they used the word was a comfort for Reap and me both.

In the evening, when the men drank beer and talked and the women joined us on the couches, the meal cleared and kitchen done, Reap sat with his son by the drapes. As a monk, Chon Vith cannot eat or drink anything other than juice after noon. Reap urged me to drink, though he could not, having forsworn alcohol the day his wife died. He smoked, drawing on the cigarette at a clumsy angle in the side of his mouth, and listened and commented to the rest of us. I thought he looked healthy and alert, even though he could barely see. I knew he was apprehensive about the surgery, both for his vision, which the hospital thought could be restored, and for the further work to be done on his jaw, and I didn't blame him—another hundred-day dream, this time in a cold and strange land.

That morning before the others had risen, I had found him sitting alone on the couch near a window closed against the early fog. He was wrapped in a ski parka, his arms folded on his chest; in the little altar built high in the corner of the room, incense burned beneath the aluminum foil canopy that protected the ceiling. Reap did not see me, or if he did, did not notice me. He had withdrawn into the parka. I left him alone.

•

The truck that took him to the prison camp in May 1975 was one that was normally used to transport swine. Reap and his fellow prisoners were chained together and to the truck for a three-day trip without relief, lying in their own waste. Reap was isolated at the camp with eighteen other prisoners, among them Aziz, who were accused of working with the CIA. They were called spies, and "poison," and were told that they were to be executed. Reap and Thach Serei, another Khmer Krom, decided to risk escape and to try to make their way back to Coto Mountain where they had heard that Reap's brother Dom and other Khmer Krom who had fled after the surrender were gathering. In the escape, Thach Serei was shot in the legs and recaptured, but Reap got away. He made his way to the Tram Forest west of the villages, but became lost and was spotted by a Vietnamese patrol near the border. They chased him, firing as they went, and finally brought him down with a round through his thigh. Reap knocked one of them down with a stick to the head, but the others beat him senseless with rifle butts.

They took him to the old training camp at Chi Lang, which was now a prison camp mockingly called "New Saigon" by the cadre who had come from the North Vietnamese Interior Department. Reap was locked in a Conex container with three other prisoners. The Conex is an American metal shipping container five feet square with a small door. They were let out of the airless box once a day in the afternoon, and fed once a day. Once a week they were allowed to bathe. Most of them developed a heavy cough, and Reap said he was "nearly strangled to death" several times by the stench of their rotting shit. Many of those in the Conexes died from the heat, sickness, and torture. Occasionally when they were taken out, one prisoner was marched to the side and bound to a tree. The guards shot at him, barely missing him, then when his terror was greatest, shot him dead. They told Sith, a former professor of military psychology, that he could go home, then shot him in the back as he walked away. When the heat of the day was at its worst, the guards allowed the prisoners to cover the Conexes with grass, then later torched the grass, cooking dozens of men each time.

In 1978, as the fighting between the Vietnamese and Cambodian communists escalated at the border, the prisoners were moved from Chi Lang to another camp farther inside Vietnam. Reap had been in the box for eighteen months and was nearly blind.

The twenty thousand prisoners in the labor camp at Kontum were South Vietnamese government officials, university students, officers above the rank of colonel, and special cases like Reap, all considered "most dangerous" and the worst enemies of the Vietnamese communists. It was called the "Cow Farm" because the prisoners were so exhausted from heavy labor, so weakened from malnutrition and disease, that they crawled on their arms and legs like cows. They were forced to gather dirt to make vegetable patches a hundred meters square in the jungle; those who worked the hardest were fed better than the others and worked themselves to death, "coughing up blood"; those who worked less were fed less and died of malnutrition. Reap often wished that he had been taken by the Khmer Rouge and killed outright rather than suffer as he did in the Vietnamese camps.

"They tried very hard to reeducate us," he said. "They made us hate our friends and to hate what we had done in the past. But even then they failed to reeducate those of us who hated the communists. However, they were successful with the opportunist traitors, the ones who sought sympathy from the communists. I wish to let you know that even if the communists tried to reeducate me for one hundred more years they would never be able to change me."

Reap was released on 17 June 1982 with 250 others, "either because the Chinese were attacking Vietnam in the north or a change in American policy toward the Vietnamese. I do not know."

His home in Olam village was gone. His wife and children had fled to the forest to escape punishment for their relation to him and his brother Dom, who was still at large.

"As I arrived, I looked for my wife in the marketplace and she eventually came. She was unbelievably skinny and was not recognized immediately. She grabbed me and held me tight. We cried. The whole market cried."

She told him that two of his daughters had starved to death in the forest. Blind, crippled, and emaciated, Reap lay down next to Kim, his once-beautiful seamstress, in her parents' house in Phnom Pi. Two weeks later, Kim died in her sleep.

After twelve years of trying, his application to emigrate to the United States with his surviving children was finally approved, and they arrived in Tacoma in August, six months before my visit.

·

I noticed that when Chandha changed the videotapes, she began each new one with a slow pan of the family portraits on the living room wall, lingering at each as though for a brief visit. First Reap's parents in a faded formal photograph, enlarged and framed. They sit together on a bench before a backdrop of leaning palm trees. Sok wears a patois of clothing: sarong and sandals and a jacket with a French provincial cut. He appears solemn, perhaps shy; she unafraid. Next a stained, faded photo of Kim and their six children taken while Reap was in the camps. She is thin, her eyes sunken, but she is still beautiful; the children stand stunned before the camera. Then came the living relatives, the immediate family in various stages, and even an enlarged print of me and my family taken at Christmas. Last, my oldest son Jacob, who is a midshipman, in his choker whites. Then a stop at the high little altar, and back to the present, to those gathered in the room, with special attention to the children, before she fixed the camera in the tripod and returned to the kitchen.

While we were being filmed, we watched the videos that Kem had made of our visit to Fort Lewis that afternoon. We watched Reap getting in and out of the car, saw barracks speed by out the window, a blur of headquarters and parked tanks, and for thirty minutes coming and going the highway ahead filmed over my shoulder from the back seat. While we ate, we watched videos of ourselves eating the night before. Several of our guests brought films taken a few months earlier on visits to Olam and Wat Pratheat. Everyone over sixteen in the apartment buildings works two jobs: one for subsistence, the other for the temples and family members back in the villages. A few had been back to take money and visit relatives. We watched a water buffalo race and a temple festival in Phnom Pi. When I saw people I knew, Chandha filmed my surprise at seeing them on film, so the old friends could see a film of me being surprised to see them on film when someone next visited. We watched Kem's father's funeral. He had been bitten by a poisonous snake and had swollen horribly in death. The camera paid loving attention to his corpse and mourning daughter. Reap offered me a hand as if to shake, but instead held it in his, resting both on his knee.

"Next time you come we'll drive to the mountain with the snow on top," he said. "You can bring Captain Strait too. Before the Europeans came, the name of that mountain was Tacoma. Did you understand that?"

22

"I'M SORRY, I don't understand you very well."

Her voice was polite, but hesitant. Her English was good; I guessed she was about seventeen, schooled in the states for five years or more, a quick learner, the eldest child, the one who spoke for her parents on the phone when English was called for.

I tried again, slower this time, pronouncing carefully. I have lost most of my Vietnamese; my pronunciation was never good enough for the phone.

"I've just heard that your father's brother, Col. Thach Quyen, is alive and on the West Coast. That he escaped. I am an old friend of his from Chau Doc. I would like very much to find him, maybe even visit him."

"Chau Doc?" she asked, pronouncing it beautifully. "From the war? Oh, yes. You must mean Thatch *Quyen*. It's pronounced like 'Wing.' Yes, he's my uncle."

"I always called him Major back then—or sir."

"Yes," she said. "Please wait while I talk to my father."

Distant Asian voices.

"My father says it's OK if you contact his brother. He thinks he will be happy to hear from you." She gave me his phone number and address. "You may have to write to him. He's an old man who is living alone; he never answers the phone."

I tried three times. I let it ring and ring and ring, then finally gave up and wrote to him. I told him how happy I was to hear he had survived the Khmer Rouge holocaust and the "reeducation" camps, how I had believed him dead for sure, killed or starved like so many of the others. I found two photos from 1969 and sent them along. In one he is walking toward me from Coto Mountain, two of his junior officers following. His head is turned slightly, showing his fine features and that same expression of a man who is comfortable with authority and used to being photographed. Though he is in the field, he wears his uniform seriously: the shirt is starched and tucked perfectly, the brass shined, his holster, lifted slightly from his hip by his stride, gleaming. In the other photo, he stands with his wife and little daughter. It is evening in the courtyard between his house and headquarters; he is wearing a bright white T-shirt tucked into his fatigue pants. His wife and daughter, both as handsome as he, are wearing white silk blouses, smiling nervously at me. Colonel Quyen's arm lies across his daughter's shoulder.

I told him I had been to see Reap and was eager to see him, too, and to learn more about the Scouts and our other friends from Tri Ton. Would he please write back, if he had the time?

A short time later the reply came:

Dear Comrade in Arms,

I have just received your letter at 6:00 this morning, in the right now the time I write this letter, I still affected and I don't thinking . . . might I have chanced your news. Oh! my friend, what and how you think; in the summer of 1968—in the summer of 1994. It was twenty five years ago! . . . and we are alive, we are here . . . in USA. God bless us, we have had the faith, we believed and we lived to tell the tale, did you? In my opinion the great thing in this world is not so much where we stand as in what direction we are moving. We grow by helping to develop each other's hearts and mind.

I had memorized the map he had drawn for me, but once on the ground in San Francisco, so close to him, I kept it handy anyway, just to be sure. For each block, he gave the number of paces in parentheses as he would for a minefield or defensive perimeter sketch. Preparing it, he would have lengthened his steps to make them more like mine.

To turn the corner onto his street, I had to ease my way through a crowd of ragged, stumbling street people, smoking, drinking from brown bags, reeking of vomit and urine-soaked wool. A man who looked like he had been eating toxic foam looked me up and down, clearly disgusted by my button-down shirt, Levi's, and running shoes. He pushed around and blocked my way.

"Fucking shirt!" he said, and the others laughed.

Quyen was waiting just off the sidewalk behind a parked truck, with his hands clasped behind his back. He wore glasses now, and beneath his neat Fedora, his hair was white, his little chin whiskers the same. He wore creased trousers, a russet silk varsity jacket zipped up to the collar of a white shirt beneath.

We saw each other at the same time.

"Aah!" was all he said. We embraced, held each other at arm's length to see, then hugged again. His eyes were still the same vivid dark brown, and his laughter still high and musical. He took my elbow and guided me to his door.

"This is my friend." He presented me to a slack-jawed giant in the doorway. "He comes to visit me."

The man took no notice, did not even turn his eyes to the colonel. On the way up the stairs, Quyen explained, "That's my landlord. He's a very nice man."

Inside we removed our shoes and put them in line with his other two pair. He hung his hat and jacket on the wall and took my arm again to turn me into a little alcove, barely big enough for the two of us to stand. Before us, propped on a small stand covered with red silk, was an old water-stained photograph of a man in his middle years, framed in gold and draped with tinsel roping.

"My father," he said.

"He was a handsome man," I said.

"Yes, yes, of course."

On the other wall, beneath a shelf of neatly folded towels, was a small poster of Marilyn Monroe, her hands on the hips of a short black shoulderless dress, one knee lifted slightly, her head laid back in laughter.

The main room, if it could be called that, was perhaps twelve by twelve, with one window that looked out onto a wall and a raised parking lot. It was small but clean and comfortable. A couch for two, created by pillows and covered with a white wool blanket; a coffee table with a vase of plastic flowers, faded but washed clean; a narrow table covered with his clothes, folded and stacked in categories from shirts and sweaters to socks and cotton handkerchiefs; a little desk with a folding metal chair painted baby blue. And everywhere else books. Dictionaries, almanacs, odds and ends of encyclopedias, and histories in French filled the two shelves over the desk. On wire display racks culled from a church sale, volumes of American and Asian history were arranged in tidy ranks at the foot of the bed. You could bounce a quarter on the blue blanket that covered the bed.

"We can sit and talk here. We can talk until midnight if we want, like old friends!" he declared. On the wall calendar the month of October was bare, save that day, the 23rd, in which were printed my initials.

We settled on the little couch facing one another, our knees touching, and he asked about my family. When he asked to see a picture, I found an old one of my kids in my wallet and we held it together; he pointed to each one in turn, oldest to youngest, repeated their names and made quiet noises of appreciation as I described them.

"You are very lucky," he said.

"What about your family?" I asked.

He held onto my photo and looked at me. "My wife died while I was in the prison camps; I didn't know it until I came home. I also didn't know about my son. In 1977, in April, when he was ten years old, he went out at night to catch fish for the family. They were not allowed to fish because of me. The communists caught him and shot him. It was one A.M. He died next to our family's cemetery. My daughter—do you remember her in your photo on the desk there?—she is in Oakland now and she is all right. I see her with her husband sometimes."

"How did your wife die?"

"The communists, you know, because of me. She got sick and could have no medicine or enough food." He turned away slightly, "No grave."

Outside on the street someone shouted over the noise of a boom box; another man swore and a bottle was smashed.

·

Quyen and the three other officers who were taken from their homes that morning in Can Tho after the surrender were transported across town to a holding area for prisoners. The camp was crowded with thousands of officers of all ranks up to brigadier and Protestant ministers, priests, and Buddhist monks, "all of the ecclesiastical people." There Quyen saw Aziz. After ten months, the senior officers and clerics were led away to ships, which carried them to the work camps in North Vietnam.

The labor camp at Son La, where he spent most of his nine years of penal servitude, was an old French political prisoner camp thirty kilometers from the Chinese border. He and thousands of others living in connected camps cut trees and broke ground for planting rice, manioc, and sweet potatoes. They were fed bite-size pieces of manioc or potato, some rye or wheat seed, and two spoonfuls of salt water each day. On Independence Day they got a bowl of rice, a piece of meat the size of an egg, and soup. Escape was impossible as no one could stay alive in the jungle without salt.

"I didn't know about other prisons, but in mine there was no teaching, no 'reeducation,' only hard labor and unceasing hungry. That 'reeducation' was a play on words by the communists, to joke."

In May 1984, he returned to his native village in Tra Vinh Province, having traveled most of the 250 miles by foot. "Empty-handed, penniless, nothing but skin and bones," he built a small thatch hut with the help of his brother and sister. Twice a week he had to present himself to the communist village chief, and he was watched carefully by cadre disguised as peddlers on bicycles. Like the others who had found their way home, he was not permitted any occupation but rice farming, "to follow the plow for life." It would take him two years to put on flesh again, he thought, but only if he could escape.

On the night of 27 July 1986, he and his daughter Lang, then twenty-one, set out together on foot for the Thai refugee camps, 420 miles away. Through Vietnam, then Cambodia, they walked at night, avoiding the roads and villages where they might be arrested again or arbitrarily murdered. They ate roots and leaves, paddy crabs, and grubs. His daughter carried all they owned, a few photos and an oilcloth, in a small pack on her back.

"In one place near the Thailand border, they killed ten thousand people!" He was still amazed. "Yes! Ten thousand. Nobody accepts this, but I've seen it with these eyes. Even now."

"Who killed them? Why?"

"I don't know. I don't know who would do that. I don't know why."

They spent two years in refugee camps and there he began writing a book about the Khmer Krom, called *The Race with No Place to Go.* He and his daughter made it to California in 1988. Since she had married two years before, he had lived alone in the apartment where he intends to stay until he joins his wife.

Now he eats at the Grace Methodist Church nearby. Each morning at 11:30 a line begins to form at the side door; by noon, when the door is opened, the line has stretched around the block. On Mondays, Wednesdays, and Fridays, he joins the line at the end because he works on the cleanup crew those days. Almost every day, he said, they serve potatoes and gravy, and there is always plenty to eat. They are given a bag lunch to take home when they leave. At six o'clock he sits at his little kitchen table, unrolls the bag, and takes out its contents an item at a time, arranging each on the table: a sandwich wrapped in foil, a napkin, a container of juice with a straw attached, a pack of cookies, and a nice red apple.

After twenty-five years, most of my memories of him had eclipsed into single images, black-and-white stills. But one remains in motion. I do not remember when it was, only that it was late at night in the rainy season. They hit the Tri Ton compound with rockets first, 107s, whose explosions deafened us and impacts threw men and debris in every direction. Then they began to walk in the mortars, each dull explosion answered by the screams of wounded and terrified mothers crying out for their children in the darkness. I was frozen in fear next to the commo bunker, and behind me, somewhere, an American was yelling: "They're in the wire! They've broken through! They're in the fucking wire!" The small arms fire on the south wall was so heavy it made a roaring noise like Puff the Magic Dragon. And toward it moved Quyen at a brisk walk, only slightly slowed by the drag of the terrified militiaman he pulled along by the collar. He appeared and reappeared in the flashes of the exploding incoming rounds. He slowed as he passed me. He did not look around, but spoke clearly, in English, above the terrible noise.

"Come this way, please," was all he said.

•

"About your other Khmer Krom friends, ours, and your desire to find about them. In my competence domain, I'll help you in everything I knew and recall, with all one's heart of my conscience, with heart and hand, with heart and soul."

I brought out the notebook in which I had pasted photos of the Scouts. All of them, I had assumed, were dead, but now I hoped to hear otherwise, or at least learn what happened to them.

But first, he said, we should have a beer, if I would like. I would like, I said. He went through the beaded curtain into the little back room and returned with a can of beer, which he set before me. I said I hoped he would have one with me. He laughed nervously and said no. When I insisted, he returned with a can that had been opened and covered with foil. He removed the foil and raised the can, which I touched with mine. I opened the notebook and spread it across our knees.

"Chau Got," he said. "They shoot him at the football field, in front of everybody."

"Did he suffer?" I imagined the beatings, the gauntlet of families and friends of his victims scourging him with clubs and sharpened sticks on the long walk to the playing field.

"Yes, of course. But we learned that he showed them no fear."

On the next page, a laughing Krech with a gold-capped tooth, and Cop, standing in the foreground of a group by the flagpole. He pointed at each and named them. "Both killed." He stabbed, as if with a dagger, and twisted it, making a squishing noise in his cheek.

Behind them stood Uchs in his soft beret. Quyen placed a finger on Uchs's chest and said his name. I told him that while visiting Reap I had heard that Uchs was still alive, had survived somehow and was still at large. Quyen said he was not surprised.

In the next photo, Con, looking up at the camera. "Ah, the musician!" The same stab, the same squishing noise.

"But someone told me he thought Con might have escaped," I said.

"Maybe," he patted my knee, "but I don't think so, you know."

Outside a car alarm went off; someone shouted, another laughed cruelly.

I turned the pages slowly. On each he whispered the man's name, covered his picture with his palm, and shook his head.

"You know, Peter, the communists. They kill, kill, kill, kill." Each "kill" to me was a remembered friend lost, each to him the sight and sound of a loved one going down in a bloody struggling heap.

Only Chom, the youngest Scout, may have escaped. Rumor among the Khmer Krom in Tacoma had it that he was living in Tapor village with his surviving family. Like Quyen, he had not fled to Cambodia to be butchered by the Khmer Rouge, but had stayed in Vietnam, where he served ten years in a labor camp. While the phone rang and rang, and we both pretended not to hear it, he explained that Chom did not want to come to the United States, only wanted to stay with his people, in his village where his ancestors are buried.

"Maybe I could go see him," I said.

"They will punish him after you leave. Don't do that."

He held his hands over his ears, grimacing, until the phone stopped ringing, and I closed the notebook.

·

When it came time to leave, I said he did not need to come with me to the airport, but he insisted. Before we left, he undid his trousers and re-tucked his shirt, then straightened his gig line. In the doorway by his father's little shrine, I said something about the Marilyn Monroe poster.

"My father had four wives: one Chinese, one Cambodian, two Vietnamese. He loved them very much, and he loved Marilyn Monroe, too. They didn't let him have a picture of her. Now he's with them, and also he can see her all the time he wants."

The bus stop was on a corner in front of a little market that sold anything. A half-dozen street people were congregated there, some sleeping, some drinking, others carrying on an excited conversation with full body dance. Quyen and I stood shoulder to shoulder on the curb, watching down the street for the bus. A tall black man, wearing a soiled lab coat over several layers of other coats, was waving a pair of new work gloves at the passersby. He held the gloves by the wrist so he could flap them open to show what was pinched between them. Finally a young man stopped, examined the contents, argued briefly, paid the man, and walked on.

But he had not gone ten feet before he shouted, "Mother fucker!" and spun around. The street people moved over against the wall. The man in the lab coat stood his ground next to us, while his customer, high-stepping, waving his fists, spitting outrage, closed on him. Colonel Quyen did not turn around or move aside, but watched serenely for the bus.

"Come on, you piece-a-shit," Lab Coat snarled, reaching inside the layers of clothes to his left hip. The customer stopped and swore. He hesitated for a second, then turned on his heel and strode away.

When we had found a seat together on the bus, I asked him if he was not scared back there. We almost got caught in a gunfight, I told him. Jesus Christ, I thought we had had it for sure.

"Only last week, in that same place, a man got shot. Boom! Here in the chest. Boom! Two times. Dead, right there at the bus stop."

He looked out the window at the passing buildings.

"It's very hard here for Negroes," he said.

Epilogue

Sa Abdul Aziz spent nine years in prison camps. His incarceration was "not as bad as for some others." He was moved from camp to camp and "saw much of the whole country." After his release in 1984, he and his wife and daughters moved to Ho Chi Minh City (Saigon) and began a pharmaceutical and beauty aids business near the central bus station that did very well until government regulation and "other difficulties" began to impede their efforts and deplete their resources. In 1996 he applied to the High Commissioner for Refugees in Bangkok to emigrate to the United States, with me as his sponsor. His application was denied.

Lon Nol never returned to Cambodia. He settled in California with the remains of the million dollars he had been given when he left Phnom Penh, and died in 1987.

Reap underwent two more operations in Tacoma to further repair his jaw. Most of his vision was restored by surgery in 1996. Since then he has been attending English language school, where he is a quick learner. He hopes to find a job when he graduates.

Sem Lý and those of his company who refused to surrender flew the flag of the FLKK atop Coto Mountain for two weeks. The communists made no attempt to capture or kill them: no assaults, no probes, no messengers with surrender demands. But the relatives and friends who brought them food and water begged them to come down for the sake of their families and the villages on whom the communists would take their vengeance. Those of his men who would rather starve or die fighting he released to join Reap's brother and the other Khmer Krom hiding in the mountains across the border. He and his NCOs and those who feared for their families waited two days, then in a "sad ceremony" buried their flag on the summit and came down off the mountain. Sem Ly spent nine years in prison, then escaped with his family to the Philippines and eventually San Francisco, where he recycles cardboard. It was he who sponsored Quyen when he came to the United States.

Son Ngoc Thanh was taken to the Chi Hoa prison in Saigon six hours after he returned from Phnom Penh. His bodyguard, whom Quyen met in the

Thai refugee camp, said that Son Ngoc Thanh never mentioned seeking asylum in the United States or France. His brother Son Thai Nguyen was incarcerated with him. Thanh died in prison.

Socheat Som graduated from high school in 1989. He attended Muskingum College and Cleveland State University, where he earned a bachelor's degree in 1997.

John Strait commanded a rifle company in the 82nd Airborne Division for two years after he left Tri Ton. He wrote to Reap twice, but got no reply. His last four years in the Army were spent as a recruiting officer in Pittsburgh, "a miserable goddamn business." He and Reap were reunited in Toronto in 1995 when they attended the fifth World Convention of Khmer Krom. They sat at the head table at the banquet and ate uncomfortably before video cameras. At night their room was crowded with their former friends and soldiers; during the day they took long walks together or sat on the veranda in the sun to plan their next meeting. Strait is a mail carrier in Jonesville, Michigan.

ABOUT THE AUTHOR

Peter Scott was born and raised in Washington, D.C. From 1967 to 1970 he served in the U.S. Army with the 82d Airborne Division and was an advisor to the Phoenix Program in Vietnam. He has taught in private schools for more than twenty years and is the author of dozens of articles and stories. He lives in Ohio with his wife and children.

The Naval Institute Press is the book-publishing arm of the U.S. Naval Institute, a private, nonprofit, membership society for sea service professionals and others who share an interest in naval and maritime affairs. Established in 1873 at the U.S. Naval Academy in Annapolis, Maryland, where its offices remain today, the Naval Institute has members worldwide.

Members of the Naval Institute support the education programs of the society and receive the influential monthly magazine *Proceedings* and discounts on fine nautical prints and on ship and aircraft photos. They also have access to the transcripts of the Institute's Oral History Program and get discounted admission to any of the Institute-sponsored seminars offered around the country.

The Naval Institute also publishes *Naval History* magazine. This colorful bimonthly is filled with entertaining and thought-provoking articles, first-person reminiscences, and dramatic art and photography. Members receive a discount on *Naval History* subscriptions.

The Naval Institute's book-publishing program, begun in 1898 with basic guides to naval practices, has broadened its scope in recent years to include books of more general interest. Now the Naval Institute Press publishes about 100 titles each year, ranging from how-to books on boating and navigation to battle histories, biographies, ship and aircraft guides, and novels. Institute members receive discounts of 20 to 50 percent on the Press's nearly 600 books in print.

Full-time students are eligible for special half-price membership rates. Life memberships are also available.

For a free catalog describing Naval Institute Press books currently available, and for further information about subscribing to *Naval History* magazine or about joining the U.S. Naval Institute, please write to:

Membership Department
U.S. Naval Institute
118 Maryland Avenue
Annapolis, MD 21402-5035

Telephone: (800) 233-8764
Fax: (410) 269-7940
Web address: www.usni.org